818
MC

McManus, Patrick F.

Rubber legs and
white tail-hairs

$14.45

DATE			
NO 4 '87	JAN 26 '99		
NO 23 '87	AUG 03 '99		
NO 30 '87	MY 07 '99		
JE 21 '88	JA 17 '00		
JY 05 '88	MY 03 '00		
AG 30 '88	JY 19 '00		
SE 16 '88	JY 09 '01		
SE 20 '89	OC 21 '04		
NO 3 '90	AG 04 '05		
AP 22 '91	AP 10 '06		
FEB 4 '98	JY 24 08		

© THE BAKER & TAYLOR CO.

Rubber Legs and White Tail-Hairs

Also by Patrick F. McManus

Kid Camping From Aaaaiii! to Zip
A Fine and Pleasant Misery
They Shoot Canoes, Don't They?
Never Sniff a Gift Fish
The Grasshopper Trap

Rubber Legs and White Tail-Hairs

Patrick F. McManus

Henry Holt and Company • New York

Published by Henry Holt and Company, Inc.,
521 Fifth Avenue, New York, New York 10175.
Published in Canada by Fitzhenry & Whiteside Limited,
195 Allstate Parkway, Markham, Ontario L3R 4T8.

Library of Congress Cataloging in Publication Data
McManus, Patrick F.
Rubber legs and white tail-hairs.
I. Title.
PN6162.M35   1987   814'.54   87-8494
ISBN: 0-8050-0544-7

First Edition

Designed by Jeffrey L. Ward
Printed in the United States of America
10 9 8 7 6 5 4 3 2 1

All stories in this book appeared previously as follows: In *Outdoor Life*: "Shooter";
"The Belcher" (originally titled "The Sharps"); "To Filet or Not to Filet"; "A
Really Nice Blizzard"; "The Last Flight of Homer Pidgin"; "What's in a Name,
Moonbeam?"; "The Big Fix"; "A Boy and His (Ugh!) Dog"; "Throwing
Stuff"; "Muldoon in Love" (originally titled "Show and Gawk"); "Letter to
Santa" (originally titled "Dear Santa"); "Nude, with Other Wildlife" (originally
titled "Gummy"); "Claw of the Sea-Puss" (originally titled "Mutiny on the Sea-
Puss"); "The MFFFF"; "The Mountain"; "Pigs"; "Not Long for This Whirl";
"Cry Wolf"'l(originally titled "The Bridge"); "Outdoor Burnout"; "Advanced
Duck-Hunting Techniques" (originally titled "The No-Fail School of Duck
Hunting"). In *Outdoor Life Hunting Guns, 1985–86*: "Gun-Trading" (originally
titled "A Trader in Our Midst"). In *Reader's Digest*: "Muldoon in Love." In *Field
& Stream*: "Angler's Dictionary"; "Rubber Legs and White Tail-Hairs"
(originally titled "Getting Hooked on Fly-Tying"); "The Cabin at Spooky Lake"
(originally titled "A Strange Occurrence at Nowhere Lake"). In *Field & Stream
Hunting Annual 1981*: "The Fine Art of Delay" (originally titled "Art of Delay").
In the Spokane (Wash.) *Spokesman-Review*: "Summer Reading" (originally titled
"Books for the Beach"). In *Chrysler-Plymouth Spectator*: "Loud Screeching and
Other Tips on Getting Lost."

ISBN 0-8050-0544-7

To my mother,
Mabel McManus DeMers

Contents

Rubber Legs
and White Tail-Hairs

Muldoon in Love

Afterwards, I felt bad for a while about Miss Deets, but Mom told me to stop fretting about it. She said the problem was Miss Deets had just been too delicate to teach third grade in our part of the country.

Besides being delicate, Miss Deets must have also been rich. I don't recall ever seeing her wear the same dress two days in a row. To mention the other extreme, Mr. Craw, one of the seventh-grade teachers at Delmore Blight Grade School, wore the same suit every day for thirty years. Once, when Mr. Craw was sick, the suit came to school by itself and taught his classes, but only Skip Moseby noticed that Mr. Craw wasn't inside the suit. Skip said the suit did a fair job of explaining dangling participles, which turned out to be a kind of South American lizard. I would have liked to hear the suit's lecture, because at the time I was particularly interested in lizards. But I digress from Miss Deets.

No one could understand why a rich and genteel lady like Miss Deets would want to teach third grade at Delmore Blight, but on the first day of school, there she was, smelling of perfume and money, her auburn hair piled on top of her head, her spectacles hanging by a cord around her long, slender, delicate neck. We stood there gawking at her, scarcely believing our good fortune in getting this beautiful lady as our very own third-grade teacher.

We boys all fell instantly in love with Miss Deets, but none more than my best friend, Crazy Eddie Muldoon. I loved her quite a bit myself at first, but Eddie would volunteer to skip recess so he could clean the blackboard erasers, whether they needed cleaning or not. For the first month of school, the third grade must have had the cleanest blackboard erasers in the entire history of Delmore Blight Grade School. For me, love was one thing, recess another. God had not intended the two to interfere with each other. But Crazy Eddie now skipped almost every recess in order to help Miss Deets with little chores around the classroom. She was depriving me of my best friend's company, and bit by bit I began to hate her. I wished Miss Deets would go away and never come back.

Worse yet, in his continuing efforts to prove his love for Miss Deets, Eddie started studying. He soon became the champion of our weekly spelling bees. "Wonderful, Edward!" Miss Deets would exclaim, when Eddie correctly spelled some stupid word nobody in the entire class would ever have reason to use. Then she would pin a ridiculous little paper star on the front of his shirt, the reward for being the last person standing in the spelling bee. It disgusted me to think Eddie would do all that work, learning how to spell all those words, for nothing more than having Miss Deets pin a ridiculous little paper star on his shirt.

Then one day Miss Deets made her fateful error. "Now, pupils," she announced, "I think it important for all young ladies and gentlemen to be able to speak in front of groups. So for the next few weeks we are going to have Show and Tell. Each day, one of you will bring one of your more interesting possessions to school, show it to the class, and then tell us all about it. Doesn't that sound like fun?''

Three-fourths of the class, including myself, cringed in horror. We didn't own *any* possessions, let alone interesting ones! Miss Deets looked at me and smiled. "Patrick, would you like to be first?"

I put on my thoughtful expression, as though mentally sorting through all my fascinating possessions to select just the one with which to enthrall the class. My insides, though, churned in terror and embarrassment. What could I possibly bring to Show and Tell? The only thing that came to mind was the family post-hole digger. I imagined myself standing up in front of the class and saying, "This is my post-hole digger. I dig post holes with it." No, Miss Deets probably had a longer speech in mind. I glanced around the room. Several hands of the rich kids from town were waving frantically for attention.

"Uh, I need more time," I told Miss Deets. Like about fifteen years, I thought, but I didn't tell her that.

"All right, then, Lester?" Miss Deets said to one of the rich kids. "You may be first."

The next day Lester brought his stamp collection to Show and Tell, and held forth on it for about an hour. An enterprising person could have cut the tedium into blocks and sold it for ice. But Miss Deets didn't seem to notice. "That's wonderful, Lester!" she cried. "Oh, I do think stamp collecting is such a rewarding hobby! Thank you very much, Lester, for such a fine and educational presentation. Would you like to clean the blackboard erasers during recess?"

I glanced at Crazy Eddie. He was yawning. Eddie had a habit of yawning to conceal his occasional moments of maniacal rage. Good, I thought.

At recess, Eddie refused to play. He stood with his hands jammed in his pockets, watching Lester on the third-grade fire escape, smugly pounding the blackboard erasers together. "Did you ever see anything more boring than that stupid stamp collection of Lester's?" he said to me.

"I think I did once," I said. "But it was so boring I forget what it was."

"I've got to come up with something for Show and Tell, something really good," Eddie said. "What do you think about a post-hole digger?"

Lester's stamp collection, however, was merely the beginning of a competition that was to escalate daily as each succeeding rich kid tried to top the one before. There were coin collections, doll collections, baseball-card collections, model airplanes powered by their own little engines, electric trains that could chew your heart out just looking at them, and on and on until we had exhausted the supply of rich kids in class. We were now down to us country kids, among whom there were no volunteers for Show and Tell. Miss Deets thought we were merely shy. She didn't realize we had nothing to show and tell about.

Rudy Griddle, ordered by Miss Deets to be the first of us to make a presentation, shuffled to the front of the class, his violent shaking surrounding him with a mist of cold sweat. He opened a battered cigar box and tilted it up so we could see the contents. "This here's my collection of cigarette butts," he said. "I pick 'em up along the road. You'll notice there ain't any shorter than an inch. If they's an inch or longer they's keepers. Some folks pick up cigarette butts to

smoke, but I don't. I just collect them for educational pur-
poses. Thank you." He returned to his desk and sat down.

The class turned to look at Miss Deets. Her mouth was
twisted in revulsion. Suddenly, someone started clapping!
Crazy Eddie Muldoon was applauding! And somebody else
called out, "Yay, good job, Rudy!" The rest of us country
kids joined in the applause and cheering and gave Rudy a
standing ovation. He deserved it. After all, he had shown
us the way. From now on, Show and Tell would *really* be
interesting.

Farley Karp brought in the skunk hide he had tanned
himself and gave a very interesting talk on the process, even
admitting that he had made a few mistakes, but after all, it
was the first skunk hide he had ever tanned. He said he
figured from what he had learned on the first one, the next
skunk hide he tanned he probably could cut the smell by a
good 50 percent, which would be considerable.

Bill Stanton brought in his collection of dried wildlife
droppings, which he had glued to a pine board in a tasteful
display and varnished. It was a fine collection, with each
item labeled as to its source.

Manny Fogg, who had been unable to think of a single
thing to bring to Show and Tell, was fortunate enough to
cut his foot with a double-bitted ax three days before his
presentation and was able to come in and unwrap the ban-
dages and show us the wound, which his mother had sewed
shut with gut leader. It was totally ghastly but also very
interesting, and educational too, particularly if you chopped
firewood with a double-bitted ax, as most of us did.

Show and Tell had begun to tell on Miss Deets. Her face
took on a wan and haunted look, and she became cross and
jumpy. Once I think she went into the cloakroom and cried,

because when she returned, her eyes were all red and glassy. That was the time Laura Ann Struddel brought in the chicken that all the other Struddel chickens had pecked half the feathers off of. Laura Ann had set the chicken on Miss Deets's desk and was using a pointer to explain the phenomenon. The chicken, looking pleased to be on leave from the other chickens, but also a little excited at being the subject of Show and Tell, committed a small indiscretion right there on Miss Deets's desk.

"Oh, my gahhh . . ." Miss Deets gasped, her face going as red as dewberry wine, while we third-graders had a good laugh. This, after all, was the first humor introduced into Show and Tell. From then on, those of us who still had to do Show and Tell tried to work a little comedy into our presentations, but nobody topped the chicken.

So many great things had been brought to Show and Tell by the other country kids that I had become desperate to find something of equal interest. Finally, I went with my road-killed toad, explaining how it had been flattened by a truck and afterwards had dried on the pavement, until I came along and peeled it up to save for posterity. The toad went over fairly well, and I even got a couple of laughs out of it, which is about all you can expect from a toad. Even so, Miss Deets chose not to compliment me on my performance. She just sat there slumped in her chair, fanning herself with a sheaf of arithmetic papers. I thought she looked a tad green, but that could have been my imagination.

Now only Margaret Fisher and Crazy Eddie were left to do their Show and Tells. I knew Eddie was planning to use several pig organs from a recent butchering, provided they hadn't spoiled too much by the time he got to use them. But Margaret changed his plans.

She brought in a cardboard box and proudly carried it to the front of the room. Miss Deets backed off to a far corner, her hands fluttering nervously about her mouth, as Margaret pried up the lid of the box. A mother cat and four cute baby kittens stuck out their heads. Everyone *ooh*ed and *aah*ed. Miss Deets went over and picked up one of the kittens and told Margaret what a wonderful idea she had had, to bring in the kittens, and would Margaret like to clean the blackboard erasers at recess?

At recess, Eddie was frantic. "I can't use the pig stuff now," he said. "I got to come up with something live that has cute babies."

"How about using Henry?" I suggested.

"Yeah, Henry's cute, all right, but he don't have no babies."

"Hey, I've got an idea!" I said. "I know some things we can use and just *say* they're his babies. But you'd better call Henry a girl's name. Heck, Miss Deets won't know the difference."

Eddie smiled. I knew he was thinking he would soon have back his old job of cleaning the blackboard erasers for Miss Deets.

Everyone in third grade counted on Crazy Eddie Muldoon to come up with a spectacular grand finale for Show and Tell. An air of great expectation filled the room as Eddie, carrying a lard pail, marched up to make his presentation. Even Miss Deets seemed to be looking forward to the event, possibly because it was the last of Show and Tell, but no doubt also because she expected one of her favorite pupils to come up with something memorable.

With the flair of the natural showman, Eddie deftly flipped off the lid of the lard pail, in which he had punched air holes. "And now, ladies and gentlemen," he announced, "here is Henrietta Muldoon . . . my pet garter snake." He held up the writhing Henry.

Miss Deets sucked in her breath with such force she stirred papers on desks clear across the room.

"And that's not all," Crazy Eddie continued, although it was plain from the look on Miss Deets's face that Henry all by himself was excessive. Beaming, Eddie thrust his other hand into the pail.

"Here, ladies and gentlemen, are her babies!"

He held up the squirming mass of nightcrawlers we had collected the evening before.

At first I thought the sound was the distant wail of a fire siren, a defective one, with a somewhat higher pitch than normal. It rose slowly and steadily in volume, quavering, piercing, until it vibrated the glass in the windows and set every hair of every third-grader straining at its follicle. We were stunned to learn that human vocal cords could produce such an unearthly sound, and those of a third-grade teacher at that.

Mr. Cobb, the principal, came and led Miss Deets away, and we never saw her again. We heard later that she had gone back to teach school in the city, where all the kids were rich and she could lead a peaceful and productive life.

As the door closed behind her, I turned to Eddie and said, "I think you've cleaned your last blackboard eraser for Miss Deets."

"Yeah, I suspect you're right," he said sadly. Then he brightened. "But you got to admit that was one whale of a Show and Tell!"

Cry Wolf

Sometimes it seems I can scarcely turn around nowadays without being entertained. I am surrounded by TV sets, radios, videocassette recorders, video games, stereos, and assorted other electronic home entertainment. Then there are movies, plays, concerts, and the symphony. (True, I only attend the symphony when my wife can rent the straitjacket that looks like a tuxedo, which, too, is considered by many people an entertainment.) Spectator sports exist in such copious variety and number that I can scarcely find time for matters of more consequence, such as my hunting and fishing. In short, I live in a veritable sea of entertainment. But it was not always so.

During the years I was six and seven, my mother taught all eight grades in a little log schoolhouse tucked back into a remote valley of the Rocky Mountains. There was no electricity, no running water. Our stove had been constructed out of an old steel barrel by a local madman. Countless fires had burned little holes through the metal of the stove. Sparks popped through these holes to provide our only home

entertainment, which consisted of stomping out the fires
they started. The closest newspaper route ended forty miles
away. Our mailbox was sixty miles away, which was all
right, because we didn't have any magazine subscriptions
or anyone to write to us. We didn't have a radio. Our only
source of news was the Ouija board, and it wasn't reliable,
always trumping up phony illnesses in healthy but distant
members of the family or giving accounts of those who had
passed on. The departed generally seemed to be having a
better time than we were.

I did what I could to create my own entertainment. Once
I affixed a pry pole to the girls' privy and hid in the brush
until my victim entered, a foxy eight-year-old by the name
of Opal. Then I leaped out and pushed up and down on the
pole, causing the privy to rock precariously to and fro. (This
was one of my earliest experiments in physics, and, I believe, quite a successful one.) The rocking produced im-
mensely satisfying screeches from inside the privy, thus
proving my hypothesis as to that effect. Little did I realize
that this innocent prank would typify my future relation-
ships with women, all of whom would regard me with suspicion, even when I wasn't carrying a pry pole.

Winter bored me most, with the roads to town blocked for
months by snowdrifts, and the privies frozen solidly to the
ground. Aside from stomping out stove-spark fires, our family's only other entertainment during the winter occurred on
Tuesday evenings. Although we had no radio, our nearest
neighbors did. Their cabin could be reached only by hiking
three-quarters of a mile on a narrow trail cut through thick
second-growth forest. The trail began with a long, winding,
decaying bridge once used by a logging operation to cross
several meanders of a creek and a swampy area. The bridge
consisted largely of gaping holes suspended high in the air

caught up with them at the bridge, where they stood ing and gathering their wits for crossing this last but or obstacle to safety. I stared glumly at the lacework of , whitened by snow and ice, outlining the dark and gap- holes.

Remember," Mom said, her voice shaky with barely rained terror, "just one step at a time. Keep your bal- e and take it nice and slow. I'll go first and—"

t that instant, from the darkness of the trees right above came the loud hoot of a wolf!

'Wolf! Wolf!" I screamed. "They got us!"

As a mist of snow settled around my small, defenseless dy, I vaguely made out the darting, hurtling, leaping, unding figures of Mom and the Troll midway across the idge. They sailed over an open expanse of darkness, arcely touched down on an icy log, then took off again, gging and zigging in midair, picking out occasional foot- olds as if by radar, and elbowing each other for position the turns.

The wolf hooted again above me.

"Wolves don't hoot," I said to myself, smiling with sat- sfaction over the proof of another of my hypotheses about uman motivation. "Owls hoot." Everybody knew that, ut Mom and the Troll had momentarily forgotten it when ubjected to the proper stimulus. Interesting. I felt a little guilty, conducting experiments on live humans, but still, a small boy snowbound in a remote valley of the Rockies had to invent his own entertainment as best he could.

and roughly defined by rotting timbers. A cautious person would think twice before crossing it in daytime and summer. Only desperate fools would consider the possibility of crossing the icy structure in the dark of a winter night.

"Watch where you step," my mother said one wintry Tuesday night. "This log is really slick."

She carried a torch made of a length of broomstick and a cloth dipped in kerosene. Huge shadows of ourselves leaped and played among the trees as the Troll and I, in single file, followed Mom inch by inch along the log.

"Hurry," the Troll said. "We don't want to be late."

"There's plenty of time," my mother said. "Careful! Lord save us! I nearly slipped off the bridge! Here, Trudy, grab my hand and pull me back up, so I can hook my other leg over the log. Ah, thank you, dear. Whew!"

"C'mon, Ma," I said. "Stop foolin' around. Now you've gone and dropped the torch in the crick. We're gonna be late for sure."

"Would you stop your eternal whining! Reach back and whack him one, would you, Trudy dear? Thank you. All right, now just another four hundred feet and we'll be off the bridge."

Exactly what was this entertainment for which we risked crossing the bridge? Why, nothing less than the "Henry Aldrich" radio program, a joyous half hour of unrelieved laughter and entertainment. I remember that the show opened with the teenager's mother calling out, "Hen- reeeeeeee! Henry Aldrich!" Even now, the recollection of that parental cry gives me a warm feeling of joyous antici- pation. I have a soft spot in my heart for dumb ol' squeaky- voiced Henry Aldrich, for without him to look forward to each Tuesday night I surely would have died of boredom at age six in a remote valley of the Idaho Rockies.

The rich people who owned the radio, the Burfords, were a family of woodcutters: a stringy little father, a plump mother, and four sons the size and intelligence of pickup trucks. We would all gather around the radio and listen to the hilarious predicaments Henry was all the time getting himself into, and we would laugh until our sides ached, which was what everybody said every Tuesday evening, "I laughed till my sides ached!" After the program was over, someone would repeat something Henry had said, and we would all be off again, laughing until our sides ached even more than they had before.

"I don't know how one boy can git hisself into so much trouble," Mr. Burford would say, wiping his eyes. "A week don't go by but what that Henry pulls some fool stunt."

As soon as the Henry Aldrich show was over, Mrs. Burford would clean off the kitchen table and my mother, Mr. and Mrs. Burford, and the smartest of the Burford boys would play a few rounds of pinochle. The Troll and the—it goes without saying—dumbest of the Burford boys would sit in a corner and giggle. I would curl up with the dogs by the stove and try to get a bit of sleep, if for no other reason than to take my mind off the fact that we still had the bridge to cross on our way home.

The pinochle game served not merely to milk more entertainment out of a Tuesday evening, but had a practical purpose as well. A wolfpack roamed the valley in those days, and the playing of pinochle gave us the opportunity to get a reading on the whereabouts of the wolves. The point of this was to improve the odds that the paths of the wolves and the McManuses would not intersect on our way home. Every so often, Mr. Burford would say to one of the boys, "Cleetus, go check on the wolves."

Cleetus would step outside the cabin and stand there in

the frosty air until he heard the wolves back inside and report, "They's mo above Wampus Crick, Pa!"

"Still too close," Mr. Burford wou is it?"

When Cleetus finally reported the wo tance away, the McManus family would Coats would be thrown on, hasty good we would charge out the door of the Burf for home.

On the Tuesday night in question, the w their usual ruckus, possibly because there the night was black as pitch. Cleetus stoo frosted over, without hearing a single wol hear 'em, Pa," he reported. "They could b

"Maybe you all should spend the night, suggested.

"Thank you, no," Mom said. "We'll go

"Wha . . . ?" I said. "We don't know w are! You gotta be kidding! Wild horses coul out that door!"

Five minutes later we were scurrying alon ward home, walls of darkness towering abo sides. The wolves, gaunt and hungry, their bla over their sharp white fangs, could be lying i anywhere, watching for any telltale signs of we panicky herd of hurrying humans. Crouche trail, the leader of the pack points to the small ging farther and farther behind the two larger or the best bet," he says.

"Wait for me," I hissed through frozen bre long legs of my mother and the Troll churned u powdery snow in the distance.

Pigs

Retch Sweeney, Al Finley, and I were returning from a fishing trip in Finley's new station wagon, when we saw the crudely lettered sign nailed to the gatepost of a ramshackle farm: PIGS $7.

"Holy mackerel!" Retch said. "Did you see that? Pigs for only seven dollars!"

"Just keep driving," Finley mumbled peevishly. Exhausted, irritable, and still shivering from a little tumble he had taken into the river, he had ordered me to drive us home, while he sprawled pouting on the rear seat. He claimed Retch had bumped him off the log on purpose.

Still, the drop into the river couldn't have been more than fifteen feet at most, although from Finley's long, quavering screech you might have supposed he had fallen off the Matterhorn. Also, if he had just relaxed and collected his senses, he would have realized that there was no point in trying to swim upstream in rapids, thus saving himself a lot of wasted effort. The waterfall he went over was nothing to brag about either, but, typically, Finley had to create practically a ma-

jor drama before he was swept over the brink. I think what
irritated him the most, though, was Retch's yelling, "Stop
thrashing about, Finley, you're scaring all the fish!" That,
of course, was inconsiderate of Retch and even untrue, because I caught a nice rainbow just a few seconds after Finley
washed by me.

"Pigs for seven dollars apiece!" Retch cried. "Stop the
car! Listen to me! I got an idea!"

"Will miracles never cease," Finley grumbled.

"Here's what we'll do," Retch went on. "You guys buy
two pigs for each of us, that's two times three times seven
which comes to . . . uh . . ."

"Forty-two dollars," I said, since I didn't want to grow
old waiting for Retch to work out the arithmetic.

"That's right," Retch said. "So here's what we'll do.
You guys buy the pigs and I'll raise 'em. Then, come fall,
we'll have them turned into smoked hams and bacon and
sausage. Don't that sound good?"

"That's the dumbest thing I ever heard of," I said.

"Wait a second," Finley said, using his shrewd tone.
"You mean next fall I end up with two full-grown hogs for
a total price of twenty-one dollars? You'll do all the work
and pay all the cost of raising them, Sweeney?"

"Yeah," Retch said. "I'll just gather up all the spoiled
food the supermarkets throw away. Won't cost me nothin',
except maybe for some grain."

"Sounds good to me," Finley said. "But we can't haul
six pigs in my station wagon. You'll have to come back and
get them with a truck or a trailer."

"That's over two hundred miles round trip," Retch said.
"No, we got to take them now. What we'll do, see, is fold
down the backseat. They'll just be little pigs, so we can tie
'em up in gunnysacks. No problem."

"Well, okay," Finley said, ever alert for a bargain. "I just don't want pigs messing up my car."

My own reluctance remained intact. Unlike Retch and Finley, I'd had actual experience with pigs. I was but seven years old when my friend Crazy Eddie Muldoon asked me if I wanted to ride one of his family's pigs. "Why not?" I said, never one to spend much time contemplating consequences. We walked out to the pigpen and Eddie pointed to three huge hogs snoozing in the odorous mire.

"That one's Champ, next to him is Trigger, and the biggest one, that's Silver. Ol' Silver, he'll give you the best ride, 'cause I ain't broke him yet. Just climb up on the fence there and plop down on Silver's back and grab him by the ears. You can be the Lone Ranger and I'll be Tonto."

"Which one is Tonto going to ride?" I asked.

"Tonto ain't gonna ride. He's gonna sit here on the fence and keep a lookout for my pa."

Caught up in my anticipation of trotting about on Silver, I had forgotten about that standard precaution. Ninety percent of the things Eddie and I did required keeping a lookout for his pa.

I climbed the fence and plopped down on Silver's back, grabbing him by the ears in a single smooth movement, and started my Lone Ranger yell: "Hi . . . !" In one second flat, two hundred pounds of furious pork sizzled around the pen like a piece of ice on a hot griddle. Champ and Trigger joined in the general ruckus, but without anywhere near the enthusiasm of Silver. I quickly tired of the ride and began looking for a way to dismount, finally deciding that the next time Silver tried to scrape me off on the fence, I would make a jump for it. Intelligent beings that pigs are, however, Silver made a few quick calculations in elementary physics, arriving at the conclusion that if he was to stop suddenly, whatever was on his back would continue on at the same momentum until the pull of gravity counteracted the original force. He instantly put this theory to the test, and with great success. The hog's sudden stop launched me like a torpedo off his back and sent me streaking headfirst through six-inch-deep residue of pig.

I got up and shook off as much muck as I could, carefully wiping a couple of eyeholes so I could see. Tonto sat unperturbed on the fence, nibbling a straw as he studied the situation. Without speaking to him, I climbed out of the pen and headed for the creek. I knew what Tonto wanted to say, that it was building up in him, demanding to be said, because an opportunity like this might never arise again in his lifetime. When I was a safe distance away, but not so far that I couldn't make out the words uttered in a small, pleased voice, he said it:

"Who was that masked man, anyway?"

From that moment on, I never had any use for pigs. They had left a bad taste in my mouth.

"I don't want to have anything to do with pigs," I told Retch and Finley. "They're nothing but trouble."

"No trouble for you and me, though," Finley said. "We won't even see them again until they're hams and bacon."

He had a point there. I swung the car around and we drove back to the farm. A grizzled little man came out of the house picking his teeth and rubbing his rounded belly as though he had just finished a large dinner.

"Let me handle this," Finley said out of the corner of his mouth. "This guy looks like a sharpie. That seven-dollars sign was probably just a come-on. Guy probably thinks he's lured some dumb city slickers into his snare. Ha!"

I was glad we had a shrewd person like Finley along to handle the deal.

"Howdy," the farmer said. " 'Spect you fellas want to buy some pigs."

"Might be," Finley said. "If the price is right."

The farmer appeared a little puzzled, and I could see that Finley had got in a deft stroke.

"If you seen the sign, you seen the price," the farmer said. "Seven dollars."

"Uh-huh," Finley said shrewdly. "Now, we're not talking about the runts of the litter, are we? We're talking good, healthy pigs?"

"Yep," the farmer said. He pointed to a large, fenced area where about fifty little pigs ambled about. "There they are. You can take your pick."

"Well, that seems fair enough," Finley said. "You got a deal. We'll take six pigs."

"Good. That'll be forty-two dollars. I'll throw in some gunnysacks for free to haul 'em in."

Finley handed him the money. The farmer counted it and tucked it into the bib pocket of his overalls. "They're your pigs now," he said. "Go catch the ones you want."

"We have to catch them ourselves?" Finley asked. "How do we do that?"

"Don't know," the farmer said, turning to walk back to his house. "Ain't none of 'em been caught yet. But you fellers might be faster than most folks."

"Uh, I don't suppose you would be interested in buying the pigs back?" Finley said, now more nervous than shrewd.

"Nope. I already got a surplus of pigs."

Our first tactic consisted of each of us selecting a pig and trying to run him until he tired out. But all the pigs looked pretty much alike. So when one of the chased pigs got tired, he would charge into a crowd of other pigs, and a fresh pig would race out the other side, so that we were competing individually against what amounted to a pig relay. Another problem was, the pigs stood only about a foot high on all fours. When we closed in on one, we had to run stooped over in order to grab at it, the posture not unlike that of a person doing a toe-touching exercise while sprinting. After an hour of this fruitless—or pigless—effort, we met for a consultation.

"I think we should all three of us concentrate on one pig at a time," I said. "That way we can run it into a corner, grab the bleep-of-a-bleep, and dump it into a gunnysack."

"Good idea," Retch said. "Now, can any of us straighten up enough to hold the sack?"

"I can raise my hands to my knees," Finley said.

"Close enough," I said. "You hold the sack."

Only a few minutes after midnight, we cornered the sixth of our pigs and sacked him. We folded down the backseat of Finley's station wagon, spread out a couple of plastic rain slickers, dumped our sacks of little porkers on them, and headed for home.

"I still say it's cheap hams and bacon," Retch said, his body still curled in the shape of a question mark. "What say, Finley?"

"I say, 'Owww owww ooooooh ah oh my aching back,' that's what I say! And I better never lay eyes on these pigs again until they are hams and bacon!"

"You got nothing to fear," Retch said, thereby proving his inadequacy as a prognosticator.

The pigs, apparently content in their gunnysacks, occasionally emitted a quizzical grunt but otherwise caused no commotion. Retch and Finley dozed off. I hung on the steering wheel, sucking an occasional drag from a vacuum bottle of cold coffee to keep my eyelids from sneaking shut.

After half an hour or so, we hit the freeway and had a straight shot home. Tired and aching, I paid little attention to a scuffling noise behind me. Suddenly, on the back of my neck, I felt a moist snout, bristly little whiskers, and a hot panting breath. I must have been dreaming with my eyes open, because for a second I thought it was my old high school girlfriend, Olga Bonemarrow. I quickly realized, however, that the cause of these sensations wasn't chewing bubble gum, which ruled out Olga.

"A pig's loose!" I yelled.

"Ye gads!" Finley said. "He's off the rain slickers too! Don't scare him! If he does anything on the carpeting, I'll kill him now with my bare hands!"

Alas! The shrill tone of Finley's voice prompted the pig to commit an act of hygienic indiscretion right on the station wagon's new carpeting, even as the culprit stood blinking his little pig eyes at his would-be assassin. The resulting wail from the carpeting's owner sent the pig tearing about the rear of the station wagon in a frenzy almost equal to that of Finley. This alerted the other prisoners to the festivities, and in a matter of seconds they had torn loose from their sacks and joined in the bedlam. The hysterical squealing was deafening.

"Would you please stop squealing, Finley?" I said. "You're giving me a headache."

"Stop the car!" Finley ordered. "We've got to get the pigs back in their sacks!"

"Shucks," Retch said sleepily. "They won't hurt nothin', Finley. You can hose out the back of the station wagon tomorrow and it'll be good as new. Let the little porkers have their fun."

"I said stop the car!"

"I can't stop," I said. "You can only stop on the freeway

if you have an emergency. You know that, Finley. Now calm down.''

"Then someone's got to climb back there and stuff the pigs back in their sacks!''

"Be my guest,'' Retch said.

"Oh, good heavens, I should know better than to hang out with you nitwits,'' Finley said, climbing into the back and grabbing at a pig.

The station wagon rocked and swayed as Finley thrashed about, stuffing pigs into sacks, only to have them escape when he lunged after another one. I turned up the radio in an effort to drown out the hideous sounds. Distracted as I was, and possibly because of strong motivation to end the drive as quickly as possible, I pressed down on the accelerator pedal a bit too hard. At that moment a pig leaped over my shoulder and into my lap, only to be pursued by a sweating, snarling Finley, who dragged the squalling beast over my face and into the back. The car swerved. No sooner had I got it back under control than a pulsing blue light filled the interior of the vehicle, followed by the wail of a state patrolman's siren rising ever so slightly above the din of Finley and the pigs.

"Cripes,'' Retch said. "Now you gone and done it, Finley.''

A fragrant hush fell over our little group as I pulled the station wagon to the edge of the road and stopped. The patrolman walked cautiously up to my lowered window, his right hand resting on the unbuttoned flap of his holster. The man knew a wild bunch when he saw one.

"I can explain, officer,'' I said, handing him my driver's license.

"I bet,'' he said, not at all friendly. "Had a bit too much to drink, right, sir?''

"Haven't had a drop," I replied. "I'm waiting until I get home to have too much to drink."

"Oh, yeah? Well let me just take a whiff of the inside of your vehicle, sir. Whewwweeeeee! *Choke! Gag!*" He staggered back, barely catching his balance and almost falling into the ditch.

"As I tried to explain, officer," I said, "we have a man in back here trying to stuff pigs in sacks and—"

"That's enough of that, pal. I don't put up with wise—" The patrolman flicked the beam of his flashlight into the back of the station wagon. Six pigs and Finley returned his stare. Smiling weakly, Finley held up a gunnysack, apparently as proof that he was engaged in a legitimate activity.

"You see," I continued, "what happened was—"

"Okay, okay, stop explaining," the patrolman said. "I'll let you off this time. But don't ever let me catch you guys driving while stuffing pigs in sacks again!"

"Rest assured, officer," I said. "You never will." Seldom have I been so confident in one of my predictions.

The MFFFF

No matter what you may have heard, hunting is a competitive sport. The competition, of course, comes not from seeing who can shoot the most or biggest game, but from the display of one's physical fitness. How often have you been taunted by your hunting companions when you've suggested taking a rest after a steep climb to the top of a hill? I myself once regularly underwent such humiliations, even when the climb up the hill wasn't made in a vehicle.

Finally, I said to myself, "You must do something about your rotten physical condition. You must get in shape once and for all." As it happened, I wasn't listening to myself at the time, and thus I was saved endless hours of boring exercise.

Most of my exercise has come from strenuously avoiding all forms of physical fitness, although I do find it amusing to run the Jane Fonda workout cassette at fast speed on the VCR. But, you ask, how do you avoid being taunted by your hunting companions for being out of shape? I'm glad you asked that, because otherwise this article would end right here. The answer is the McManus Formula for Fitness Fakery. By carefully following the MFFFF, you too can be a winner in the Great Outdoors.

First, you must instill in your hunting partners the belief that you have hidden reserves of supernatural strength that can be called up at any moment. Here's one ruse that works very well. Conceal your lunch somewhere on your person, such as in the game pocket of your jacket. Then, when you are a couple miles downhill from your hunting vehicle and in need of extensive rest, you say, "Oh-oh, I forgot my lunch. I'll just run back to the car and get it. You fellas wait here."

Naturally, this announcement is going to be greeted by hoots and hollers and a few threats of bodily harm from your companions, but you must persist. Charge off into the brush. As soon as you are out of sight of your companions, slow to a walk—this goes without saying—for the next fifty yards or so. Make sure you are far enough away so you can't hear their comments about you, because that would depress you unnecessarily. Sit down on a log and rest for fifteen or twenty minutes. Then return to your companions, bursting out of the brush at a speed sufficient to impress them but not enough to make you breathe hard.

"You back already?" one of them will say. "Ha! You didn't go back to the car for your lunch after all!"

"I did so," you say. "But the car was locked and you forgot to give me the keys, Harold!"

Now repeat the entire performance, this time with the car keys, and return with your lunch. Works like a charm. Your friends will be so impressed by your superhuman feat that they will not want to risk humiliation by challenging you to a race up a mountain with a hindquarter of elk on your back, or some similar form of suicide. You will become a legend in your own time, or at least someone might mention your feat in a bar sometime during the following week, but, of course, don't hold your breath.

Next we have the Nature Lover ploy. Recently I was on a three-state turkey hunt that outfitter Ron Dube (pronounced "Doobee") conducts out of Buffalo, Wyoming. Ron runs the spring hunt up where the corners of Montana, Wyoming, and South Dakota meet. Thus, during a typical week-long hunt, you can shoot a turkey in each of three states, provided you're not as selective about turkeys as I am. (I select only slow, dumb, nearsighted gobblers, in my dedicated effort to improve the gene pool of the North American wild turkey. But what thanks do I get?)

After I had followed Dube around the hills for a couple of hours, I became more than a little impressed at the speed with which he moves up vertical ground.

"How many states *wheeeeeeze* have we covered so far?" I asked him.

"Jeepers criminy," Ron said, using his most serious cussword. "We're still in South Dakota. Why, you getting tired?"

"Me? Are you *wheeeeeeze* kidding? Heck no."

"Good," Ron said, pointing to a mountain that must have been an offspring of the Grand Tetons. "Because there's a big gobbler hangs out on the other side of this rise."

"My lunch *wheeeeeeze!*" I cried. "I forgot my *wheeeeeeze* lunch! Back at the *wheeeeeeze* car."

"Don't worry about your lunch," Ron said. "I always carry plenty of food in my pack."

Always expect any single ploy in the McManus Formula for Fitness Fakery to be countered by a companion, especially an experienced outfitter like Dube. Now, note carefully how I moved smoothly from the Lunch gambit to the Nature Lover ploy.

Ron and I started up the Teton, his legs gobbling up a yard of altitude at every stride while mine nibbled on inches.

"Hey, hold up a second, Ron," I called. "What's this little *wheeeeeeze* flower here?"

Dube came back down the mountain, ready as always to impart some bit of exotic nature lore to an interested client. He stared at the little flower.

"Why, that's a buttercup," he said. "Jeepers criminy, haven't you ever seen a buttercup before?"

"I guess not this close," I said, since my face hovered mere inches above the ground, watering the little yellow flower with dribbles of sweat.

A few yards more up the mountain, I ran out of breath again. "Hey, Ron, what's this *gasp* flower?"

Dube loped back down the mountain. "Still a buttercup," he said.

"Oh," I said. "It's a little different shade of *gasp* yellow. What *gasp* makes it a different shade of yellow?"

Thus cleverly did I slow our ascent of the hill, engaging Dube in a discussion of each species of flora on the mountainside, including everything from lichen to ponderosa pine, some of them three and four times. Never once did Ron catch on to my clever tactic, even when I led him into the realm of geology.

"What's this *choke gasp* odd protrusion?" I asked, pointing at the object with my tongue.

"A rock."

"Well, *gasp* I'll be darned. A rock."

Clare Conley, the editor of *Outdoor Life* magazine, also hunts with Ron Dube, usually for elk. He refers to a trek

with Ron as a "Dube death march." He claims that since
Dube always carries a backpack, the best method for slowing him down is to sneak a bunch of rocks into his pack
when he isn't looking. I consider such conduct unsportsmanlike, mean, and contemptible, and besides, as far as I
could tell, Dube didn't even notice the rocks. As I told Conley, if you are going to use an unsportsmanlike, mean, and
contemptible method of slowing down your hunting partner,
use one that's guaranteed to work.

Such is the Picture-Taking ploy. This is a truly wonderful
gimmick. When the point of exhaustion is arrived at where
your feet are no longer taking orders from your brain and
each is just wandering around on its own, then you call out
to your partner, who may be but a speck on the horizon
ahead of you, "Hey, Harold! Come back here! This will
make a great shot!"

"So shoot it!" the speck on the horizon calls back.

"No!" you yell. "I want you in the picture!"

The speck on the horizon then scuttles back toward you
until finally it becomes Harold. It is a well-known truth that
no outdoorsman can resist having his picture taken against
a wild and rugged backdrop.

Naturally, when Harold arrives he immediately realizes
that the scenery here is absolutely identical to all the other
scenery within a fifty-mile radius.

"What's so great about this shot?" he asks.

"Good gosh, don't you see it?" you say, putting Harold
on the defensive, because he has always been insecure in the
area of art appreciation. (It helps to have a companion who
had trouble coloring inside the lines back in elementary
school. In fact, I make this one of my main criteria in selecting a hunting companion.)

"Man," you continue, "look at the rare quality of light

on the snow (water, grass, sand, dirt, mud) here. Stand over there so I can get this light on your face. Take off your hat. No, put the hat back on. Take off your jacket. Hold your rifle in your left hand. No, right. Good, hold that pose while I put a roll of film in the camera." And so on. With any skill at all, you can stretch the Picture-Taking ploy into a good thirty-minute rest.

Warning! Merely feigning to take a picture under these circumstances may cause your partner to break off your friendship, not to mention various parts of your anatomy, because he will insist on seeing and having copies of each of the two dozen shots you took of him on the trip. ("And here's the one of you standing in a field of gray snow. Oh, this is a good one of you standing in a field of gray snow. Look at this one of you in the field of gray snow. And this one . . .")

Finally, we come to the Sock-Changing ploy. Most of your companions won't catch on to the fact that you're sneaking a rest if you sit down to change your socks every so often, particularly if you comment, "Blisters can incapacitate an outdoorsman faster than anything. The best precaution against blisters is to change your socks frequently." The one problem consists of having to leave most of your gear behind in order to have enough room in your pack for socks. But a night or two in the wilds without a sleeping bag can be an invigorating and memorable experience, particularly if you have the right attitude and aren't exhausted from charging up and down mountains all day without sufficient rest stops. I have tested this ploy thoroughly and have found that you can get away with one sock-change per mile of terrain covered, if you have sensible and considerate companions. But how often does that happen? Right. I have some hunting partners who change their own socks only

once a month on the average, so with them I go directly to
the Picture-Taking or Lunch ploy. The Nature Lover ploy
doesn't work well with them, either, because if you ask one
of them to identify a plant for you, he's likely to say,
"That's just your regular old weed. Now quit foolin'
around and get a move on."

One further cautionary note on the Sock-Changing ploy.
It should be carried out expeditiously. For example, I have
found that if you try to extend the rest period by playing
"this little piggy went to market" on your toes, some hunters will become irritated and attempt to throw you off a cliff.

Well, those are all the tips I have for sneaking a rest on
hunting trips without suffering ridicule from your macho
friends. If you don't like the tips, however, you can always
go to an extreme and start getting in shape. Just don't ask
me to hunt with you.

Summer Reading

Of all the classifications of literature, the only one distinguished by season is "summer reading." Why is that? Do you really care? I thought not. Nevertheless, I have put a good deal of work into this essay and you had better darn well pay attention.

The phrase "summer reading" seemingly reeks of literary permissiveness. Many readers interpret this to mean they can read anything they please between May and September. Not so. A set of rules governs summer reading, and the consequences of ignoring them can be serious. For example, a man was arrested recently for reading Proust's *Remembrance of Things Past* on a public beach while naked. If you have any sense, you'll leave Proust in the library where he belongs.

Now for the rules. First of all, books containing any of the following disqualify themselves as summer reading.

Ideas—Nothing so provokes disgust in a summer reader as suddenly coming upon ideas in a seemingly innocent book. This is why my own books are often recommended for summer reading. An idea occasionally will creep into something I write, but usually I catch it before the book goes to press. An editor once found a small idea in one of my stories and nearly suffered an infarction. "Listen, McManus," he snarled, "we pay you to write, not think." Thinking and summer reading are incompatible. If the book has caused either you or the author any thought, then it is probably regular reading and not fit for summer consumption.

Socially Redeeming Qualities—I'm reading a book right now in which medieval monks are being murdered by someone or something. At first I thought this in itself might be a socially redeeming quality, but apparently it isn't. Although this book does contain some ideas, the author had the decency to introduce them with Latin phrases, so they can be easily recognized and thus skipped over. Several times I've caught myself almost thinking while reading the book, so I doubt I would recommend it for summer reading.

Self-Improvement—Summer is the time of degeneration, if not degeneracy. We readers of summer have no interest in improving our minds, bodies, sex, children, pets, lawns, manners, mileage, etc. We are loath to read anything that might improve us in any way. Generally, we prefer summer books that leave us a little bit worse for having read them.

Dust-Jacket Blurbs—The perfect summer book lacks even one dust-jacket blurb. This means that reviewers could not find a single favorable thing to say about the book. Also, any book containing blurbs with the words *sensitive, intelligent,* or *brilliant* should instantly be rejected. Blurbs containing the words "gross," "disgusting," "insipid," and "truly rotten'' suggest the books might make good summer reading, but they are hard to find.

Any summer-reading book should contain one or more of the following.

Sharks—If a shark doesn't show up someplace in a book, it's probably not worth summer reading. I just finished a police action novel in which the villain gets eaten by a shark in the final chapter. I thought it was great. My wife tried to read the book but said she thought it would have been better if the author had been eaten by a shark in the first chapter. She lacks the necessary credentials of a summer reader, however, and her judgment can't be trusted in these matters.

Illicit Sex—Combine sharks and illicit sex and you have a darn good summer read. The sex scenes should not be too graphic, of course. Otherwise, they are offensive or, worse yet, fall into the category of self-improvement.

Murder—A murder or two should occur early in the book, unless a shark is present, in which case a minor character can be eaten. By early, I mean no later than the first half of the second page. *Gorky Park* opens with three murders on the first page, which is about the maximum number you can expect in that limited space. The murders should be tastefully done, preferably in the manner of the early British mystery writers. They should also be fairly tidy and conventional. Summer readers don't like their victims turning up as pot roasts or that sort of thing.

Cardboard Characters—Nothing ruins a good summer-reading book faster than well-rounded, complex characters. They slow the action. The plot sits there idling while the hero ponders some moral dilemma. There should be no moral dilemmas in summer fiction. If the hero must ponder, he should ponder sharks, illicit sex, or the villain. Ideally, he will ponder nothing and get on with his pursuit of one of the above.

That pretty well sums up summer reading. Now hop to it. Summer doesn't last forever, and before you know it we'll be back reading the heavy thinkers—Fyodor Dostoyevski, Herman Melville, Sigmund Freud, Shirley MacLaine. . . .

Angler's Dictionary

Note from the lexicographer: In my continuing effort to compile a dictionary of uncommon angling terms for use by newcomers to the sport of fishing, I have recently defined the following words and phrases as they are commonly understood by experienced fishers. You will note that the dictionary is not in alphabetical order. This is a labor-saving device. I have never been very good at the alphabet anyway, and have come to regard it as a frightful nuisance, useful only for soup. If some critics see this as a shortcoming in a lexicographer, I have only this to say to them: Picky, picky.

Here, then, is the "Angler's Dictionary."

Wicker creel—This is a lively folk dance often performed by a fisherman on the occasion of slipping the point of a No. 4 hook under a fingernail. While the dancer performs the wicker creel, his companions typically will clap rhythmically and encourage him with shouts of "Go, man, go!"

Kitchen table—Of all the dangers that confront an angler, the one seldom mentioned to beginners is the kitchen table. It is a repository of various essential fishing tackle that never makes it out to the fishing site. As a personal example, I laid a brand-new, ninety-dollar, 6-weight flyrod on our kitchen table one day last summer, and it was never seen again. This is an extreme case, of course. Usually the item can be found still on the kitchen table upon the angler's return, although it often has been buttered and drenched with maple syrup.

Car roof—This is a deadly variation of the kitchen table. Car roofs are to fishing what black holes are to outer space. Whatever is placed on them even for a few seconds gets sucked into another dimension. "Where's my fly book?" one angler will say to another. His companion will reply, "I saw you place it on the car roof at our last stop!" The two anglers look at the car roof. It glares back at them with smug emptiness. I have had cameras, fly reels, sack lunches, and numerous other items sucked into the void by car roofs. Never place any fishing gear on a car roof, and, even more important, never sit on one yourself.

Spinning reel—This is a form of comical walk performed by anglers who have spent an evening around the campfire exchanging stories and sipping 150-proof rum. The spinning reel is usually attributed to excessive consumption of night air, although a doctor friend of mine claims that theory is nonsense. He speculates that the true cause is altitude. "We're only three hundred feet above sea level," I told him once. "Well, that's altitude, isn't it?" he replied. "In every instance of the spinning reel that I've ever witnessed, there has been altitude present." I for one am certainly not going to argue with scientific evidence.

Cast—There are almost as many kinds of casts as there are kinds of anglers. There's the foot cast, the leg cast, the arm cast, the full-body cast, and many more. One of the common methods of achieving a full-body cast is by following the advice of a fellow fisherman who yells, "Take a running jump, Stan! You can make it!"

Sinker—An angler who steps off a dock with a ten-horse outboard motor in his arms is referred to as a *sinker*. Some athletic anglers claim they have actually swum fifty or sixty feet to shore while dragging a ten-horse motor, but it is generally believed that they simply walked along the bottom until they reached shallow water. Since the other anglers present continued to concentrate on putting their tackle together, no eyewitness accounts exist as to what actually may have been the case.

Split-shot sinker—An angler who suddenly drops into the water while standing with one foot on the dock and the other in a drifting boat and holding a ten-horse motor in his arms is known as a *split-shot sinker*. First he splits, then he sinks like a shot. The split is usually accompanied by a hideous screech, so horrible in fact that other anglers present have been known to look up briefly from sorting their tackle boxes.

Purist—An angler who doesn't catch any fish, because he uses only dry flies the size of dandruff, often conceitedly refers to himself as a *purist*. Other anglers refer to him as a *loon*.

Fresh air— This is what the purist claims he enjoys getting out in, even though he doesn't catch any fish.

Fishing journal—An imaginative work of sub-literature in which the angler records the weight, length, and species of fish he didn't catch.

Rock—This is a tool used in the field to make delicate repairs on expensive fishing reels, because the tool kit was sucked into the void by the car roof.

Pink nighty—Dry-fly purists enjoy coming up with colorful names for the various bits of fluff they employ not to catch fish. However, when they see a lunker brook trout that they really want, they will often tie on a No. 10 Pink Nighty, which usually does the job. Also known as a *ten-inch nightcrawler*.

New car—An expensive dehydration chamber that ten-year-old boys use to dry out strings of perch on hot July days.

Blue upright—Although primarily the name of a dry fly, it also denotes ice fishermen in Wisconsin.

Blue darter—Refers to a Wisconsin ice fisherman who has just stepped through a hole in the ice.

Best fishing time—Yesterday or last week.

Worst fishing time—Now.

Gaff—What old gaffers do when they have a young fisherman trapped in a boat with them. Fatal only if the young angler leaps out of the boat and attempts to swim three miles to shore while carrying his tackle box.

Fishing tackle—This is an extreme but useful maneuver for preventing a fellow angler from reaching the best fishing hole before you do.

Carp—This is a form of immature behavior displayed by fishing partners, often consisting of whining, after you have clipped off the tips of their flyrods by inadvertently pressing the switch on your car's automatic windows.

Forked stick—Stylish fishermen often use forked sticks to carry their catch, after a sixty-dollar creel has been claimed by the kitchen table.

Who wants raw egg in their beer?—A little joke that charter-boat fishing captains wish they had never called out to their clients after the boat has been tossing about in rough seas for six hours.

Fair-to-middlin'—This is the standard reply used by

fishing resort owners to describe the worst fishing in fifteen years.

Good—Fishing resort owners use this word to describe fishing that's fair-to-middlin'.

Awesome—A favorite word of resort owners to describe fishing, it is based on the fact that they heard of some kid who caught two small perch the previous week.

Let's tell Mommy I caught some of the fish—This is a pathetic plea that comes up anytime a father takes his little son or daughter fishing for the first time. The situation is delicate and should be handled with utmost care. One way is to promise the youngsters ice cream or candy. Then there's a good chance they'll let you get away with the ruse.

The Mountain

"April," the poet wrote, "is the cruelest month." Boy, no kidding! If I had read that poem while in third grade at Delmore Blight Grade School, I might very well have said, "How true! How true!" Although it's more likely I would have said, "Do I really have to read this stupid poem?"

Outside the grimy windows of third grade, April was dissolving the last lingering stains of winter. Inside, however, Miss Goosehart was stretching us pupils on the rack of the multiplication table, a fiendish device once used to torture young children. April was slipping from our grasp. Flowers were bursting into bloom, trees were leafing out, and the sap was rising, namely one Milton Clinker, to give the answer to four times seven. Who cared about four times seven, anyway? Only a sap like Clinker would want to multiply while all outdoors filled up with April.

Miss Goosehart cranked up the rack another notch. "Pat, would you take one of your wild guesses at three times six?"

I scratched my head in a show of concentration. Crazy
Eddie Muldoon, who sat behind me, leaned forward and
whispered something. I thought maybe it was the answer.
But it was, "Saturday, let's climb the mountain."

Eddie was so far gone with April he didn't even realize it
was my turn on the rack. He wasn't called Crazy Eddie for
nothing.

"Give me a hint," I said to Miss Goosehart. "How many
letters does it have?"

Had Eddie really said, "Let's climb the mountain"?
What a terrific idea! My heart did a handspring at the very
thought. "Okay," I whispered back. Eddie groaned. Miss
Goosehart now had him on the rack, trying to wrench out
the answer to seven times seven. It was ghastly.

The mountain Eddie and I intended to climb reared up
abruptly from the valley about a mile from our farm. At
night, in the glow of the moon, the mountain took on the
shape of a sleeping dragon, the high, ragged peak forming
the hump of its back; a long, descending ridge was its neck,
and another knob of mountain was its head. The head of
the dragon rested on the valley floor not far from Delmore
Blight Grade School. It was easy to imagine the dragon
awakening one night, stretching out its neck, and gobbling
up the school in a single bite. In the morning the only evidence of what had happened would be a gaping hole in the
ground and the smile on my face.

The dragon lived only at night. Daylight revealed a solid,
no-nonsense mountain, with a craggy granite peak, sheer
cliffs, a crosshatching of crevices and ledges, and, lower
down, thick forest.

The mountain talked to me. I don't mean to imply that
we held long philosophical conversations, but even as a

small boy, sitting on the back steps of my house, I could hear it calling: "Pat! Pat! Come climb me! It will be fun! And I won't try to kill you, as I do some folks!"

On an April Saturday at the age of eight, I learned that mountains don't always tell the truth.

Before setting out for the mountain, Crazy Eddie and I told our mothers that we were going for a hike. It seemed like the only decent thing to do.

"Don't you go barefooted," my mother ordered. "It's too early in the year, and you'll catch your death. Stay away from the crick, because it's too high and you might fall in and drown. Don't tease the Guttenbergs' bull, because he might gore you to death. Don't cut yourself with your jack-knife because you might bleed to death. Don't wander around in the woods, because you might get lost and starve to death." She stopped to catch her breath and search her memory. "Oh yes, don't climb any tall trees because you might fall to your death."

Mothers can be depressing. Mom couldn't recall any disasters with me and a mountain, and I saw no reason to give her further cause for worry by going into a lot of unnecessary detail about the hike. My mother was downright permissive compared with Eddie's parents. On Saturday mornings at his house, the family had to get up an hour early to run through the list of don'ts for Eddie and still have time enough to get the milking done by eight.

Eddie, as I expected, was late getting to my house. He looked good, swaggering into the yard, his eyes bright with the anticipation of great adventure. His broken arm had healed nicely. I envied the scar at his hairline, the result of his not having ducked quite low enough as we threw ourselves under the Guttenbergs' fence, and just in time, too. (There's nothing quite so disgusting as getting bull slobber

sprayed all over you.) I thought maybe Eddie was conceal-
ing his limp from me, but apparently the fall from the cottonwood tree hadn't done any lasting damage. He seemed
fit, which was more than I could say for his parents, the two
most nervous people I'd ever known. As Eddie said, they
probably drank too much coffee.

"Your folks skipped 'Don't mountain climb,' didn't
they?" I said, grinning.

"Yep," Eddie said. "Never even occurred to them. They
hit everything else, except dirt-clod throwing. The lump on
your head go away?"

"More or less," I said. "It was my fault. I would have
ducked faster if I'd known you were gonna charge my fox-
hole. You ready?"

"Sure," Eddie said. "Let's go!"

An hour later we were working our way up the lower
slope of the mountain. Here and there the April sun had
slipped in among the trees and incited a riot of buttercups.
We each picked a handful of the little yellow flowers and
put them in our shirt pockets to take home to our mothers.
For some reason, mothers seemed thrilled by these little
squished balls of withered flowers. So what the heck. The
effort more than paid for itself with the PR spinoff. Say
you were found guilty of getting home five hours late and
had been sentenced to some whacks, the number to be determined by how long it took the parent's arm to feel as
though it were about to fall off; the idea was to haul out
the pitiful little bouquet and present it to your mother just
before the penalty was to be executed. Nine times out of
ten the bouquet got you a stay of execution. Wilted bou-
quets of wildflowers were not only good PR but excellent
insurance.

"You got enough buttercups?" I asked.

"Yeah," Eddie said. "These should do the trick. Anyway, we probably won't get home that late."

We climbed the mountain for an hour, expecting always to reach the top at the next rise. But there was always another rise and another after that and still another. Finally we broke free of the sloping forests and could survey the valley down below. The familiar fields and pastures had taken on a new look, shaping themselves into intricate rectangular patterns of spring browns and greens. Mouse-size cars scurried up and down the roads.

The climbing had now become more difficult. Eddie, a born leader (the worst kind), took charge of planning our ascent. It seemed to me his motive was not to find the easiest route but to test our character. When we came to a rocky knob we could just as well have walked around, he insisted that we make a frontal assault on it, finding little cracks and protuberances with which to pull ourselves upward. When I complained, he said, "This is the way mountain climbing is done. Any sissy could walk around."

Now we were high up on the mountain. The cars below had shrunk to the size of ladybugs; cows and horses appeared no larger than ants.

"It's getting steeper," Eddie said, panting.

"And colder," I said, shivering.

"That means we're nearly to the top," Eddie said.

"I don't know," I said. "We've been 'nearly to the top' fifteen times already. Maybe we should turn back."

"Only a sissy would turn back," Eddie said.

"I'm not turning back," I said.

"Okay," Eddie said.

Among the patchwork of fields below, I could see my own little tiny warm house. It called to me in the same way the mountain had. "Turn back," it called. "Turn back."

"I'm not turning back," I muttered.

"Okay, okay," Eddie said. "I didn't say you were."

Eddie no longer had to seek out difficult routes. *Every* route had become difficult. Once we had to drop into a deep ravine, losing altitude we had already paid for, only to have to buy it again, inch by inch, foot by foot. On the shaded side of a ridge we encountered deep drifts of snow, streams of ice water gushing from beneath them. The April sun had rotted the drifts, and at every step we sank in almost to our waists, the gritty snow stinging our legs raw.

Once, as we stopped to rest against a gnarled, stunted tree, my pants freezing to my legs, my lungs aching, I stared out over the empty space to where Delmore Blight Grade School snuggled up against the edge of town. Old Delmore Blight Grade School, I thought. Well, this is a heck of a lot better than being *there*. The thought gave me strength to go on.

Late in the afternoon, finally, the jagged peak of the mountain came into view. There was no mistaking it. A few hundred yards more and we would reach the ridge that led up to the peak. After that, the summit would be as good as ours!

But our ascent now appeared to be blocked. A twenty-foot cliff rose directly above us. To get around it we would have to drop far back down the mountain and climb up again by another route. I knew now that we would have to turn back. Only a crazy person would try to scale the cliff.

"Boy, this looks dangerous," Eddie said. "Great! I bet a lot of guys would chicken out right now. Here, let me give you a boost."

I hauled myself over the lip of the cliff only to discover a great expanse of rock sloping steeply toward me. Water bright with sunlight trickled in tiny streams down the face of the rock. There was no going back now. I began to crawl on my belly up the slippery slab of granite—five feet, twenty feet, fifty feet. I thought: *Just about got it made. Then I can watch ol' Eddie climb up here. Ha! Bet he'll be scared. Just a bit more and I can reach for the upper edge of the slab. Only ten inches to go! Six inches! Three inches! Oh-oh, I slipped back an inch. Better get a foot in a crack or something. Still slipping. Still slipping! Dig my fingernails into the rock! No! Wait! What's happening? I can't stop sliding! I'm going too faaaaaaaaaaaaaaast!*

Buttons flew off my jacket and shirt like shrapnel. The knees ripped out of my pants. I felt as though I were leaving a streak of hide all the way down the rock. I whipped over on my back to see where I was going. Then I saw where! I tried to whip back on my stomach so I wouldn't have to see. But it was too late. I shot off over the edge of the cliff.

WHUFFF!—I saw green. I had flown spread-eagle right into a scrawny but merciful fir tree. It bent over and deposited me with a plop on a patch of snow.

I lay on my back, eyes closed, letting life drain back into me. Except for a few miscellaneous patches of missing clothing and hide, I seemed all right. Presently I heard a scrabbling in the rocks off to one side. I knew it must be Eddie. So I played dead to teach him a good lesson. He didn't say anything, but I could sense him looking down at me. I held my breath so he couldn't see me breathe. I could feel him studying me intently, wondering how he could explain the fatal accident. ("I tried to talk Pat out of it, but he wouldn't listen. Can I go play now?") Peeking from beneath my eyelids, I saw him bend over me. What was he doing? Checking to see if I might still be alive? Eddie set a large rock on my chest. He put another rock next to it, and then another. He was burying me.

"Stop!" I yelled. "I'm alive!"

"I knew you were still in there," Eddie said. "I saw you peeking out from under your eyelids. I just wanted to practice burying a person, in case I ever have to. Did you know you're bleeding through your shirt?"

"Just a scratch," I said. I had always wanted to say that.

"Good," Eddie said. "But next time you get up near the top of that slab of rock, grab hold of a branch or something. Otherwise, you'll just slide off again. C'mon, I'll give you a boost to get you started."

I stared hard at Eddie. "Forget it," I said. "I'm not climbing back up there."

"But we're so near the top!" Eddie cried. "You can't quit now. Look, you can even see the peak."

Against my better judgment, I looked at the peak, that ragged, twisted point of granite gleaming against the dark blue of the April sky, so beautiful and majestic that the mere sight of it could make a person dizzy with awe. Suddenly I knew what I had to do, and I did it.

"Cripes!" Eddie wailed. "Not on my shoes!"

I wiped my mouth on my torn, bloody sleeve. "Sorry about your shoes, Eddie, but I'm going back down the mountain. You can climb to the top by yourself if you want."

"I will, too!" Eddie said.

I limped back the way we had come. Then I heard Eddie running after me. "But I'll climb it some other time," he said. "Now I'd better help you."

"To do what?" I asked.

"To pick buttercups," Eddie said. "When your mom sees those clothes, you're going to need a whole lot more buttercups than you've got."

Not Long
for This Whirl

As at the beginning of every spring in our part of the country, water invaded the world and ruled over it with a cold and merciless hand. It drizzled out of the murky sky, oozed up from the saturated ground, and roared in torrents from the melting snow in the mountains, filling the creek and river channels to overflowing, washing out bridges, pump houses, and any other structure within its grasp. Water that could find nothing more enterprising to do with itself turned the dirt roads of the country into sloughs of mud the color and consistency of butterscotch pudding.

It was not a fun time for a teenage outdoorsman. More or less trapped in the close confines of our farmhouse with my mother, grandmother, and sister (the Troll), I grew increasingly frustrated and irritable that my weekend had been washed out by the water. Seeing her chance, my grandmother rushed to aggravate my sorry state of mind.

"Your grandpap wouldn't let a little water keep him all wrapped up in the house like a festering sore, I can tell you that!'' Gram said smugly, barely containing her glee. "He'd be out there right now, cutting down trees and skidding 'em to the mill. I can't even get you to go cut a pile of kindlin' wood. Nope, your grandpap shore wouldn't let a little water keep him in the house."

"Yeah, I can see why," I said meanly, trying to cut right to the quick. But Gram had tough, quick, thick skin, and a stirring spoon with which she bonked me on top of the head.

"You're practically as worthless as that old reprobate Rancid Crabtree," she probed. "I ain't seen hide nor hair of him since the melt came, which is one good thing. You and him are both pantywaists, lettin' a little dampness make you hole up by the fire like a couple of sick pups."

"Arrrrh!" I yelled, bringing a burst of delight to Gram's face. "I am not a pantywaist, whatever that is. And besides, Rance is sick. He says he's dying."

Gram activated her scoff to full power. "You believe that? Well, let me tell you, Crabtree is too mean and ornery and dirty and smelly to die. And he's so lazy, nobody could tell if he did. What ails him is probably somebody offered him a job and scared the old windbag so bad he took to his bed."

I yawned to show her how bored I was with the debate, but I hoped Gram was right. My heart had welled with grief ever since the old woodsman told me, "Ah ain't long fer this whirl." I assumed he meant "world," but on the other hand he loved a good whirl as much as any man I've ever known, so I couldn't be sure. Rancid had taught me everything I knew about woodcraft, hunting and fishing and trapping and numerous other manly arts. Now my mentor in all things I valued most seemed to be dying. I had hesitated for several days even to visit him, for fear I might find him dead. Gram's subtle attempt to cheer me up had helped a little. I began to accumulate enough gumption—one of Gram's favorite words—to make a watery trek to the Crabtree shack, just to see if Rancid still lingered among the living.

"Why don't you heat up some of that chicken noodle soup we had for supper?" I said to Gram. "Maybe I'll take some over to Rancid. It can't make him any sicker than he already is."

"You think I'm going to waste good soup on old Crabtree, you must be tetched in the head!" Rancid was not one of Gram's favorite *Homo sapiens,* or even, for that matter, vertebrates. She stomped off to the kitchen, muttering to herself.

Turning back to the window, I practiced my melancholy stare, getting it perfected for the time I became a writer. All writers have melancholy stares, because they have seen so much misery. I couldn't wait to leave home so that I could start seeing misery.

Through the sheets of rain, I noticed a cloud of smoke moving down the mud road toward our house. It was accompanied by a series of explosions, like a tiny war advancing across the country in search of a truce. I recognized the phenomenon immediately—Mrs. Peabody. Mrs. Peabody was a mountain car that my friend Retch Sweeney and I had built ourselves and named after our favorite high school teacher.

Retch sloshed up the walk to our door. "You ain't gonna believe this," he said. "But I got Mrs. Peabody with me."

"I know that," I said. "I'm not blind and deaf, you know."

"I mean the first Mrs. Peabody, our teacher!"

I wouldn't have believed it, either, except for the beaming of Retch's big ugly face with the rain dribbling off the wispy chin-whiskers. As Retch hurriedly explained, Mrs. Peabody had telephoned the Sweeney house and asked Retch if he could drive her out to a friend's house in the country, where she had been invited for the weekend. With the roads so bad, she said, she thought it would be safer if she had a man drive her. I guessed that she hadn't been able to find a man, so she called Retch. Although Retch probably could have borrowed the family sedan for such an important mission, he thought this would be a good opportunity to show off the mountain car to Mrs. Peabody.

"Want to go along?" Retch asked me. "Mrs. Peabody's friend lives up past the Market Road junction. Shouldn't take more than an hour both ways."

"Hey, Gram," I yelled. "I'm going out with Retch. I'll have him drop me off at Rancid's to see how he's doing. You don't mind, do you, Retch?"

"Naw. That road up to Crabtree's will really show Mrs. Peabody what the mountain car can do."

"Well, you just hold your horses," Gram yelled, "till I get this hot soup poured in a jug."

Gram poured the soup in a little crockery whiskey jug we kept in the kitchen for decoration. I thought Rancid would probably appreciate the appropriateness of the container, since he had several just like it that he didn't use for decoration.

Mrs. Peabody sat hunched over in her namesake, a bit of wet hair plastered to her forehead. "How do you like our mountain car, Mrs. Peabody?" I asked, climbing in beside her.

"Oh, it's fine, fine," she said. "Quite lovely."

"I thought you'd like it," I said. "Retch and I built it ourselves."

"Really? I never would have guessed."

"Yep, what we did was, we left off everything that wasn't essential, like fenders and the exhaust pipe and muffler."

"And seats," she said, smiling tightly.

"Yeah, well, actually we couldn't find any seats. I hope that apple box isn't uncomfortable."

"Good heavens, no! Shall we go now, boys? The fumes in here are beginning to corrode my nasal passages."

"Wasn't me," Retch blurted.

"The exhaust fumes," I said. "That's one of the reasons we didn't put any windows on the car. The fumes dissipate to the outside. How'd you like the way I tossed in that vocabulary word, Mrs. Peabody—'dissipate'?"

"Very nice," she said, wiping a drop of water from the tip of her nose. "Very nice."

"Did you know we named the car after you?"

"Yes, I know," she said. "It's a rare honor."

I noticed a distinct lack of enthusiasm on the part of Mrs. Peabody when I asked Retch to swing by Rancid's shack so I could drop off the jug of soup. Her lack of enthusiasm became even more pronounced as we started slipping and sliding down the mud road that led to the Sand Creek bridge.

"Stop! Stop!" she shrieked. "There's no bridge! No —— bridge!"

Later, Retch and I vaguely recalled that Mrs. Peabody had inserted into her shriek a bad word, but decided that couldn't possibly have been the case, she being a teacher.

Retch and I laughed. "Sure, there's a bridge," Retch said. "You just can't see it because it's about a foot underwater. Now I got to stop talking, so I can concentrate on exactly where the bridge is supposed to be, 'cause I sure wouldn't want to miss it. Har dee har!''

The mountain car crept slowly across the flooded bridge, the current trying to get a hold on the vehicle and hurl it and us into the maelstrom. Mrs. Peabody snatched a cigarette out of her purse and lit it with a trembling hand.

"I didn't know you smoked," I said, smoking not being common among the ladies I knew at that time.

"Only on occasion," she said. "This happens to be one of the occasions."

Having safely traversed the bridge, we ran out of luck on the steep slope of mud leading up the hill to Rancid's shack. Its tires spinning wildly, the mountain car suddenly lurched sideways into a ditch of rushing water, where it stuck fast.

Mrs. Peabody heaved a sigh that could have knocked a bird off a fence post, if the bird had been stupid enough to be out in the driving rain. "What'll we do now?" she asked, her voice quavering only slightly.

"No problem," I said. "I'll go get my friend Rancid Crabtree and have him tow us out with his truck. I just hope he's not dead yet, because then we'll be in a real fix."

"Dead?" Mrs. Peabody said, digging frantically in her purse for another cigarette. "What do you mean, dead?"

I didn't waste any time explaining, because the car seemed to be sinking deeper into the ditch by the second.

Splattered with mud halfway to my neck, I bounded through Rancid's door.

"Knock! Knock!" he croaked, his hand reaching for a shotgun beside his bed. "How many times Ah got to tell you?"

He didn't look well, wrapped up with a blanket all the way to his stubbly chin. His energy seemed drained out of him by the long winter, the watery spring, and, of course, his fatal illness.

"Good," I said. "You're not dead yet."

"Not yet," he growled feebly. "Ah'm gettin' thar, though."

I held up the whiskey jug of chicken noodle soup. "Look here! I brought you a little something."

Rancid's face broke into his big, snaggletoothed grin. "My, my! Ah knew thar was some reason Ah let you hang out with me all these y'ars. Mighty thoughtful of you. Now hand me thet jug. Iffen Ah got to die, Ah might jist as well die happy."

"Don't you want a bowl and spoon?" I asked. "It's chick—"

Rancid tilted the jug back and took a big swig. His eyes popped wide in horror. A huge shudder convulsed his body, and he spat the chicken noodle soup from one side of the shack to the other. "Gol-dang a-mighty!" he cried. "It's spiled! It's got dead worms in it!"

"No, it's not spoiled," I said. "It's not whiskey, for gosh sakes. It's chicken noodle soup. Gram sent it."

"Ah shoulda known!" he said. "Why, thet ornery old she-critter. I wasn't dyin' fast enough to suit her, so she put thet soup in a whiskey jug to disappoint me to death."

I quickly explained about the stuck mountain car to Rancid and suggested that he tow us out with his truck. "I hate to bother you while you're dying, but we've got to get the car out."

"Cain't," Rancid said, taking a tentative sip of the soup. "Ah'm too sick. Jist leave her be till the ground dries out. Thet's what Ah'd do."

"I know. But we got our teacher, Mrs. Peabody, in the car," I pleaded. "She can't wade through mud all the way back to our house."

A thoughtful expression came over Rancid's face. "This Mrs. Peabody, what's she look like?" Even fatally ill, Rancid still had a strong interest in good-looking women, a promising sign.

"She's beautiful," I said, without lying much.

"Whar's Mr. Peabody?"

"I don't think there is one. I never ever heard him mentioned."

"Hmmmmmmm," Rancid said. "Mebbe Ah could tow you out. This hyar soup seems to be bringin' some of maw strangth back."

He whipped off the blankets and climbed out of bed, fully clothed right down to his boots.

"You don't take your clothes off when you go to bed sick?" I asked.

"What fer?" he said. "If Ah got well, Ah'd jist have to put 'em back on again."

It made sense to me.

After much fussing around, finding chains and ropes and Rancid's cranking his old truck to life, we arrived back at the scene of the accident. He parked the truck at the top of the hill, since he didn't want to get it stuck, too. If he didn't die right away, he said, he might need the truck again before the mud dried out. Rancid slogged down the hill and peered in at the huddled forms of Retch and Mrs. Peabody—particularly Mrs. Peabody, I was sure, because he had told me many times he had seen all he ever wanted to see of Retch.

"Howdy, ma'am," he said. "What seems to be the trouble here?"

It was a dumb thing to say, since any fool could see what the trouble was. I knew Rancid was just making conversation, even if Mrs. Peabody didn't. From the look on her face, I suspected she doubted the solution to the problem had just arrived.

"We're stuck," Mrs. Peabody said.

"Yep, and pretty good, Ah'd say. Ah'll tell you what we's got to do hyar. You and the animal has got to git out of the car, 'cause maw truck won't pull it out with you in it."

I poked Rancid in the back. "You don't expect Mrs. Peabody to wade in mud all the way up to her knees, do you?"

"Nope. Ah'll carry her up the hill and put her in maw truck."

"Uh, you think that's wise, you dying and all?"

"Sheddep and mind your own bidness."

At that moment, I realized that Rancid possessed the soul of a romantic, and that right here, on a mud-choked, rain-splattered mountain road in a remote corner of Idaho, chivalry was about to be resuscitated by a grizzled old woodsman. I was embarrassed.

As soon as the plan was explained to Mrs. Peabody, Rancid scooped her up in his arms and, ignoring her embarrassed protests, began tromping heavily up the slope to his truck. I soon ascertained that Mrs. Peabody was a bit plumper, the distance to the truck greater, and the mud deeper than the old woodsman had judged.

To conceal the strain on him, Rancid began to hum: "Hmmmm mmmmm mmmmm." Presently, however, the hum turned into more of a rhythmic and sustained grunt: "Mmmmm mm mmunh uuunh UNNNNNGH UNNGH UNGH!" And slowly his shoulders began to cave in and his back to bend, with Mrs. Peabody swaying precariously above and ever closer to the mud that sought to claim her.

"You're dropping meeee!" Mrs. Peabody wailed.

With a herculean effort and a hideous groan, Rancid wrenched the lady back up and plodded on, his boots making great long sucking sounds with every slow step he took in the mud. My teacher looked as if she was on the verge of hysteria, and I began to wonder how this might affect my grade in sophomore English. I also wondered if what I was witnessing might qualify as a misery, just in case I ever wanted to write about it.

At last Rancid reached the truck, and plopped Mrs. Peabody on the seat. He collapsed on the running board, alternating between wheezing and sucking in great gasps of air.

"Well, thank goodness," Mrs. Peabody said. "I certainly never thought we would make it. I did get some mud splattered on my coat, but it will probably brush right off when it dries. Now maybe you should hurry and get the car out of the ditch, Mr. Crabapple."

"Wheeeeze GASP Wheeeeze GASP," Rancid replied.

Presently, he pushed himself up and started dragging the heavy logging chain back down the hill to the mountain car. After a good deal of work, we finally got the chain hooked up and the car pulled out of the ditch, turned around, and headed back in the direction of the invisible bridge.

Rancid and I unhooked the tow chain and tossed it in back of the truck.

"Well, all that's left to do now is carry Mrs. Peabody back down to the car," I said. "Maybe you should just let her walk, you dying and all. I think my grade in English is already shot anyway, so it wouldn't hurt much."

"Nope," Rancid said. "Ah wouldn't feel right, lettin' her

walk through this slop. What a man's gotta do, a man's gotta do, even if he is dyin'."

"I'm ready for another ride," Mrs. Peabody called. "But please do try to be more careful this time."

"Yes, ma'am," Rancid said. Suddenly he turned and staggered backwards up to the door of the truck, where Mrs. Peabody stood on the running board. He bent over and put his hands on his knees. He seemed to be suffering some kind of attack. The exertions of carrying Mrs. Peabody and towing the car out of the ditch had taken their toll on him, and now seemed to be hastening his departure from this whirl even sooner than he'd expected. I was almost paralyzed with shock and grief.

"Good heavens!" cried Mrs. Peabody. "Are you all right, Mr. Crabapple?"

"Ah ain't exactly feelin' chipper, if thet's what you mean," Rancid said. "So Ah'd 'preciate it if you'd climb aboard before Ah sink any deeper in the mud."

It was astonishing. In one afternoon I had seen chivalry suddenly reborn and just as suddenly snuffed out again. And chivalry was not the only thing snuffed out. Watching Rancid carry my English teacher piggyback down the hill to the mountain car, where the genetic accident known as Retch Sweeney howled in delight, I knew for certain that my slight hope of ever passing sophomore English had also just expired.

Tagging along behind Rancid and his human backpack, I could not help but feel sorry for Mrs. Peabody. All she had wanted was to be driven out to her friend's home in the country, where the two dignified ladies would spend the day sipping tea and discussing great literature. Now here she was, suffering the humiliation of being carried piggyback through the mud and rain by a smelly old mountain man.

Rancid turned and backed up so that Mrs. Peabody could dismount into the open doorway of the car. I braced myself for the lash of sarcasm for which Mrs. Peabody was famous.

But to my astonishment, she was laughing. She held out her hand to the dumbfounded mountain man. "Rancid, you dear man," she said. "That was wonderful! I haven't ridden piggyback since I was a little girl! How can I thank you for all you've done?"

Rancid made some strange sound as he tried to untie his tongue.

"Oh, I'll tell you what," Mrs. Peabody went on. "I'll have you over to my house for tea. I'll bet you're a wonderful conversationalist."

"Yup," Rancid said.

Retch cranked up the mountain car's engine. Mrs. Peabody, coughing only slightly, stuck her head out of a cloud of exhaust smoke. "Remember the tea, Rancid. I'll give you a call."

The rain had stopped. Rancid and I waved at the departing mountain car, he thinking he was waving good-bye to a new lady friend and I knowing I was waving good-bye to a passing grade in sophomore English.

All at once, the sun broke through and set all the water and even the mud to gleaming as far as the eye could see. The new buds in the birch trees sparkled like emeralds, the mountains emerged from mists, and somewhere off in a meadow, a lark warbled.

"Shucks, Ah feels pretty good," Rancid said, grinning his snaggletoothed grin. "Ah reckon Ah won't die after all." His grin vanished. "Dang it! That Miz Peabody didn't ask for maw number!"

"Even if she had asked for your number, Rancid, it wouldn't do any good. You don't have a phone."

"Ah knows that, but she don't. Probably when she tries to call me and Ah don't answer, she'll write me a letter." His grin revived.

"Yeah," I said. "She'll probably write you a letter."

I chose not to remind Rancid that he didn't have an address, either.

Claw of the Sea-Puss

One day some years ago, I awoke to find myself washed up on a beach in Hawaii. I made a mental note never again to partake of happy hour at a waterfront bar in Seattle.

Then it all came back to me. In atonement for some minor indiscretion, I had agreed to accompany my wife thousands of miles over the Pacific Ocean for the purpose of lying on sand, which is a popular pastime in Hawaii. Considerate husband that I am, I tried to conceal from Bun that I rank lying on sand well up on the list of the World's Ten Greatest Tediums.

"Boy, this sure is fun," I said. "Feel that sand, Bun? It's made out of pulverized diamonds. That's why the hotels have to charge the rates they do. Maybe later we can tour the diamond-pulverizing plant, what say? Wow, have you tried pouring the sand through the cracks between your toes? Fantastic! When I tell the boys back at Kelly's Bar & Grill about this, they'll be amazed. 'Tell us again, Pat, about pouring the sand between your toes,' they'll beg, but I won't tell them right away. I'll just tantalize them with . . ."

Bun propped herself up on an elbow and shot me a glance that missed by a hair and knocked an innocent seagull head-over-tailfeathers into the surf.

"I've got an idea," she said. "There was a dark little alley we passed yesterday. I saw a sign down there for a deep-sea charter office. I don't know why I didn't mention it then. Anyway, why don't you go see if you can charter a fishing trip for yourself?"

"What!" I said. "And give up lying on sand with you? A man would have to be an inconsiderate lout to do something like that!"

The sand was still spraying out of my thongs as I scurried down the alley in search of the charter office. A crudely lettered sign identified the establishment as Scroom & Scram Deep Sea Fishing Charters.

A sporty-looking chap extended his hand. "Welcome to Scroom & Scram! What can I help you with, pal?"

"Marlin," I said, shaking the hand.

"Biff. Good to meet you, Marlin."

"My name's not Marlin."

"I understand. My name's not Biff, either."

"What I mean is, I want to fish for marlin."

"Hey, no problem, pal. I can fix you right up."

The one-day charter cost me scarcely more than a two-week cruise on the Love Boat, but Biff said he was able to give me a discount because I would be sharing the boat with three strangers, provided they all made bail, ha ha. "Have a good time, Marlin."

Early the next morning I drove my rental car down to the lagoon where the fishing fleet moored, and began looking for the *Sea-Puss,* the boat I had chartered. It occurred to me that the owner of the boat must be of literary bent, for I recalled that the author James Thurber had somewhere written about a *Sea-Puss*. I think the line went, "The claw of the Sea Puss will get us all in the end." Although I hadn't known him personally, Thurber did not seem the fishing type, and I doubted that he had ever chartered the actual *Sea-Puss*. Still, one never knows. In any case, I was to recall the Thurber quote several times during the day.

At last I spotted the *Sea-Puss*, and was relieved to see that it was a large and nifty craft. There had been something about Biff that gave me the uneasy feeling my charter boat might turn out to be a nautical hybrid achieved by crossing the communal bathtub of a skid-row hotel with a sieve. This excursion might turn out all right after all, I thought. Since the captain and crew had not yet arrived, I sat down on the dock to wait. "No doubt," I muttered to myself, "the catch here is that my three charter partners will turn out to be mobsters, homicidal maniacs, or life insurance salesmen."

Presently, a taxi pulled up and three mild-looking individuals got out. They appeared legitimate and sane enough, and none carried a briefcase. They came over, shook hands, and introduced themselves as Ron, Bill, and Ed, a dentist, a college professor, and a minister. Much to my surprise, they were not old friends but had met only the day before on the *Sea-Puss*.

I said, "You fellows must have had a pretty good time yesterday, since you're going out on the *Sea-Puss* again today."

They smiled inscrutably, although none appeared to be an Oriental. When a non-Oriental fisherman smiles inscrutably, it means only one thing—he knows where to catch fish and he's not telling anyone. "Hoo-boy," I said to myself. "Today's my lucky day."

Soon afterwards the captain showed up, followed by a clothed primate of indeterminate species. The captain had a narrow, pinched face, with mean little eyes. The primate was the crew. Its name was Igor. The captain's name was Bly.

"So, back for some more," Bly greeted my three companions, who nodded meekly. The captain laughed evilly. Igor made guttural sounds of amusement.

"You!" Bly yelled, pointing at me.

"Wha-what?"

"Clean off those shoes. You think I want you tramping dirt all over my deck?"

"Uh, no, sir. I mean, yes, I'll clean them."

"One more thing. I hope you're not one of those posies who get seasick, although you certainly look the type. If you are, don't use the head."

"Don't use the head?"

"No—over the side. And another thing. NO BA-NANAS!"

"No b-bananas?"

"Right. Bringing bananas aboard a fishing boat is bad luck. Boats have been known to go for years without catching a fish after someone ate a banana on board. I catch you eating a banana on board, I'll keelhaul you! Now clean those shoes and go aboard."

Igor made threatening noises as I wiped off the soles of my sneakers with my handkerchief. Bly then ordered us aboard. My fellow charter partners scurried up the ladder to the deck ahead of me. I could tell from their frightened demeanor that they were intimidated by the captain and Igor. They were also insane. Otherwise, why return to a boat like this?

I had previously encountered rude charter captains, but

only rarely. This fellow and his crew took the prize as the worst I'd ever run afoul of—real nasties, if you get my drift. How, I wondered, could a boat like this stay in business, given its customer relations? Then I caught a whiff of a familiar odor. It was the sweetish smell of a tax shelter. Bly's only interest in clients was to snooker enough of them aboard to qualify the boat as a business and thus make it tax-deductible! The captain may have been rude and surly, but he wasn't dumb.

Still, why had my companions returned for a second outing? Perhaps the boat really did catch fish.

"How'd you do yesterday?" I asked Bill.

He glanced around to see if the Bly or Igor might overhear him. "Terrible," he whispered. "Didn't get a single strike. Captain spent half the day letting the boat drift to save fuel. It was horrible, worst day of fishing I've ever had."

"Oh."

Before putting out to sea, the captain lined us all up and gave us orders. "Don't touch any of the tackle! Don't ask a lot of fool questions! Don't get in the way of the crew, because Igor will run you over and squish you on the deck! Anyone thus squished on the deck must clean it immediately. Don't . . ."

I wondered vaguely where I might find a secondhand mast from which to hang the sporty Biff of Scroom & Scram Deep Sea Charters. I even thought about the size of the splash the scrawny captain would make if someone inadvertently threw him overboard. The sight of the hulking Igor quickly erased the thought from my mind.

The four of us charter clients cowered in the cabin as the boat put out to sea. I did not much care to be in such close quarters with three lunatics, even though they were nice enough. Besides lunacy, they all seemed to have in common a peculiar meekness.

After four hours of alternately trolling and drifting, we were overtaken by a dense cloud, which I thought at first was fog but which turned out to be boredom. The boredom sat on me like a foggy elephant. Two things I can't stand are work and boredom. I drifted off into merciful sleep.

Suddenly—POW!—one of the lines snapped from its outrigger. The reel screamed. Bly had assigned each of us a fifteen-minute section of the hour in which a fish hooked on any line would be that of the person assigned that time slot. The marlin had chosen my time slot in which to strike.

I ran toward the fighting chair, only to be squished by Igor, who was rushing to tangle the lines. I immediately leaped up, wiped all signs of the squishing from the deck, bounded into the fighting chair, strapped on the fighting harness, and waited for Igor to hand me the rod with my marlin on it. And waited. And waited. The primate was still busy tangling the lines.

"Lines tangled," Igor informed the captain, who quickly came down from the bridge to help tangle the lines even more.

"Oh-oh, he got off," the captain said, shrugging.

"No, he's still on," Igor said, giving Bly a wink.

"Oh yeah, right, I see that now," the captain replied. "Why did I ever think he got off while the lines were tangled?"

Bly thrust the rod at me. "Reel fast! Reel fast! Take up the slack!"

I cranked the reel furiously. But the whole line was slack.

"You lost him!" the captain shouted. "You lost him! Didn't I tell you to reel fast?"

I climbed out of the fighting chair. As I slunk back into

the cabin to join my companions, I noticed a change in them. Tension crackled in the air.

"Ask him if he's going to throw in with us," Ed whispered, indicating me. "After all, they did lose his marlin. That should be reason enough."

"We're going to scuttle Bly, Igor, and the whole damn boat," Ron whispered to me. "We've had enough of these louts. This is our revenge for the way we were treated yesterday. We sat up all night in a bar making plans. Are you with us?"

"You guys really are crazy!" I hissed. "Igor will kill you! Even if he doesn't, this is mutiny on the high seas—a hanging offense!"

"They'll never catch us," Bill whispered. "Are you in?"

I thought of the only marlin I had ever had a chance for in my entire life. Igor and the captain had lost it and then blamed me. I watched Ron open a satchel and begin taking out the blunt instruments. I didn't know if I was up to this kind of violence.

"You want one?" Ron asked.

"Yeah," I said. "Give me that eight-incher."

"Know how to use it?" Bill asked.

"Sure." I wiped my sweaty palms on my pants.

"Okay, let's do it!" Bill cried. "Now!"

Savagely, we ate the bananas. Bly and Igor never knew what hit them.

A Really Nice Blizzard

Henry P. Grogan, proprietor of Grogan's War Surplus, glanced up from his cash register as Crazy Eddie Muldoon and I bolted through the front door of his establishment.

"Quick, Mr. Grogan," Crazy Eddie shouted, "we need to buy a parachute!"

"A parachute? What you boys need a parachute for? And why ain't you in school? You fellas playin' hooky?"

"No, we're not playing hooky," I said. "They let us out early when the blizzard got too dangerous for us kids to stay at school. We've got to hurry because the school bus leaves to take us home in fifteen minutes."

"I don't know about sellin' a parachute to two fool kids," Grogan said. "You probably got some notion about jumpin' off a barn roof with it, ain'tcha? Gitcher selves killed or worse doin' something like that. No, I wouldn't feel right about it."

"We got over seven dollars between us," Crazy Eddie said, looking the proprietor right in the eye.

68

"But I've been wrong before," Grogan said. "Lemme see your money."

That was one of the things I liked about Crazy Eddie and Mr. Grogan. They both knew how to do a deal.

As Eddie and I hurried toward the door with our parachute, Grogan called after us. "Just out of idle curiosity, boys, what *are* you gonna do with that parachute?"

"Oh," I said, "because we got out of school on account of the blizzard, Eddie and I thought we could rig a sail with the parachute on a sled and sail across a field. This is the only good blizzard we might get this year, and we don't want to waste it."

"Sounds reasonable to me," Grogan said. "I always did like a good blizzard myself."

When we got home and tried to hook up the sail to my sled, we discovered that rigging a mast with an old two-by-four and a broom handle wasn't easy. We struggled with the contraption until we were both half frozen. Finally I said, "We'd better go get Rancid to help us. He'll know how to hook up a sail. Rancid knows just about everything."

Crazy Eddie and I tramped through the blizzard to Rancid's shack and, covered with a snow veneer, burst in without bothering to knock. The old woodsman was standing by his barrel stove, stirring something in a frying pan with a hunting knife. He leaped back with the knife raised in a stabbing position, and yelled, "Aiiigh! Aiiigh!" (Later he told us that yelling "Aiiigh! Aiiigh!" in a shrill voice is a good way to confuse evil forest spirits until you can think of a good way to deal with them.)

"Gol-dang an' tarnation, ain't you fellas ever heard about knockin'? Why, in another second Ah mighta had both of you chopped up into itty-bitty pieces! Ah got lightnin' relaxes.''

Eddie and I shook off our coating of snow onto Rancid's floor and rushed over to warm our hands by his stove.

"Why cain't the two of you shake off thet snow outdoors? Now it'll just melt and turn to mud. Ah'll be slippin and slidin' on it all day. You raised in a barn?"

"Sorry," I said. "We were just about frozen. Anyway, what we want is to have you help us build something we can use to sail on the snow. We've got a parachute for the sail. It'll work great in this blizzard."

"Hmmmm," Rancid said. "Let me thank about it a spell. You boys want somethin' to eat? Ah got plenty to go around."

"I don't think . . ." I said.

"Sure," Crazy Eddie said. "I'm starved." He had never yet had the experience of eating with Rancid.

Rancid blew the dust off a couple of tin plates he kept for guests and scraped out a glob for each of us from the skillet. He ate his share out of the skillet with the hunting knife.

"This is pretty good, Mr. Crabtree," Eddie said. "What is it?"

"As best Ah can recall, it's some chopped up b'ar meat, b'iled taters, beans, a chunk of hog fat, and, uh, let's see, oh, some dried wild mushrooms and a couple of squirrels. Why, you thank your momma might want the recipe?"

"She might," Eddie said. "She wouldn't use the wild mushrooms, though, because she can't tell the difference between the good ones and the poison ones." He chuckled, presumably at his mother's ignorance of wild mushrooms.

Rancid joined him in the chuckle. "Thet's okay, Ah cain't tell them apart neither."

"You *can't?*" Eddie croaked, staring down at the few little bites left on his plate.

"Nope, Ah cain't. But don't you worry none. Ah always tests wild mushrooms out on maw dog, Sport. If he likes 'em and don't drop daid, Ah eats 'em mawsef. Fed him a batch of these mushrooms a couple hours ago. Here, Sport, come show Eddie here you ain't daid. Sport! Here, Sport! Sport! Where is thet dang dog? He always comes when Ah calls him."

Eddie rose slowly from his chair, wild-eyed and suddenly pale. I stared uneasily at him as he selected a finger to put down his throat.

"Don't do it, Eddie," I said. "I'm still eating. Besides, Rancid doesn't have a dog."

After we'd all had a good laugh over the mushrooms and Rancid's mythical dog, Eddie and I presented our idea about the sailing parachute to the old woodsman.

"If thar's one thang Ah knows about, it's parachutes," he said authoritatively. "Ah done a lot of parachutin' in the Great War. General used to have me dropped behind enemy lines to do spyin' work. Ah ever tell you about the time—"

"Yeah," I said. "But what about using the parachute as a sail in the blizzard?"

"A sled won't work," Rancid said. "The sled will cut through the snow crust and you'll be stuck tighter'n a fly on a stirrin' spoon. You needs somethin' flat on the bottom, somethin' like a big pan."

"Shoot!" Eddie said. "There ain't no pan that big. Right now we've got this great blizzard and no way to use it!"

"Hold on a sec," Rancid said, putting on his thoughtful expression. "Hot dang, Ah thank Ah got just the thang!"

He stomped outside and soon returned with a large, curved metal object. He banged the snow off it onto the floor, in his enthusiasm apparently having forgotten about turning the floor to mud.

"What is it?" I asked.

"A fender off an old wrecked truck. Been keepin' it out in the yard. Figured some use would turn up fer it, and one has."

Eddie and I shouted with joy and relief. We would be able to put the blizzard to good use after all.

Rancid was a person who could never take a good idea and leave it alone. He had to improve on it. Eddie's plan had been for us to sail across the open fields on the icy crust burnished to a high polish by the wind and driven snow. Rancid, however, said the best idea would be to hike over to the Old Market Road. "It's just one long strip of shiny ice," he said. "It's so slick thar won't be nobody drivin' on it, thet's fer shore. We can have it all to ourselves."

"But what about a mast?" Eddie said.

"Won't need a mast," Rancid said. "Ah'll show you how it's done."

We cut through the woods to the Old Market Road, and sure enough, there was not a vehicle on it as far as we could see through the driven snow. Off in the distance, an undisturbed snowdrift slanted across the road. We had to lean into the wind in order to stand, and even then our feet skittered along on the snow-polished ice. It was slick.

Rancid threw the fender down with a metallic *ker-whump*. "Which one of you boys wants to go fust?"

"Let me try it," Crazy Eddie said.

Getting no argument from me, he climbed into the cavity of the upside-down fender and lay down on his belly.

"Thet ain't no way to do it," Rancid said. "Git up out of thar and let me show you how."

Rancid got in the fender, sitting upright. "Now hand me the parachute harness." For an old experienced parachuter, he didn't seem to know much about putting on the harness, but I suppose so much time had passed since the Great War that he had forgotten. Finally, he simply tied various straps of the harness around his waist and let it go at that. Then he grabbed a cluster of shroud lines in each hand like so many reins.

"Now here's the idear," he said. "Eddie, you take the bundle of parachute out in front. When Ah gives the signal, you throw the chute open so the wind can catch it. Pat, you push on the back of the fender to get me goin' so's the chute can pull me along. Ah'll show you how it's done. Then you fellas can give it a try."

Crazy Eddie and I, slipping and sliding on the icy roadway and fighting against the fierce wind, took up our assigned positions.

"Okay, ready?"

"Yeah!" Eddie and I yelled against the pounding wind.

"On the count of three!" Rancid yelled. "One! Two! ThreeEEEEEEEEEEEEE . . . !"

Eddie and I skated along the road, driven by the wind at our backs. There was no sign of Rancid, except an occasional blasted-out snowdrift marked by a spray of tobacco juice and claw marks that looked as if they might have been made by human hands.

After a while we stopped at a farmhouse and knocked.

A skinny old man in bib overalls and a flannel shirt opened the door and stared down at us.

"What in tarnation you boys doin' out in a storm like this? You look half froze. Come in by the fire and thaw out."

"Thanks," I said. "But we were lookin' for our friend, Rancid Crabtree. He went by here on the road about half an hour ago."

The farmer scratched his jaw. "Nope, can't say I seen anybody go by. You're lookin' for Crabtree, you say. What was he drivin'?"

"An upside-down truck fender," Crazy Eddie said.

"Yes," I said. "And he was wearing a parachute and—"

"Oh, Mavis," the farmer called out to his wife. "Better put some hot chocolate on for these boys. I think the cold's about got 'em. How do you fellas feel, anyway?"

"I don't feel so good," Eddie said. "But I think it may have been some poison mushrooms I ate for lunch."

"I see," said the farmer. "Poison mushrooms. Hurry up with that hot chocolate, Mavis."

After the hot chocolate, and not knowing anything else to do, Eddie and I returned to Rancid's shack. Much to our relief, the old woodsman came in a short while later, looking like a tattered icicle in more or less human form. The cut ends of the parachute harness dangled from his snow-caked waist.

"You don't look too good, Mr. Crabtree," Crazy Eddie said with rare understatement.

Rancid sank down on a chair and dug some snow out of his whitened ears with a blue finger. "Oh yeah?" he snarled. "Wal, you wouldn't neither if you'd been blowed halfway 'cross the gol-dang county in a truck fender. Ah'd still be goin' iffen Ah hadn't had the good fortune to get snared by a barbwire fence and torn dang near to shreds and . . ."

As he ranted on, I heard a sad sound from outside. With one last thrust at tearing the shakes from the roof, the wind dropped away with a rattling moan. The blizzard was dying. It had been a fine blizzard, and I was sorry to see it pass away.

Rubber Legs
and White Tail-Hairs

Caught up in the media craze of placing one-hundred-dollar bills end-to-end to see if they reach to the moon and back, as a way of making the national debt more understandable and poignant to the taxpayer, I recently laid all my fly-tying books end-to-end to see how far they reached. They reached from my writing desk to the cat box in the utility room. How far is that? Not nearly far enough, believe me.

"Look," I said to my wife, Bun. "I laid all my fly-tying books end-to-end to see how far they would reach. What do you think?"

So who cares what she thinks? The point I wished to illuminate with this comparison is simply that an unfathomable copiosity of fly-tying books exists, and I possess most of the copiosity. I have been studying fly-tying books for forty years and have yet to succeed in tying a single fly that resembles anything more than a hair ball.

The fault lies with the books and not with me, despite my childhood nickname of "Thumbs." Here is the problem.

Fly-tying books all contain a powerful spring in the binding. Whenever I reach Step 15 in the tying of a fly, with both hands fully engaged in maintaining a cat's cradle of thread in the vicinity of a wad of feathers and fur clinging precariously to a hook, the powerful spring is activated and snaps shut like a bear trap. I lean over and open the book with my ear. Using my tongue, I flip pages back to the instructions for the fly. Holding the book open with my chin, I read Step 15 with my nose while telescoping my eyes around to watch what my hands are doing. When the fly is finally finished, I remove it from the vise and place it in my fly box. You never can tell when the fish might go for a hair ball.

The other problem with fly-tying books is that the author has deliberately designed each fly so that it will contain one material that the fly-tyer doesn't have on hand. This requires the tyer to drive forty miles around town looking for a shop that hasn't sold the last of the material to some guy who came in fifteen minutes before the tyer arrived. Recently I was tying a fly that called for rubber legs. I rushed down to the nearest sporting goods store, hoping to get there before the guy who always arrives fifteen minutes ahead of me. The lady clerk stared at me wearily, as she always does, her fat elbows propped on the counter.

"You got rubber legs?" I asked.

"No, just tired," she snarled. "So whatta ya want?"

"I mean rubber legs for fly-tying. You know, the little—"

"Guy come in here just fifteen minutes ago and—"

"Yeah, I know him," I said. "Thanks anyway."

Boy, I just hope that guy is fifteen minutes late someday, and I'll show him a thing or two.

When I reached Step 18 of my latest fly, I could hardly

believe my nose. "Next take a pinch of white tail-hairs of calf . . ." it began. I repeated these words aloud, causing our cat to rise screeching like a banshee from the cat box. "White tail-hairs!" I repeated in a more moderate tone. "Who's got white tail-hairs of calf?"

Just then my finicky neighbor Alphonse Finley barged into my den and demanded to borrow his lawn mower.

"Oh, all right," I said irritably. "Just remember to return it."

"You sound irritable," he said. "What's the matter?"

"It's just this stupid fly-tying book," I said. "The instructions for this fly I'm tying call for white tail-hairs of calf. Now, where am I going to find white tail-hairs of calf?"

Finley studied the makings of the fly in my vise. "Odd," he said. "Why would a No. 16 hair ball need white tail-hairs? However, I may be able to help you out. I was driving in the country a few miles from here and noticed some calves in a barnyard. If I recall correctly, and I do, they had white tail-hairs, or fairly white, calves being what they are."

"Great," I said. "Let's drive out right now and you can show me where they are. I'll ask the farmer if we can clip a few tail-hairs from his calves."

"I assure you, my good man, that I have much better things to do than to assist you in clipping hairs from the tail of a calf."

As I say, Finley is a finicky character. Even so, I was surprised he would dress in a pinstriped suit to mow his grass, as I deduced from the fact that he was thus attired when he came begging to borrow his lawn mower. I called this perversion to his attention.

"Dear boy," he said, "I have no intention of mowing

my lawn in a suit and tie or any other way. I'm going to
hire young Raymond down the block to handle the chore
for me. I'm wearing a suit and tie because I'm speaking at
a luncheon this noon.''

"You're going to pay Raymond real money to mow your
lawn? What will the other bankers think? They might drum
you out of the union. Listen, you go out and show me where
the white-tailed calves are, and I'll mow your lawn for free.
Actually, I'll have Raymond do it, since I've already advanced him the money for approximately twelve hundred
lawn mowings.''

"Really? And I don't have to do anything else but show
you where they are? I just wait in the car?''

"Yep.''

"Gosh, I don't know. Every time I get involved in
one of your escapades, I end up in some humiliating pre-
dicament.''

"What could happen to you, Finley? All you have to do
is wait in the car.''

Twenty minutes later we drove into the farmer's yard.
Sure enough, Finley had been right. Half a dozen calves
with white tails were moseying about in the goo of the barnyard. They were quite a bit larger than I had expected,
more the size of adolescent cows than calves, but they did
have white tails. How would fish know where the white hairs
came from? Would they care? They probably would, at least
if they had ever seen a calf mucking around in a barnyard,
paying little or no attention to proper hygiene, but that
wasn't my problem. My problem was how to ask the farmer
if I could clip some tail-hairs off one of his calves.

I decided on a direct approach: "Sir, this may seem like
an unusual request, but I could use a few of your white tail-

hairs to tie flies with. You have plenty of them and I doubt
if they're of any use to you. I'd even be glad to pay, and
I'll clip them myself.''

Unfortunately, the farmer failed to respond to my knock
on his door, and I assumed that he must have gone to town
to buy feed or barbwire, or whatever it is farmers do away
from the farm. It seemed unlikely to me that the farmer
would miss a few tail-hairs or that he would care one way
or the other about the loss. I scribbled out a hasty note
informing the farmer of my intended acquisition and inserted three one-dollar bills as payment. Having no idea
what tail-hairs go for these days, I guessed that three dollars
would be more than adequate. Perhaps, I told myself, the
note and the money would alert the farmer to a whole new
market, the tail-hair market, which in the long run might
prove more profitable than the calves themselves. Not a little
pleased with myself over this contribution to the economics
of agriculture, I headed for the barnyard.

I climbed through the barnyard fence and extracted from
a pocket my folding fly-tying scissors, looking around for a
promising candidate. Much to my somewhat nervous surprise, for I had expected the calves to be suspicious of strangers, the herd of a half-dozen or so converged upon me and
began nuzzling my clothes with their slimy muzzles. I attempted to shove away the friendliest of my assailants, but
they were a stout and aggressive lot. Apparently disappointed that I didn't conceal a feedbag somewhere on my
person, they began to bump me about in a rather rude fash-
ion. Trying my best to ignore their brazenness, I selected
one of the nasty beasts and began to work my way down his
back in the direction of his tail, but the calf, suspecting that
I was up to something not in his best interest, quickly swung
his rear end away from me. He had repeated this maneuver

several times, when I heard a supercilious chuckle from Finley. He was standing there, one foot propped on a fence board, thoroughly enjoying my lack of success.

"C'mon, Finley, be a good sport," I said. "Give me a hand here."

"You must be mad," Finley replied. "Do you think I want to get calf slime or worse all over my new suit?"

At that instant, the other calves lost interest in me and wandered off to other parts of the barnyard, while the one in my embrace amused himself by trying to suck the buttons off my shirt.

"It'll only take a second, Finley," I said. "Just come over here and hold the calf, while I clip off some tail-hairs. Then I'll drive you back to town for your luncheon."

"Oh, all right." Finley tiptoed through the barnyard ooze, complaining about its effects on his shiny black oxfords. "What shall I grab on to, the ears?" he asked in a whiny tone scarcely conducive to arousing confidence in his skill as a calf-wrangler.

"No, I'll hold him by the ears until you can get a good grip on his tail. Leave the white hairs hanging down, so I can slip back and cut some off."

A grimace puckered Finley's face as he gingerly took hold of the calf's tail.

"Got a good grip?" I asked. "Okay, I'm letting go of the ears."

"Just hurry, that's all I—!"

The calf had lunged forward. Finley's feet spun in the muck. Flailing his legs wildly in an attempt to regain his balance, he pulled the tail straight back from the point where it was hooked onto the calf, thus saving himself from a disgusting fall. The calf, deciding it had had enough of Finley's uncouth intimacy, charged across the barnyard.

Finley sailed after it in the angled posture characteristic of water skiing, a sport at which luckily he is proficient, for the calf's tail made an extremely short tow rope.

I rushed after the two of them, hoping to get my white tail-hairs while Finley still had the calf in hand. Upon glimpsing me in hot pursuit, the calf, alas, broke into a frenzied gallop, with the result that Finley's shoes now sent up two curling and overlapping wakes of barnyard muck. The other calves, caught up in the excitement, stampeded ahead of Finley and his calf, all of them bellowing and bawling and in general creating an uproar typical of the bovine species. I must say the whole hullabaloo was beginning to get on my nerves, particularly the bellowing, not the least of which came from Finley.

I wondered briefly if perhaps Finley might be enjoying himself, since as a child I had often played grab-the-cow-tail in our own barnyard. As the calf rounded the corner of the barn, however, and as Finley cut a wide arc and jumped the curl of his own wake in the classic manner of the expert water skier, I was disabused of the notion that the man was having fun. His spectacles were askew on his nose, his eyes protruded like soft-boiled eggs from egg cups, and his pin-striped suit had acquired a splattered effect not unlike that of a Jackson Pollock painting, only in a bland monotone lacking aesthetic appeal.

It was upon rounding the corner of the barn myself that I discovered that the farmer was home after all. In a nearby field, two men, one of them presumably a hired hand, were tinkering with the innards of a tractor. They straightened and turned to determine the cause of the commotion, namely Finley's skiing, rather stylishly I must admit, behind one of the farmer's calves. Naturally I can't say for sure, but judging from the expressions on their faces, I would venture to guess this was the first time the farmer and his hired hand had witnessed an event of this sort.

Approaching the far end of the barnyard, the calf gunned itself into a right-angle turn, at which moment Finley let go of its tail and skied gracefully into the fence, to which he clung in an attitude that suggested extreme agitation. The farmer and his hired hand moved somewhat cautiously in Finley's direction, each carrying a large wrench, and neither perhaps entirely dismissing the possibility that, instead of a mere prankster in a business suit, they might be confronting a lunatic.

At this point I decided that Finley, after all, was an articulate person and fully capable of explaining the situation as well as I. Just in case that wasn't well enough, I returned to the car and revved up the engine, pausing only briefly to remove from the farmer's door my note and the three dollars. As I told Finley when next I saw him, I certainly wasn't going to pay for white tail-hairs I didn't get.

Nude,
with Other Wildlife

In my youth, there were two things I wanted to be when I grew up: either a mountain man or an artist. Deep down, I had a strong preference for mountain man, but even at a young age I realized that course in life was closed to me because of a severe handicap—acute fear of the dark. I had given much thought to inventing a portable night-light suitable for mountain darkness, but its bulk would have been impractical. It was too easy to imagine a band of hostile Indians closing fast on me as I galloped uphill, towing my night-light. So I opted for artist.

From age seven to ten, I worked very hard at becoming a wildlife artist. My first efforts revealed enormous talent, recognized only by my mother. I would show her one of my drawings, and she would say, "Very nice maybe you'll be an artist when you grow up have you seen my car keys?" Without such encouragement, I surely would have given up, if for no other reason than the ridicule directed at my art by my sister, the Troll. Once I had the bad judgment to show her a picture I had drawn of a mallard duck in flight.

84

She turned the drawing this way and that, studying it intently.

"I've got it!" she exclaimed, as if I had asked her to solve a puzzle. "It's a dead chicken run over by a car and flattened out on the road, right?"

"Right," I said.

"But why did you put that dog collar around its neck? Chickens don't wear collars."

"It's a pet chicken," I said.

"What's the dead chicken got in its mouth? Looks like a piece of toast."

She was referring, of course, to the duck's bill. I was still in my straight-line phase, and I suppose it was possible for a person ignorant of art to mistake a duck's bill for a rectangular piece of toast. Later I would experiment with curved lines.

Although I worked exclusively on wildlife art, I also wanted to paint nude women. I never mentioned this to my mother, and certainly not to the Troll, since our family was devoutly religious and probably would have been upset by a ten-year-old boy bringing home nude models to paint. With the exception of my dog, Strange, I was the only deviate in the family.

Ideally, when I was grown up and had my own studio, I would be able to combine my two great interests—nudes and wildlife—in paintings titled *Nude with Grazing Elk* or *Nude Hunting Ducks*.

Lacking any instruction in art, I had to make my way as best I could through trial and error. The problem was, I couldn't tell which was the trial and which was the error. Furthermore, I had no idea what a nude woman looked like, never having seen one. I asked my friend Crazy Eddie Muldoon if he had ever seen a nude woman, and he claimed he had. Eddie tried to describe her to me while I drew, but just as I was finishing up the details, my mother walked by and glanced at the picture. Both Eddie and I were scared, but she said only, "Oh what a nice duck maybe you'll be an artist when you grow up have you seen my car keys?" It was a close call but also made me suspect that Eddie had never seen a nude woman either.

The only artist I knew in our area was a logger who whittled interlocking chain links out of boards. Whittled chains are nice, but once you've seen one, you've pretty much seen them all. Besides, I didn't have the patience to whittle even one link, which is scarcely enough to impress anyone, let alone an art critic. Then one day Eddie and I discovered a real, honest-to-goodness artist, an old man by the name of Gummy Johanson.

Gummy Johanson got his nickname not because he lacked teeth—he had a fine set—but because he constantly chewed gum. Gummy looked after a ranch for the banker who owned it but who lived in town. Crazy Eddie and I occasionally passed by Gummy's little white house on our way to fish a stream that wound through a meadow on the ranch. One day Gummy was sitting out on his porch, and we exchanged a few pleasantries with him. To anyone who didn't know him, Gummy might have appeared a bit weird and even a little scary. His eyes bulged, giving him a look of extreme intensity, and his white-stubbled jaws worked ferociously at the ever-present wad of gum, which he snapped, crackled, and popped in a frenzied manner. Ranch hands claimed they would rather be beaten with a stick than have to work beside Gummy and listen to his gum-chewing. But Crazy Eddie and I didn't mind it, particularly since Gummy usually offered us sticks of gum, and we would stand around and chew ferociously with him.

On this particular day, Gummy said to us, "If you got a minute, boys, c'mere. I wanna show you something." We followed him into the house, which was usually neat and clean but now was a total mess. Dirty clothes and piles of rubbish covered the scant furnishings, the dishpan and stove were heaped with unwashed dishes, and strewn about the floor like silvery leaves were hundreds of empty gum wrappers. A whole case of chewing gum rested on the kitchen table. Eddie and I had never seen so much gum, and we thought that was what Gummy wanted to show us. But he walked into the bedroom. "In here, boys," he said. We followed him.

While I wondered what possibly could have happened to the tidy old man I had previously known, Gummy led us over to his grungy, blanket-tangled bed. The metal bedposts were painted a dull blue, except for one, which was covered from top to bottom with a strange, grayish glob, something that looked as if it might have been deposited by insects.

"This is it," Gummy said, pointing at the glob.

Crazy Eddie and I backed away. "What is it?" I asked.

Gummy beamed. "My sculpture."

He turned on a bedside light and tilted the shade so that the light threw the glob into relief. We gasped in astonishment and delight. The glob had been transformed into a cluster of tiny deer, elk, bears, ducks, and various other fauna and even flora. It was magnificent!

"Holy smokes!" I said.

"Wow!" Crazy Eddie said. "It's beautiful! It's all made out of—"

"Yep," said Gummy, his bulgy little eyes twinkling with pride. "Chewing gum!"

Gummy explained how the sculpture had come about. Every night just before he went to sleep, he said, he took out his wad of gum and stuck it on the bedpost. Over the years, the gum had accumulated until it became the glob. The oldest layers of gum had turned almost black with age, with each successive layer lighter than the one before, the gradation from dark to light producing the illusion of depth sought by all the great classic artists, in whose company Gummy Johanson must certainly have belonged.

One morning, Gummy went on, he had awakened early and was lying in bed thinking about nothing in particular, when he glanced at the glob, backlighted as it was by the rising sun in the window. He imagined he saw the shape of a deer's head in the glob, much as Michelangelo saw the figure of David in a block of marble. He got a kitchen match and began to poke and mold with it, until the deer head emerged in relief from the glob.

Gummy was so excited by his newly discovered talent that every moment he had free from ranch chores he spent sitting by the bed chewing gum as fast as he could and molding it with the match into all the wonderful creatures that had so awed Crazy Eddie and me with their exquisite and delicate beauty.

"Where did you learn to do this?" I asked.

"Never had an art lesson in my life," Gummy said, giving his suspenders a pleased snap with his thumbs. "I'm self-taught."

"Gosh, you're the best artist I've ever seen," Eddie said.

"Thank you," Gummy said modestly. "Say, how would you boys like to watch me do some sculpture work? You can help me chew up a batch of fresh gum."

"We'd love to," I said. At long last, I had found someone who could teach me fine art. I imagined apprenticing myself to Gummy Johanson, first serving as a chewer for him, then maybe doing some of the detail work on the flowers and animals, and finally, after years of study, being given the opportunity to create my own chewing-gum sculptures. Maybe someday I too would have my own glob of gum on a bedpost, and people would come from miles around to look at it. It was not too difficult to imagine my bedpost displayed in an art museum. I shivered with excitement at the awesome opportunity suddenly opened up to me.

Eddie and I hauled some chairs into the bedroom and began to chew sticks of gum for Gummy as he worked on his sculpture of a Canada goose in full flight. Every so often he would lean back and hold the kitchen match up and sight along it at the sculpture. Apparently this helped him get the right proportions for the goose, and I could tell it was a very professional thing to do. In practically no time at all the goose was finished, and it was one of the finest geese I'd ever seen. Eddie and I shouted and applauded, and Gummy looked as if he would burst from excessive pleasure, he was so pleased.

"Well, boys," he said, "I got time for just one more before I have to get back to chores. What would you like to see next?"

The room filled with silence. I could practically hear Crazy Eddie's brain cells clicking together as he thought about what he wanted to see next, and I knew it was the same thing I wanted.

"Oh," I said casually, "how about a nude woman?"

"I was thinkin' the same thing," Eddie said.

Gummy looked startled. "Well, I don't know. I ain't never done a woman before, nude or not. All I ever done is other kinds of wild critters."

Our shoulders sagged. Well, what the heck, it was worth a try.

"Shoot!" Gummy said, apparently noticing our disappointment. "If I can do a nude goose, I should be able to do a nude woman."

Finally—I said to myself—I get to see what a nude woman looks like!

Crazy Eddie and I began to chew gum like mad, cramming stick after stick into our mouths, until our jaws ached. Gummy hunched over his sculpture, working furiously with the matchstick, molding and carving, poking and smoothing, as Eddie and I tried to peer around him. We chewed and chewed and chewed.

"More gum! More gum!" the artist cried feverishly, and we boys feverishly passed him our wads of chewed gum and crammed more sticks into our mouths. Beads of sweat formed on the back of Gummy's neck, and his long gray hair stood out at all angles. "More gum! More gum!" he croaked.

Slowly the sculpture began to take shape. Aha, I thought, a nude woman looks a lot like a moose. Then the artist wiped out his creation and started over. Oh, I thought presently, I see now, a nude woman looks like a bunch of grapes. Once I even thought that a nude woman was going to look like one of my own drawings of a duck. I began to suspect that Gummy didn't know any more about what a nude woman looked like than Crazy Eddie did.

Gummy suddenly stopped working. He slumped down in his chair and held his face in his hands. Eddie and I glanced at each other.

"What's wrong?" Eddie asked.

The artist didn't answer. He got up slowly and walked to the window, where he stood for a long while, looking out over the meadow.

"I guess I can't do nudes," he said after a bit. "I just can't seem to do them!"

NUDE, WITH OTHER WILDLIFE

Eddie said, "You do good geese."

"Thanks," Gummy said sadly. He seemed enormously disappointed by the discovery of this major void in his talent, although, I must say, scarcely more than Eddie and I.

We got our fishing poles and walked out across the meadow toward the creek, rubbing our aching jaws. There was still enough light left for us to catch a few fish.

"What do you suppose was wrong with Gummy?" I asked.

"He was just tormented," Crazy Eddie said. "All artists are tormented. Didn't you know that? If you want to be an artist, you got to learn how to be tormented."

"I don't want to be tormented," I said. "Maybe I'll be a mountain man after all."

I knew mountain men weren't tormented, at least not if they had night-lights. The next day I started inventing a very large portable night-light.

The Belcher

While I was making a minor adjustment on my muzzle-loader one day last fall, several parts fell off. I thought maybe I hadn't tightened the doohickey enough or maybe had allowed too much play in the thingumajig. In any case, while I was banging the barrel on the concrete floor in the garage, all these parts fell off. So much for amateur gunsmithing.

Fortunately, I have a friend who is a certified gun nut, one Gary Roedl by name. (Rhymes with *yodel.*) For a living, Roedl teaches metal shop in a high school, as is evident from his wild, darting eyes and facial twitch. To calm his psyche after school, he goes home and tinkers with his guns. He even writes about guns. His gun articles are so technical they don't have any words in them, but only numbers, abbreviations, and a smattering of punctuation. The average gun nut probably finds them interesting, but to me they're deadly. I read his "Origins of the Cleaning Patch" aloud in the garden to bore insects to death. It makes a wonderful pesticide.

I threw the parts of my muzzle-loader in a box and rushed them over to Gary's house. "Can you fix it?" I asked him.

Roedl looked at the gun and almost burst into tears. "What did you do to it?" he cried. "Beat it on a concrete floor?"

The man's intuition is eerie.

At first he said he thought the gun had been damaged beyond repair and probably should be put to sleep. I begged him to save it. He agreed to try, and finally got all the parts reassembled.

"Looks good as new," I said.

"Not quite," Roedl said. "When you shoot it in the future, I recommend you trip the trigger a little differently."

"How's that?"

"With a long string."

"But that will ruin my accuracy."

"Not all that much," Roedl said. "Not all that much. Say, did I tell you, I bought that Belcher I've been looking for."

"You've already got a dog," I said. "What do you want with another one?"

"It's not a dog, it's a gun. Belonged to a famous old buffalo hunter. I'm writing a book about him and the gun."

"No kidding. Going to use words in this one, or just go with the abbreviations and numbers?"

Ignoring my protests and skidding feet, Roedl dragged me into his gun vault, which is fashioned after the gold bullion room at Fort Knox. He held up the Belcher. "Now there is a gun!"

Why he told me this, I don't know. Even I, non-gun

nut, could identify it as a gun at a hundred paces with one eye blindfolded.

"Right," I said. "Well, I've got to be running along. Thanks for fixing my muzzle-loader."

Before I could move, Roedl deftly kicked shut the door of the vault and set the time lock for two hours. If there's one thing gun nuts love to do more than tinker with guns, it's talk about them. "Now here's something you'll find interesting," he began. "This .50-70 M-1874 Belcher blaw blaw 12 lbs. blaw blaw .50 cal. 2½-in. straight case blaw blaw 70 grn F or FFG & 370 gr. PP. . . . "

I immediately took off on an out-of-body experience, my consciousness floating gently up to the ceiling. Looking down, I could see my own body seated in a chair listening to Gary, the head nodding and saying, "Yeah, uh-huh, right, fascinating." I saw two bugs race across the floor, trying to get out of hearing range, but they were overcome with boredom before they could escape. They rolled over on their backs, kicked a few times, and were still. What a rough way to go, I thought, even for an insect. I vowed never again to read Gary's "Origins of the Cleaning Patch" aloud in the garden. A bug bomb would be more humane.

Finally, I heard Roedl say, "And that's about it for the .50-70 M-1847 Belcher. Pretty fascinating, what?"

Instantly, I was sucked back into my body.

"Kept me on the edge of my chair the whole time. Can I go now?"

"One more thing. When we go hunting in Montana next week, I'm—are you ready for this?—going to hunt with the Belcher! What do you think about that!"

My jaw hinges cramped up from stifling a yawn. "Wow.

I can hardly wait. But please don't tell me any more. I'm already hyperventilating from excitement.''

Thus it was that on the following week I found myself trapped in the cab of a pickup truck on a five-hundred-mile journey into the wilds of Montana with not one but two gun nuts, the second being the outdoor writer Keith Jackson. Jackson, by the way, is a wonderful fisherman, possessing the rare ability to make fish materialize out of thin air. On several fishing trips I've taken with Jackson, I have been under the misapprehension that we both had got skunked, only later to read his accounts of the expeditions and learn that Jackson had done very well indeed, landing numerous monstrous fish on No. 28 dry flies, whereas I, failing to follow his advice, had landed only a single fingerling with a bait consisting of a nightcrawler, a kernel of corn, and a pink marshmallow.

As might be expected, Keith and Gary droned on endlessly about calibers and grains and muzzle velocities and trajectories and other boring gun stuff. I tried to ignore them by leaning back in the seat and catnapping, but they wouldn't allow it, often resorting to screaming and calling me vile names. I told them if they didn't like my catnapping, they could just stop talking about gun stuff. Otherwise, one of them could drive.

True to his word, Roedl hunted with the ancient Belcher. On the first day of the hunt, a mule deer buck strolled out of some brush about fifty yards ahead of us. This was Gary's first opportunity to try out his prized possession in an actual hunting situation. From what I had been told about the power and accuracy of the Belcher, I expected the first shot instantly to transform the buck into a pile of venison steaks and chops ready for the freezer.

Roedl raised the Belcher and fired. A rather longish *BOOOOOM!* and a plume of smoke issued from the muzzle. The deer was stopped in his tracks. Apparently the ruckus raised by the Belcher had aroused his curiosity, because after stopping in his tracks he stared intently at us for a few moments. Then he noticed the slug traveling in his direction. He watched the slug for some time and then, becoming bored with it, nibbled some grass, occasionally glancing up to check on the progress of the slug. When the slug was nearly to him, he stepped aside and let it plop onto the ground at his feet.

Roedl was demolished. I tried to comfort him, but without much success, possibly because I was squealing with mirth. Upon recovering, I advised Roedl that on his next shot he should lead the deer by about twenty yards.

"He's not even moving," Roedl snarled.

"Yeah, I know," I said. "If he starts moving, you'd better lead him by at least eighty yards! Har har!"

"Here's the problem," Roedl said. "I loaded that shell at sea level. This higher altitude is affecting the ballistics. Fortunately, I brought along some shells with a little more oomph to them."

"Sea level!" I cried. "Oh, my aching sides! Har har heee!"

"Okay, wise guy," Roedl said. "You get the honor of taking the next shot with the Belcher."

"Har . . . what? No, I don't wanna."

"Hush! This is not a request. You will take the next shot."

I always hate it when Gary uses his teacher voice. It's so intimidating. I get the feeling that if I don't obey, I'll be sent to The Office.

"Oh, all right," I said, "If it will make you feel any better. Hand me the Belcher."

Instantly, my hand sagged to the ground from the weight of the rifle. I now knew why it was called a .50-70 Belcher. It was .50 caliber and weighed 70 pounds. I wondered if the famous old buffalo hunter had killed the buffalo by shooting them or by dropping the Belcher on them. It should have been equipped with wheels—and a team of draft horses to pull it.

In the meantime, the buck, grinning and shaking his head in disbelief, had retreated to a little grove of pine trees. Roedl claimed it was still within easy range of the rifle, and handed me one of his handloads. The shell was about the size and shape of a wiener—a .50-caliber wiener. I slipped it into the breech and snapped the gun shut. Staggering about under the weight of the Belcher, I tried to set the sights on the deer. My finger brushed the hair trigger.

When my vision cleared, the deer was gone, possibly vaporized but more probably merely escaped. A mature ponderosa pine had been shot in two near where the buck had stood. Beyond it, a smoldering gravel pit had been gouged out of the hill. Aftershocks rolled under my feet. Echoes of the deafening blast boomed up and down the valley.

"Dib I miss hib?" I asked, feeling about my face in search of my nose.

"Eh?" Roedl said.

"Eh?" Jackson said.

"I think you loaded that shell a might heavy with the FF or the PP," I said. "Probably it was the PP. Well, no harm done. I suppose Bozeman has a doctor who can surgically remove the stock of a Belcher from a person's shoulder. By the way, anyone seen my shoulder around?"

On the ride back home, Roedl continued to insist that his Belcher didn't kick. "It was the way you were holding it," he explained. "Technically speaking, there's going to be 14 psf of recoil, but with a .50-70 straight-case Belcher shell with 85 XYZ cubed to 400 PF blaw blaw MV 40,000 FPS blaw blaw 52 IRAs blaw blaw 87 BBDs. . . . Are you listening to what I'm telling you, McManus?"

"Eh?"

Shooter

Retch Sweeney and I fished the little creek up on the old Bone place one day last summer for the first time in thirty years. Weeds had grown up shoulder-high in the meadow, and a ragtag army of volunteer pine trees had invaded the pasture. On the hill above us, a weary privy stood sentry amid an orange explosion of honeysuckle. A short distance away, a brick chimney poked up from a pile of blackened rubble that had once been the Bone house.

"I can scarcely believe it," Retch said, unhitching his creel and flopping down on the bank to rest. "The fishing here hasn't changed one bit since we were kids!"

"You're right," I said. "I remember it was lousy back then, too. That's probably why we haven't fished here for thirty years."

"Yeah," Retch said. "Thirty years. The last time was before that house burned down. The folks who lived there, what was their name?"

"Bone," I said. "Mr. and Mrs. Bone, and they had a

boy our age. His name was, uh, uh, oh yeah, Henry. You remember Henry Bone.''

"No, can't say as I do.''

"Sure you do. He went to school with us in the sixth grade.''

"Couldn't have! I'd remember him. Oh, wait a minute . . . was he kind of . . . of . . . well, uh . . . ? No, I can't place him. You certain he went to school with us?''

"He was the Shooter.''

"The Shooter! Henry Bone was the Shooter? Good gosh almighty!''

I could easily understand why Retch might have trouble remembering Henry Bone, even though he had gone to school with us for a whole year. Henry Bone was one of those people so totally average that they're almost invisible. He was neither smart nor dumb, rich nor poor, ugly nor handsome, polite nor rude, dirty nor clean, just average everything. Shy and unobtrusive, Henry blended so perfectly into his surroundings that he scarcely seemed to occupy space.

If Henry had played sports, of course, he would have been noticed. A person could be terrible in sports, as I was, and still have a public identity, such as being the person always chosen last for a team. Everyone in school knew that I had laid claim to that particular athletic distinction. In softball, the advice given to a batter on the opposing team was always, "Try to hit to McManus.'' In football it was, "Okay, we'll run the next series of plays over McManus.'' Being the worst athlete wasn't much of an identity, but it was at least an identity—something Henry Bone lacked. For one brief moment, though, Henry was to emerge from obscurity and achieve the fleeting fame of the grade-school playground. He was to become the Shooter.

During much of the school year, Delmore Blight Grade School was held in the icy fist of North Idaho winter. The ball fields and the basketball court lay under two feet of gray, gritty snow packed hard as concrete. Then, in late March, the sun warmed the brick walls of the school and the snow began to recede, leaving an irregular margin of bare dirt along the south side of the building. Bare dirt! No field of wildflowers ever looked so beautiful to us as that naked piece of earth. Marble season began.

I was a fair marble shot and could hold my own against most of the other guys. There were three top nibslingers, though, with Retch Sweeney being about the best of the three. The other two were Elwood Scopes and Lonnie Custer. By the end of the marble season, these three would have won all the marbles in the school. They kept their winnings in quart jars on shelves in their rooms. I remember that Retch had seven or eight jars of marbles in his bedroom, arranged on a shelf like trophies. The rest of us would supply marbles by buying little netting bags of them for ten cents apiece. After school each day, a big marble tournament would be held in which Retch, Lonnie, and Elwood would win all the marbles. The next morning all of us losers would go out and buy more bags. I think there must be a lesson in economics here, but I've never understood what it is.

One March afternoon, we regulars had all anted up for the first marble game when a shy voice said, "Can I play?" We looked at the owner of the voice. He was vaguely familiar, but none of us could place him right off. After a bit, Scopes said, "Hey, ain't I seen you someplace before?"

"I sit across from you in the back row in sixth grade," the boy said.

"Oh," Scopes said. "I knew I'd seen you someplace."

"Is it all right if I play?"

"Sure, kid," Retch said. "The more the merrier, heh heh."

The kid took some marbles from his pocket and anted up. The "pot," drawn on the soft dirt with a stick, was a good six feet in diameter and contained at least a hundred marbles. We lagged with our laggers, marbles about the size of ping-pong balls, toward a line some distance from the playing circle. The stranger's lagger stopped right on the line, giving him first shot. Next in the shooting order were Elwood, Retch, and Lonnie. Well, at least the kid would get a shot, which was more than the rest of us could expect.

While the top nibslingers stood around warming and limbering up their trigger fingers, the kid took out his handkerchief and began to unfold it, revealing a beautiful agate shooter.

Scopes eyed the kid's aggie. "Shooters are up for grabs, too," he said.

"Okay," the kid said.

I didn't know much about him except that he had to be really dumb to risk that beautiful aggie in a game with these marble sharks.

"No way," I said. "Shooters are safe."

"Forget that," Scopes said, making a threatening move in my direction.

I smiled and stepped over next to my good friend and protector, Retch Sweeney. "Tell him shooters are safe, Retch."

"Forget that!" Retch said.

"It's all right," the kid said. "I don't mind."

He knelt down and studied the arrangement of marbles in the pot. Apparently satisfied, he made a little tripod with the fingers of his left hand, placed his right hand atop the tripod, loaded the beautiful agate shooter between the tip of his forefinger and his thumb knuckle. Snack! We all jumped at the sound of the kid's first shot. Three marbles had flown out of the pot like shrapnel, with the aggie stopping dead still at the point of impact on the target marble. Dumbfounded, we all leaned forward to watch the kid's next move. Snack! Snick! Pop! Snap! Crack! Marbles began flying out of the circle in all directions. Within a few minutes the pot was bare.

New pots were anted up. The kid cleaned them, one after another, until darkness fell. Then he pulled a long brown cotton sock out of his pocket and placed his winnings in it. The sock looked like a lumpy sausage hanging over his shoulder as he walked off into the darkness.

"Hey, kid!" Scopes yelled after him. "What's your name?"

"Henry Bone," came the reply.

"Tomorrow I'll take him," Scopes said.

"If I don't," Retch said.

"Or me," said Custer.

"You've got to get a shot first," I said.

"Shut up," Scopes said irritably.

I looked at my protector.

"Yeah," Retch said. "Shut up for once."

In the days that followed, the marble competition quickly narrowed down to Retch, Scopes, Custer, and Henry Bone. The stakes were too high for the rest of us. And day after day, Henry went home with his sock bulging with winnings.

Nearly every kid in school and even some of the teachers had become spectators at the marble shoots. Henry would make his way through the crowd, trailed by little first- and second-graders trying to touch him. "Yay!" the kids would yell. "Here comes the Shooter! Yay!" And every time Hen-

ry's beautiful agate would go sizzling into the pot to deci-
mate the antes of Retch, Scopes, and Custer, a great roar
would go up from the crowd.

One day toward the end of March, Retch took me aside.
"Tell me something," he said. "Where do you buy them
little bags of marbles?"

I was stunned. Retch Sweeney, forced to buy marbles!
He could scarcely conceal his humiliation. The Shooter had
won his whole stash, his whole hoard of marble winnings
from the eternity of years we had spent in grade school!

I helped Retch sneak down to the five-and-dime to buy
some marbles. We met Scopes and Custer coming out.
They said they had come to buy candy.

Retch handed the money to the clerk for two bags of marbles. "They're for my kid brother," he explained. Later he
said, "How embarrassing! I actually paid money for marbles! I ain't ever, as long as I live, gonna forgive the Shooter
for this!"

Although it seemed much longer at the time, I believe the
marble season lasted only about three weeks at most. In that
brief span of time, Henry Bone achieved fame and glory,
and even riches of a sort, in the form of colorful little glass
spheres. A fifth-grader who had visited the Bone home, or
so he claimed, reported that Henry "the Shooter" Bone had
lined one whole wall of his bedroom with gallon milk jars
full of marbles. Nobody believed the report. Fifth-graders
as a group were suspect in general and considered totally
unreliable.

Everyone wanted to be Henry's friend, with the obvious
exceptions of Retch, Scopes, and Custer. Kids casually
dropped his name: "I was talking to Shooter today and he
told me . . ." "I ate lunch with Bone today and . . ."
"Look at the marble Henry gave me. . . ." The Shooter

wore his new popularity well. He was still quiet and even shy, but we noticed a confidence in him that we had missed before. That was natural, I suppose, because we had never even noticed Henry himself before.

At the very peak of his fame, Henry was struck by one of those disasters that seem to stalk us all at one time or another: the last of the snow melted off the softball diamond. Marbles were instantly forgotten. Henry Bone was forgotten. Within a matter of hours he faded back into the same obscurity from which he had emerged but a short time before. What he thought of the fickle nature of fame, I don't know. I never asked him. In fact, I never even really noticed him again. I was too busy dealing with my own fame as the worst softball player in the history of Delmore Blight Grade School.

Shortly thereafter, the Bone house burned down and Henry and his family moved away. He was not missed.

Those events of thirty years ago flashed through my mind in seconds as I stared up the hill at the ruins of the old Bone place. "Hey," I said to Retch. "Let's go up and poke around in the rubble. Might find something interesting."

"Even if we don't, it'll beat the fishing," Retch said.

We kicked through the ashes for a while and were about to leave when I noticed a strange lump. I picked it up, a heavy glob of something, and brushed it off. For a moment I was puzzled. Then I held it up against the rays of the dying sun and saw that it was composed of melted glass shot through with a thousand colors.

"Wow!" I said. "You know what this is? It's a gallon jug of Henry Bone's marbles melted by the heat of the fire!"

"By gosh, it is!" Retch said. "Well, I'll be!"

We started digging through the rubble and found a half-dozen more of the melted blobs. We polished them off and

set them up in a row on the stone foundation so that the
sunlight played through them and sent the colors dancing
across the ruins. So, I thought, this is what the brief fame
and glory of the Shooter came to—a bunch of melted glass,
and colors dancing on old ashes.

"It's kind of sad, isn't it?" I said to Retch.

"What?"

"All those marbles Henry won, all those hours of shooting, all that excitement, all of it reduced to globs of colored
glass. It's sad."

Retch stared at the colors dancing on the ashes, a slight
smile on his face.

"Oh, I don't know about that," he said.

The Last Flight
of Homer Pidgin

Back during the Paleozoic era, when I was just getting started with camping, any kid who fled home from a camping trip about the time it started to get dark was known as a "homer," a term possibly derived from "homing pigeon." It so happened that the boy most endowed with this characteristic had the last name of Pidgin. Thus it was even more appropriate that he acquired the nickname of "Homer."

I should mention here something about the use of nicknames in that distant time and place of my youth. The idea, as I understood it, was to give a kid a nickname appropriate to his appearance or eccentricity of behavior, the crueler the better. A kid with warts, for example, might be known as "Toad" or "Frog" or maybe simply "Warty." In the course of time, the warts might vanish, but the nickname would remain, continuing its work of warping the kid's personality and kicking holes in his psyche. Nicknames were fun.

Often the nickname would come to dominate the kid's

whole identity, and even teachers and parents would know him by it. Coaches in particular were quick to adopt the nicknames of their charges: "Okay, here's the batting order—Toad, Pig, Goat, Larry, and Lizard." In the case of Homer, his parents soon started calling him by the nickname his friends had conferred upon him, although it's unlikely they knew that the name derived from cowardice in the face of darkness. Little did they realize that every time they said something as simple as "Homer, eat your peas," they were calling attention to a major defect in his character.

The only thing worse than being known by a monstrous nickname—say, Slug, Snake, or Wormy—was to have no nickname at all. I myself had the good fortune to be honored with a nickname by my friends and associates. Alas, time and Freudian slippage have erased it from my memory. Too bad. Let's just say that it was "Rocky."

Oddly, although I can no longer recall my own nickname or how it came about, I have a vivid recollection of the event by which Ralph Pidgin became known as Homer Pidgin. Ralph loved to plan things, particularly camping trips. To him, an hour's excursion into the wilds of the Fergussons' woodlot required all the planning and preparation of an expedition to the South Pole. An overnight camp-out on one of the creeks in the nearby mountains posed complications comparable to those of a voyage into the outer realms of the universe.

Ralph was a maker of lists. For his first overnighter with us, he called a meeting of the expedition party. "All right, guys," he told us. "First, I've made up this list of provisions we'll need. Salt, pepper, butter, lard—the butter and lard should be in leakproof containers, ditto the jam and syrup. To continue: two loaves of bread, one pound pancake flour, three cans pork 'n' beans . . ." He had a list for each of us, with the shares of the provision evenly divided. After he had distributed the individual lists, the other members of the party made paper airplanes out of them and sailed them back at him.

"Look," Retch Sweeney said, "why doesn't each of us just bring what grub he can lay hands on at home, and when we get to our campsite we'll dump it all out in a pile and see what we got. How does that sound to you, Rocky?"

"Sounds good to me," I said.

"Me too," said Birdy Thompson.

"I'll take my .22 along and shoot us some fat squirrels for meat," Retch said.

"Maybe somebody should bring wieners," Birdy said. "Last time you shot only one squirrel, and the drumstick I got looked like a burnt match. Tasted like it, too." Retch held a fist up in his face. "Good, though."

Ralph shook his head. "This trip requires planning. You guys can do what you want, but I'm going to make sure my own gear and provisions are in order."

He did, too. On the morning of the camping trip, he had all of his stuff spread out on the lawn, food items in one section, gear in another, fishing tackle in another, and extra clothes in another. He went from section to section, checking items off his lists. Not a little annoyed, we gave him a few hints that we wished to be off on the adventure without wasting any more time.

"Step on it, Ralph, or we'll leave you behind!" Retch hinted.

"Get a move on," Birdy said. "We don't have all day, Pidgin."

"Yeah," I said kindly. "Throw your junk in the pack and let's go!"

". . . extra handkerchief, check," Ralph said. "Extra socks, check. Okay, that's it. Now as soon as I arrange everything neatly in my pack, we can depart."

"ARRRGGHHHHH!" his friends said.

The hike to our camp took less than two hours. In contrast to Pidgin's tidy, compact pack, ours weighed upwards of eighty pounds each. Our reasoning was that too much time would be wasted selecting only the equipment appropriate to an overnighter. So we took all the camping gear we owned, mostly war-surplus stuff, dumping it expeditiously into our packsacks. The size of our packs also helped in selecting our campsites. The first guy to collapse from exhaustion automatically dropped onto our campsite, whether it was in the middle of a swamp or on a steep mountain slope. Even today I marvel that such an efficient process for finding a campsite should have been discovered by a bunch of fourteen-year-old boys of average intelligence, excluding Retch Sweeney, of course.

As soon as we had made camp, which consisted largely of dumping our packs on the ground, we set out to catch some fish for supper. Even at that age, we had developed a sportsmanlike attitude toward angling. The first rule was never to catch more fish than we could eat. I don't recall that we even once broke this rule, our restraint continuing to be a source of some pride to me. We were also careful to throw back "the little ones." As we set off to fish, Retch shouted, "Remember, don't keep no little ones!" This was understood to mean no fish under four inches.

Toward evening, we met back at the camp and discussed our luck at catching fish.

"I told you we should bring wieners," Birdy said.

"I'd shoot us some squirrels, but there don't seem to be

none around here," Retch said. "I wonder how chipmunk tastes."

As the first shadows of evening crept across our camp, we chopped firewood, smoothed out the ground for our sleeping bags, and generally prepared for the night. It was then that a strange look came over Ralph's face. He swiveled his head about, peering into the recesses of the forest, as though surprised by the deepening darkness. Somehow, despite all his meticulous planning, he had apparently overlooked the possibility that sooner or later darkness might occur on an overnight camping trip.

Without a word of explanation, Ralph began stuffing his gear into his pack, paying little attention to neatness. He whipped his pack on, pulled his hat down over his ears, and tore out for home, leaving behind nothing of his presence but a few wisps of smoke from the soles of his tennis shoes.

We stared after him in dumbfounded silence. Presently, Birdy said, "Cripes! What happened to Ralph?"

Retch stuck a match in his teeth and pondered the mystery. "Well," he said, "it looks like Ralph is a homer."

"A homer?" I said.

"Yeah," Retch said. "You know, a kid that runs home every time it starts to get dark."

"Ha!" I said. "Homer Pidgin!"

And that was how Homer acquired his nickname. I should mention that we did not hold his flight home against him, or even consider it extraordinary for human behavior, based on the humans we were familiar with. It never occurred to us to exclude Homer from future camping trips. He always came along. Apparently his pleasure in camping at that stage of his life consisted of planning the camping trip in infinitesimal detail, preparing his pack, hiking into the campsite, and joining in the futility of trying to catch enough fish for our supper. At that point he had acquired the maximum pleasure from camping of which he was capable. He then had the good sense to terminate the excursion before it was ruined by darkness.

We soon became accustomed to Homer's style of camping. As darkness approached and the strange look came over his face, we would matter-of-factly bid him farewell:

"So long, Homer."

"See you, Homer."

"Have a good trip."

Retch, Birdy, and I naturally assumed that Homer had no intention of camping through the night with us, but we were apparently mistaken. As we later deduced, Homer never even considered that he would flee home, until the very moment the urge to take flight came upon him.

What led us to this deduction was a trip we took twenty miles up Pack River, one of our grumbling parents driving us to our destination in the wild upper regions of the river. We were to camp out there for four days or until one of our parents remembered to retrieve us. Of course, we assumed that Homer would refuse to come, since the distance from his home was approximately thirty miles. But as soon as the proposed trip was announced, Homer immediately set about planning and making up his lists. We were puzzled by his intentions, still believing that he included the flight home in any of his camping plans.

We were dumped off at our campsite about seven in the morning, with the parent immediately roaring back toward town in an effort to get to his job on time. I could tell that Homer's intentions were much on Retch's mind.

"Uh, say, Homer," he said casually. "You know, if a

fella happened to decide he wanted to run home from here
before dark, it—uh—it might be a good idea to start right
about now."

"Are you kidding me?" Homer said. "Who would
be dumb enough to run home from here? It's almost
thirty miles."

Retch shrugged. "Just thought I'd mention it."

We went through our usual camping routine of building
a ring of rocks for our fire, chopping up three cords of firewood, fishing for our supper, and then, suddenly, without
warning, the sun slipped behind the mountain. Birdy
started preparing our supper of fried wieners, fried potatoes,
and fried pork 'n' beans. We were all joshing each other
and messing around, when I glanced up and saw Homer
standing still and silent, with the familiar strange look creep-
ing across his face.

"Don't try it, Homer," I said. "It's too far."

Birdy looked up from his frying. "You can't, Homer."

Retch threw his arm around Homer's shoulders. "Listen,
Home, it's gonna be all right. You'll see. We're gonna have
a lotta fun tonight, burn a few marshmallows, tell some
jokes, poke at the fire."

Homer didn't take off for home, but he didn't relax either, and the strange look remained. It seemed as if a huge
invisible rubber band stretched between Homer and his
house, growing ever tighter, and at any second would snap
him in the direction of home.

About ten o'clock we climbed into our sleeping bags under the lean-to we had built as a precaution against rain.
Homer hadn't said a word all evening, but at least he was
now in his sleeping bag. The rest of us began to relax a bit,
assuming that Homer's urge to flee home had given in to
reason. We were about to drift off when all at once we heard

the frantic scrabbling of Homer stuffing gear into his pack. Without further notice, he rushed off into the night.

We lay there silently for a while, thinking about Homer scurrying the thirty miles home. As we were mulling over the odds of his making it, lightning flashed and thunder boomed. Then rain began to pound down on our lean-to and, of course, on Homer, out there all alone in the night, racing madly down the road.

"Poor old Homer," I said. "Think he'll make it?"

"Yeah," Retch said. "Probably by about next Tuesday."

"We should have tried to stop him," Birdy said. "We had a responsibility to—"

"Shut up, Birdy," Retch said.

Suddenly it happened. A long, loud, quavering screech came down off the mountain above us. We had never heard anything like it before, the kind of sound that spikes your hair and raises goosebumps the size of peas.

"Cr-cripes," Birdy whispered. "Wh-what was that?"

"I d-d-d-d-don't know," I explained.

"It was s-s-somethin' b-big, though," Retch whispered. "Wh-where's my .22?"

"Y-you didn't bring it," Birdy said. "We brought w-w-wieners instead."

Then the screech came again, louder and closer this time.

"J-j-jeeeez," Retch said. "I think it's coming for us."

"M-maybe it's just s-some weird bird," I said.

"You really think it's only a b-b-bird?" Homer said.

"Y-yeah," Retch said. "Probably only a b-b-bird. A b-big b-b-bird, though."

"G-good," Homer said.

"Homer?" I said. "You're back?"

"Homer's back!" yelled Birdy.

"Hey, Homer!" Retch said. "What brought you back, Homer?"

"I don't know," Homer said. "I just thought, what the heck, I might as well spend the night with you guys."

We never did find out what made the horrible screech in the night, and we never heard it again. It did, however, make the night memorable, almost as much as did the last flight of Homer Pidgin.

A Boy and His (Ugh!) Dog

Retch Sweeney's dog, Smarts, has distinguished himself over the years as the least aptly named animal with which I've ever been associated. Retch, of course, thinks Smarts is the Einstein of hunting dogs. For example, as Retch and I were driving his old sedan out for a little bird hunting the other day, Smarts interrupted his pastime of slobbering down the backs of our necks long enough to emit an excited yelp, causing my eardrums to vibrate like bongo skins during a Jamaican festival.

Retch chuckled. "Ol' Smarts said he can't wait to get out there and start rounding up pheasants for us."

"No, he didn't," I said irritably.

"He didn't?" Retch said. "What did he say then?"

"He didn't say anything. Dogs don't talk."

"Well, *excuuuuuuse* me!"

"Don't get your tail in a knot," I said. "It's just that I can't stand all the anthropomorphizing going around nowadays."

"Me neither," Retch said, turning thoughtful. "I think

116

it gets spread by toilet seats in public restrooms. But what's that got to do with dogs talking?"

"Anthropomorphizing," I explained patiently, "means the attribution of human characteristics to animals or even inanimate objects."

"Holy cow!" Retch said. "It's even worse than I thought. I can tell you one thing, I ain't using public restrooms no more!"

"Let's forget it," I said. "All I meant was, I don't like people pretending their dogs talk, that's all."

"Oh yeah? I just so happen to recall you letting on that your miserable old dog Strange used to talk. How about that?"

"That's different," I said. "Strange did talk. He could say more with one raised eyebrow than Smarts could yelping night and day for a week. But I'll admit I didn't care much for what he had to say."

"Ha!" Retch said, as if he had just won an argument. "I don't remember you was very proud of Strange, neither."

"No, I wasn't," I said. "I tried to be, but it was impossible, particularly after we learned he was an incorrigible lecher."

"I didn't know that. I thought he was mostly mutt with a little spaniel mixed in. How come you to keep a worthless, disgusting dog like Strange anyhow?"

"We didn't *keep* him, exactly. He just sort of hung around—for about twelve years."

As I explained to Retch, when Strange first started hanging out around our place, I didn't pay much attention to him. I thought he was just passing through our farm on his way home. I fed him a few scraps from the dinner table, thinking he would be gone in a day or two. Weeks later he was still loitering around the house, hitting me up for a handout at every opportunity. When it became apparent that he was intent on establishing a permanent relationship with us, I decided I had better think up a name for him.

Since I was doing a stint in the Cub Scouts at the time, I thought at first that I might name him Scout. It soon became apparent, however, that he was untrustworthy, disloyal, unhelpful, unfriendly, discourteous, mean, disobedient, uncheerful, unthrifty, cowardly, dirty, and irreverent. I decided it wouldn't be right to name such a dog Scout.

My mother suggested Stranger, still hoping the dog might be passing through. For a few weeks, we called him Stranger, but this was soon shortened to Strange. The name fit. In the years to come, we would learn only how well.

Strange lived in a dog shack in our backyard. It was a doghouse, of course, but the rest of the family cruelly referred to it as the dog shack, because I had built it with my own two ten-year-old hands. Driven by powerful but vague ambition in those years, I had intended the doghouse to be a replica of a medieval castle, complete with towers and battlements. The project turned out to be much more complicated than I had first imagined, and I finally gave up on it, after completing only one tower (often mistaken for a chimney—but why would anyone think a dog needed a chimney?), a half-dozen battlements, and the drawbridge. Visitors sometimes expressed curiosity about the shallow ditch around the dog shack. It's surprising how many people don't recognize a moat when they see one.

The dog shack matched nicely Strange's shabby pretensions of nobility, and he seemed not to mind it particularly, although he chose to ignore my instruction on how to raise the drawbridge.

During the early part of his excessively long life with us, I still hoped Strange would exhibit some talent or characteristic to make me proud of him. None became evident. He would slouch around making rude comments, swearing, belching, burping, gagging, and in general engaging in any disgusting activity that occurred to him, and many did. Visitors would recoil at his approach, perhaps expecting not so much that he would bite but that he might try to mooch some change for a bottle of cheap wine or sell them some dirty pictures.

More than anything else at that stage of my life, I wanted to be able to brag to the kids at school about some neat trick my dog could perform. I tried to teach Strange to fetch sticks, but he would only shrug and say, "You threw it, stupid, you go get it." He refused to roll over on command, stand on his hind legs, play dead, heel, sit, or even acknowledge that he had been spoken to. Then one day a marvelous thing happened. Returning home from school, I glanced at the roof of our house, and sitting up there like a degenerate prince surveying his domain was Strange!

My dog climbed houses. Now that was something to brag about. *Why* he climbed the house, I could not even speculate. *How* was fairly easy to determine. He obviously had climbed a stack of firewood, jumped from it to the back porch roof, and from there made his way to the roof of the main house.

There was no way for me to know, of course, that my dog's learning to climb houses was not an isolated incident, but was instead a line of fate that would converge with other lines of fate upon a single point in time and space and produce what is commonly thought of as a coincidence. In this case the coincidence would also be a near-catastrophe. Somewhere it is written that any coincidence traced back far enough will prove to have been inevitable, and I'm sure that must have been the case here.

These were the converging lines of fate:

(1) The long history of genetic malfunctions that eventually combined to create Strange; his aimless meanderings that brought him to our farm; and finally his learning to climb to the roof of our house.

(2) All the genetic and societal forces that combined to shape the particular rebellious nature of my stepfather, Hank; his deciding to grow a beard; and most important, his fractious relationship with my mother's cousin Winnie.

(3) The continuum of factors that led to the creation of Winnie's haughty personality, her fractious relationship with Hank, and her peculiar compulsion to visit us for a week or two every year.

Beards were not popular in that era, and that, as much as anything else, was probably why Hank decided to grow one. He was a man who enjoyed going against the grain of society, or at least what little society existed locally. Winnie, who harbored no great fondness for Hank in the first place, associated beards with comic-strip anarchists who went around carrying bombs that looked like bowling balls with fuses. The stubbly growth of beard seemed to prove her suspicions about my stepfather.

Hank, for his part in the relationship, regarded Winnie as a "mindless twit." Her arrival for the annual visit produced considerable unease for the family, an unease that was well founded, even though Mom had browbeaten Hank to be on his best behavior on this particular occasion. Since even Hank's best behavior left something to be desired as far as Mom was concerned, the tension in our house during Winnie's visit could have been "cut with a knife," to use my mother's phrase.

"Good heavens!" Winnie greeted Hank immediately upon her arrival. "What is that horrible hairy growth on your face?"

"A beard," Hank mumbled, picking up Winnie's suitcase to lug to the upstairs guest room.

"Uh, I think the beard's kind of . . . of . . . dashing," Mom blurted out with a faint laugh, hoping to extinguish the fuse smoldering in Hank's eyes.

"Really?" Winnie said. "Reminds me more of tree moss. I suppose various flying insects might find it irresistible, though. Hee hee."

Hank scurried upstairs with the suitcase, clearly straining to be on his best behavior. Throughout the next few days, Winnie never missed an opportunity to poke fun at Hank's beard. It seemed to have become an obsession with her. Oddly, Hank never responded with any of the biting and usually off-color wit for which he was locally famous. My guess is that he took considerable pleasure in Winnie's loathing of his beard, and the more she pecked away at him about it, the keener was his enjoyment.

And then the fates converged.

After breakfast one morning, Winnie announced that she was going to take a long, leisurely bath, and departed upstairs. Hank shook his head in disbelief. "Another bath," he chuckled. "Why that's the second bath she's took in less than a week. What a twit!"

"Now, now," Mom said soothingly.

Hank and I then went out to clean the rain gutters on the roof. I held the ladder while Hank climbed it to dig away at the muck in the gutter. Strange, already perched on the roof, wandered over to breathe his road-kill breath at Hank.

Hank gasped and choked. "Git out of my face!" he snarled, taking a swipe at Strange.

Strange showed Hank his teeth, made a couple of rude remarks, and then wandered off to another area of the roof, the one containing the dormer window to the bathroom where Winnie was taking her leisurely bath.

As we learned later, Winnie, naked as a noodle, had just emerged from her bath and was drying her hair with a towel prior to putting on her spectacles, without which she was considerably nearsighted. At that very moment, Strange decided to prop his paws on the sill and peer in through the window. Winnie was staring vacantly in the direction of the window. Slowly her eyes came into focus, or as much focus as they were capable of without her glasses. There, on the other side of the glass, was a hairy, leering face—peeping at her.

As Mom said later, Winnie's shriek could have wilted the flowers on the wallpaper. It started at a high, marrow-chilling pitch and went up from there, quavering off into a range beyond human hearing. Among the members of the family, all of whom suffered temporary nerve damage, Hank was the closest to the source of the screech. Following his natural instincts, he took off running at the first high warble. He said later that he noticed right off that he was having trouble getting traction. Then he remembered he had been standing on top of a ladder. Fortunately, he had not traveled any great distance when he remembered the ladder and was able to reach back and get a hand and finally one foot on it. He said the exertion of getting back to the ladder took so much out of him that it might have been better just to take the fall and be done with it. But he said he thought Winnie was being murdered, and if he happened to get knocked unconscious in the fall, he would have missed out on it.

By the time Hank had got himself safely back to the ladder and sucked in a couple of deep breaths, and Winnie had collected her wits, her bathrobe, and her spectacles, Strange had vanished from sight. I suppose it was only natural that upon seeing a hairy, leering face at her bathroom window, Winnie would leap to the conclusion that it must belong to Hank, particularly given her opinion of his character defects. In any case, she jerked up the window, stuck her head out, and shot fierce glances around the roof. And there, to confirm her worst suspicion, was Hank's grizzled face poking up from the edge of the roof.

"You hairy pervert!" Winnie screeched. "I saw you, you . . . you . . . you peeper!"

Hank, of course, had not the slightest notion of what she was talking about, and cared even less, as he was still regrouping his senses after his recent acrobatics. Even after Winnie's head had disappeared back in the window, he clung silently to the top of the ladder.

"You gonna come down or what, Hank?" I asked.

"Yeah," he said. "Pretty quick. As soon as I can make my hands let go of the ladder."

"What was Winnie screeching about?"

"I don't know. Probably tryin' to scare me to death, the crazy twit!"

I could tell from his tone that Hank had abandoned his best behavior.

We soon got the whole mess straightened out, and Winnie had a good laugh over the misunderstanding. Hank, however, seemed depressed. He disappeared into the bathroom for a while and then returned, clean-shaven.

"You shaved off your beard!" Winnie yelped. "Why, you know, I think I liked you better with it. Covered up your weak chin."

Hank responded with a comment that indicated he was off his good behavior. Winnie laughed. Hank was back to

normal, and the tension began to melt away. He and Winnie matched insult for insult, and if I'm not mistaken, both
of them thoroughly enjoyed the rest of her visit.

But every so often, I would catch Hank staring moodily
off into the distance, and it wasn't too hard to guess what
troubled him. I'm sure he didn't care one way or the other
about being mistaken for a Peeping Tom, but it bothered
him no end to be mistaken for Strange.

As usual, the dog escaped unscathed and unrepentant,
but he kept a wary eye out for Hank the next few days, and
for good reason. Shortly after we had determined the identity of the true culprit in the troublesome affair, Hank made
a strangling motion with his hands and snarled, "Where is
that miserable mutt?"

"I don't know," I said. "Probably at the dog shack, trying to figure out how to raise the drawbridge."

Strange never again climbed the house, and it was a long,
long wait before he did anything else of which I could
be proud.

To Filet
or Not to Filet

During the years I was a college sophomore, I became interested in philosophy and signed up for several courses, hoping the intellectual discipline would improve my mind, or, failing that, help me get girls.

Even to this day, I still read philosophy on occasion. I have just been perusing Mortimer J. Adler's *Ten Philosophical Mistakes*. Surprisingly, Mr. Adler forgot the most important philosophical mistake: enrolling in philosophy courses as a sophomore. In his chapter "Consciousness and Its Objects," he cuts right to the heart of the problem: "If two persons are talking about an object that is an object of memory for both of them, or an object of imagination for both, or an object of memory for one and an object of imagination for the other, the question about whether that common object is an entity which also really exists, which also once existed, or which also may exist in the future, cannot be so easily answered."

Right! In fact, I found such problems absolutely impossible to answer. I never even knew they were problems, no one in my family ever having mentioned them.

But I have no regrets about studying philosophy. For one thing, it comes in handy for fileting bluegills. Just the other night, my friend Keith Jackson and I went out on the lake and caught a nice mess of bluegills. As is well known among pan fishermen, there is no such thing as catching too many bluegills while you are catching them. It is only when you must start fileting them that you realize that any number of bluegills is too many to catch.

Upon returning home late at night, Jackson and I were both overcome with the traditional generosity of successful bluegill fishermen the world over. "You take all of them," I told Keith. "Then when we go walleye fishing, you can pay me back."

Jackson said he would stand for nothing of the sort. "I took all the bluegills last time," he said. "No, it's your turn. You take 'em. Be my guest!" This last exclamation being expressed in the intimidating tone of Clint Eastwood's "Make my day!" and given the fact that Eastwood is but a puny shrimp compared to Jackson's six-foot-five, two hundred fifty pounds, I reluctantly acquiesced and hauled the whole mess of bluegills into my house.

My wife, Bun, was stretched out on the couch, wineglass in hand, watching the late news. "Catch anything?"

"A couple thousand bluegills," I said. "I'll just stow them in the refrigerator for tonight and get up first thing in the morning and filet . . ."

Bun's eyes narrowed instantly to the slits that thirty years of marriage have taught me mean trouble and, even worse, work. No doubt she recalled the last time I had stowed a plastic sack full of crappies in the refrigerator. Her friend Lulu had been spending the night. I had told Lulu a dozen times that a lady of her intelligence and sophistication should not watch movies like *Son of Killer Piranha*, in which a vicious fish comes ashore and eats tourists.

Futhermore, I told her, piranha are seldom if ever found lurking in the fitting rooms of chic dress shops, although that's not a bad idea. Even less are they likely to be found crouched in suburban refrigerators. All right, I will admit that a crappie does look something like a piranha. So what happened was, Lulu can't sleep and gets up in the middle of the night and goes down to the refrigerator for a glass of milk. She opens the refrigerator door, reaches for the milk carton, and a half-expired crappie flops out of the plastic bag in front of her. There is no way that it could have gone for her throat, as she hysterically claimed. I, on the other hand, would have been happy to go for her throat, a voluminous organ that no doubt instantly raised all the neighbors a good three feet straight up out of bed. I personally was raised to within a few inches of the ceiling. Hovering there, exuding cold sweat, I calmly tried to deduce the reason for the psyche-shredding screech emanating from my kitchen. The only thing I could come up with was that a burglar had broken in and was feeding Lulu through the pasta-making machine. Later, when I learned that a mere crappie had set off Lulu's alarm, I gladly would have paid a burglar to perform that service.

Rising menacingly from the couch, Bun pointed to the back porch and my fish-cleaning table. I slouched out, the bulging bag of bluegills sagging from my weary casting arm. It is at times like this that my years of delving into the quirky, quicksand depths of philosophy pay off.

I spread newspapers on the porch, then dumped the spiny, slimy pile of bluegills on them. Immediately, as I stared down at the pile, the philosophical question of guilt came to mind. Would there be any reality to the guilt I would feel if, instead of fileting the bluegills, I used them in their entirety as fertilizer for Bun's roses? Would my guilt amount to anything in the endlessly expanding universe with its trillions of stars, some of which were probably orbited by worlds containing intelligent life, one being of which was probably at that very moment staring down at the equivalent of a slimy, spiny pile of bluegills, wondering how he could get out of fileting them? That would certainly be one test of his intelligence. As to the question of guilt, I could only answer, "Yeah, probably." I had killed them. So I would filet and eat them. I picked up a bluegill and had at it with the fileting knife.

An exhausted and shivering person fileting ten thousand bluegills at midnight could easily slip into insanity and scarcely notice it. Thus, the need to invent ever more difficult philosophical questions to keep the mind firmly astride the track of rational thought. Here is one of the tougher problems I came up with: "If a wife has never expressed an interest in hunting in the past or the present and shows no inclination of doing so in the future, and if she has shown no discernible enthusiasm for guns, and indeed mildly distrusts them, would it be a relevant and significant act to give her a really nice .257 Roberts for her birthday?" In the existential sense, the answer is, of course, yes. Still, the risk must be weighed. As the great philosopher Immanuel Kant pointed out, under such circumstances one must be alert to every slight deviation in one's normal existence, such as having your oatmeal taste funny three days in a row.

Perhaps the single most difficult question that has stumped philosophers since the time of Aristotle is, "Why do men fish and call it sport?" Clearly, the act of sport fishing is absurd, lying as it does outside the realm of reason. No sport fisherman can deny the absurdity of his activity, particularly at one o'clock in the morning as he stares down at a pile of twenty thousand bluegills that he must filet. Nevertheless, one must learn not only to accept the absurdity of one's acts but to triumph over it. In one of the Greek myths, a character by the name of Sisyphus is caught by the gods in some misdemeanors involving wine, women, and song while he is supposed to be boringly dead. For his punishment, the gods force Sisyphus to push a huge stone uphill for eternity. As soon as Sisyphus gets the stone to the top of the hill, the stone rolls back to the bottom, and Sisyphus must walk back down and start pushing it up again. One version of the myth has it that Sisyphus triumphs over his fate and the gods, because, on his way back down the hill, he *laughs!* Okay, so it's not that big a triumph. Nevertheless, it appeals to me, because that is often the only triumph we have over our fates—to laugh.

Bun jerked open the back door. "Would you stop that silly cackling!" she hissed. "You'll wake the neighbors! You've got every dog in the block barking his head off!"

So much for Greek myths.

At 2:00 A.M., with the eyes of fifty thousand unfileted bluegills staring gleefully up at me, I turned to the philosophical question of identity. Say, for instance, you have wooden boat *A*. You remove a piece from it and use it to start building wooden boat *B*. You transfer each piece of boat *A* to boat *B*. Eventually, you have transferred all the pieces. Now what is the identity of the boat—is it *A* or *B?* That's a tough question to answer, unless, of course, I am doing the work, in which case boat *B* leaks like a sieve.

Finally, with 200,000 bluegills glutting the porch at three o'clock in the morning, I came to the ultimate philosophical question. Is it possible for lifeless matter, such as rock and ice swirling in space, which the world once was, to evolve eventually into intelligent life, or approximately one-sixty-fourth of the human population on the planet today? I mean, go out and look at a rock and ask yourself how long it would take that rock to become a divorced public-relations man who is three months behind in his child support. Quite a while, right? In fact, just about the same length of time it takes to filet half a million bluegills.

What's in a Name, Moonbeam?

One of my daughters and her husband were recently going through the mystical ritual of naming a new baby, which, upon its arrival, they claimed, would be either my grandson or granddaughter. They had failed to take into consideration that I am much too young to be a grandfather. As I told my wife, Bun, I'll be danged if I'll have some little whippersnapper going about referring to me as "Gramps."

"Don't be so crotchety," she said.

"Crochety!" I bellowed. "Do you realize what you said, woman?"

"I must have been out of my mind," she said. "I meant to say 'irascible.' "

"That's not any better."

"Miffed?"

"Okay. Now, do you know the name they're thinking of giving this new baby, if it's a boy? *Treat!*"

"I think Treat's a nice name for a boy."

"Nice! Why you couldn't even call the kid without sounding like a damn bird."

"So what kind of name do you think is appropriate?"

"Well, certainly not any of these nature names you hear all the time nowadays: Rain, Breeze, Sky, Snowflake, Moonbeam. What's wrong with the good, solid-sounding names we used to have? They could call him Horace, for instance. Now there's a name with character built into it."

"Horace! I wouldn't feel right about calling a little baby Horace."

"He's only a baby for a little while. He and you can put up with it for a little while. But he's going to be a man practically forever, and Horace is a man's name. I sure as heck can't imagine myself saying, 'Watch closely, Treat. I'm gonna·show you how to gut an elk.' "

"That's so disgusting!" Bun said.

"Right," I said. "Why would anyone name a kid Treat? I can tell you this, I won't call one of my grannnnn . . . grannnnn . . . one of my small relatives Treat. I'll give him a name of my own, probably Horace."

At this, I drifted into one of my dream sequences. My small relative was now ten years old, and he and I were on our way out to fish the beaver ponds on the Conckle place. Only the lad had shown any signs of aging. I looked the same as I always have for the past thirty-seven years, since the age of sixteen. The fishing trip was but another of the many lessons in the extensive outdoor education I would provide the youngster.

When we got out of my pickup truck, I locked it up tight and then put the keys on top of the right front tire.

"Pay attention to this, Horace," I said. "All outdoorsmen always hide their keys on top of the right front tire. No one would ever think to look there if he wanted to steal your vehicle.''

"That's a wonderful bit of outdoor knowledge, sir," Horace replied, his eyes shiny-bright with appreciation.

As we were climbing through the barbwire fence onto the Conckle property, Horace caught his back on a barb, tore his shirt, and cut a bloody scratch across his back. "Ha, ha," he laughed. "I just cut a very painful bloody scratch across my back, sir."

"You handled that very well, Horace," I said. "As I have taught you many times, a person cannot enjoy the outdoors unless he is willing to laugh off a few cuts and bruises. No outdoorsman ever screeches or whines over a bit of pain. Let me hear you do the laugh again."

"Ha ha, sir."

"Good. You don't want to overdo it."

We then waded into the swamp that surrounds the beaver ponds, sinking into the slimy, smelly muck almost up to our knees. Actually, since my knees were higher than Horace's, he sank in almost to his hips. Clouds of mosquitoes descended, and queued up in dozens of lines so each would get its fair turn at us. Deerflies soon arrived and tried to crowd in line. Threats were exchanged. Fights broke out.

"This is bad," I said. "Still, it is much better than some other things you could be doing. What are some of those things, Horace?"

"Lying around the house watching TV," Horace said. "And hanging out in shopping malls. Those are two of the worst things, sir."

"Right."

We soon emerged from the swamp and passed through a

grove of aspen. In the branches above us, a bird went "Tweet."

"What, sir?" Horace said.

"I didn't call you, Horace. I never call you by that name."

As we strolled along the stream bank, I suddenly did a one-legger down a beaver hole. After a bit, I smiled grimly.

"It's all right, then," Horace asked, "to screech when you do a one-legger down a beaver hole?"

"Only if you think the beaver has hold of your leg," I replied, "and has mistaken it for a cottonwood limb. That was what I surmised in this instance. By screeching the way I just did, you can often frighten the beaver into letting go."

"That is a useful bit of information, sir. Are the other words used to frighten the beaver, also?"

"Yes. However, they also frighten mothers, so I advise you not to use them around your mother or Granny. Use them only when you do one-leggers and after you are twenty-one or older. Now, if you will excuse me for a moment, I would like to say this: OWWW! OOUCH! OOOOOH! AHHHHHHHH!"

"When are you going to do the laugh, sir?"

"In about six months, Horace, in about six months."

We finally arrived at the beaver ponds, and I showed Horace how to hold large boulders over the water in the slight chance that a beaver might stick his head out. I then made several deliberately bad casts in order to show the boy how to remove a $1.50 fly from the top of a fir tree. I further demonstrated to him how to make a No. 14 dry fly splash like a diving osprey, which is a good way to excite fish from midday doldrums and get them to strike. A good outdoorsman, as I told Horace, must be a keen observer of the psychology of wildlife. Later, when he was older, I would teach him what Freud had to say about the subconscious of fish, and why Jung was ridiculed by Freud for his interpretations of perch dreams.

I did not neglect his instruction in aquatic insect life, explaining the various stages of development: egg, baby bug, child bug, adolescent bug, and finally, of course, adult bug.

"I'm sorry, sir," Horace said, "but all this is too technical for me. I'm only ten."

One of the worst things you can do while educating a youngster about the outdoors is to push him along too fast. I decided to instruct him in more practical matters, such as how to build a campfire to cook a couple of our trout. I cleared a spot on the ground with my boot, carefully arranged a handful of tinder on it, built a tiny pyramid of sticks around the tinder, and touched a match to it.

"See," I said, "if you touch a match directly to the tinder, Horace, nothing happens. First you must strike the match on something. Here is a good way to strike a match. Place the underside of your thumbnail on the head of the match. Then snap it down and back like this and . . ."

"It's all right then, sir," said Horace presently, "to say those words when you have fire shooting out from under your thumbnail?"

"Yes," I said. "Also, I hope you noticed how I grasped my thumb with my crotch and leaped about in a circle. That is an excellent way to extinguish the flames shooting out from under a thumbnail. So, anyway, that is how you build a fire. Remember, don't practice it in your bedroom. Now I will show you how to take the fish home and trick Granny into cleaning and frying them."

"That is something I would really like to learn, sir," Horace said. "It is wonderful to be your small relative."

"Thank you, Horace," I said. "You are a very fine small relative, and someday you will be a great outdoorsman."

At that moment, my dream sequence was interrupted by the ringing of the telephone. Bun answered it. She came back a few minutes later, beaming.

"Guess what. You have a new baby relative—a girl."

"Great!" I said. "Just think, in ten years I can start teaching her all I know about the outdoors. She will make a fine woodsperson. By the way, what did they name her, 'Moonbeam'? 'Snowflake'?"

"Clementine."

"All right! Now that's a name I can live with."

Loud Screeching and
Other Tips on Getting Lost

Summer is that time of year when thousands of otherwise normal citizens are overcome with the urge to rush out to the great forests and mountains of America and get themselves lost. Most of them, however, have not the slightest notion of how to get properly lost, and if they do somehow manage to achieve that exhilarating state, it is by mere accident. Since getting lost in the woods is almost always the highlight of any outdoors vacation, it should not be left to chance.

Getting lost requires planning. Otherwise, you will discover your vacation almost at an end without your having been lost even once. Then you will have to rush to get it done, and in the process you will probably botch the whole thing.

If, for example, you have a week for your wilderness vacation beginning on Saturday, set aside the following Wednesday for getting lost. That will give you Thursday, Friday, and the next Saturday to recover, to let the shakes die down and the goosebumps recede, and to sit around camp savoring the experience of, first, getting lost, and second, getting found. Some people claim that getting found is even more satisfying than getting lost, but my research shows that people tend to treasure the memory of being lost much more than of being found.

Another thing about getting lost on Wednesday is that it gives the Search and Rescue people Thursday and Friday to find you, and therefore doesn't use up their weekend. My own forty years of experience at getting lost in the woods has proven to me that it is much better not to get lost at all than to be found by Search and Rescue people who have spent their whole weekend looking for you. They are often tired and irritable and may have a tendency to regard you as a nuisance rather than as a pathetic but nonetheless heroic lost person. Actually, Search and Rescue people will regard you as a nuisance under any conditions, but more so on weekends. So plan your getting lost for midweek.

Keep in mind, also, that you will need several days to polish the account of your harrowing adventure for the folks back at work. Imagine yourself telling the people at the office, "Yeah, I got lost in the woods and sat down on a log and an hour later a park ranger came by with a nature-study group and found me." That simply won't do. To return to work without a polished and suspenseful story about getting lost deprives you of much of the enjoyment of the experience.

Now, how should you go about getting lost? Naturally, you don't want to tell the other members of the party, "Well, now that it's Wednesday, I think I'll wander off in the woods and get lost." You must appear to have some other objective in mind. Efficiency is a good one. If you are camped in a public campground, simply say that you are going to take a shortcut to the communal spigot to fill the water bucket. Since you have absolutely nothing else to do in a public campground but go for water, someone may inquire as to the need for a shortcut. You could take three hours to fill the water bucket and nobody would care or even notice. Therefore, simply ignore any inquiries about the need for a shortcut.

Shortcuts rank number one among ways to get lost quickly and thoroughly. The typical shortcut requires triple the time to traverse as the long way around. Some shortcuts to destinations no farther away than the campground restroom stretch into days and weeks, which many lost persons find excessive and even tedious.

Before starting your shortcut, take careful note of the position of the sun. This will give the impression that you know what you're doing but otherwise is absolutely useless, because the next time you try to take a bearing on the sun, it will have moved. The North Star is much more reliable, but you can only see it after dark, when you have other things on your mind, such as the strange loud snuffling noises at the foot of the tree you've climbed. Under such circumstances, I've never found that the North Star had the power to hold my attention for any length of time and was best ignored.

Always study on which side of the trees the moss is growing. Guides and other experienced woodsmen are fond of giving this advice, because looking at moss helps even them to get lost. The moss would help you get unlost if it always grew on the side of the tree facing camp or the nearest population center or some other meaningful direction. The sad truth is that moss—rather perversely, I might add—grows on any side of a tree it takes a mind to. That is why it is such an invaluable aid in getting lost.

If you have been out in the woods for an hour and still

aren't lost, you must resort to drastic measures. Start picking wild berries, for example. When I was a child, my father and mother always used huckleberry or dewberry picking for getting us lost in the woods in a quick and efficient manner. We would start out with our empty lard buckets roped to our waists, the individual berries making pleasant little plunking sounds as we dropped them on the tin bottom. The standard joke shouted back and forth, as we worked our way from bush to bush, was, "Is your bottom covered yet? Ho! Ho!" It was always good for a laugh.

"Over here," my father would call. "These bushes are loaded."

"Oh, my goodness," Mom would say. "Look up there! The berries are as big as grapefruit!"

We would charge from one berry patch to another, and in practically no time at all we would be lost. I always knew when we were lost because my parents would suddenly get into a loud and complex argument about the direction back to the car. "I know the way!" Dad would shout. "The sun was off to our right and the moss was growing on the other side of the trees, and—"

"It certainly was not!" Mom would yell. "I remember, I climbed over a big log and there was a little creek . . . !"

Both of them would have wild, desperate looks in their eyes, and I could see that it was time to introduce a little levity into the situation.

"Is your bottom covered?" I would ask, thereby learning that lost persons are the toughest audience in the world to get a laugh out of.

What should you do once you know you are actually lost and not merely standing behind some brush next to a shopping center? Well, the first thing you do is panic. Get the panic out of your system immediately, so that you can start thinking straight. Inexperienced' lost persons often try to hold the panic in until it explodes and sends them ricocheting off rocks and trees, or propels them over entire mountain ranges. Years ago, I invented the Modified Stationary Panic, which consists of madly running in place and screeching. (You may wish to substitute an inspirational song for the screeching, but you would be the exception.) The MSP has the advantage over uncontrolled panics in that when you are finished you **are** still in the same place and in one piece, thus making yourself easier and neater for Search and Rescue to find.

Once the MSP has been performed to your satisfaction, sit down and calmly carve a notch on a piece of wood. All lost persons carve notches on pieces of wood, each notch indicating another day they've been lost. Carving notches is part of the tradition. Actually, it's a good idea to carve several notches right away, just in case you get found within the next fifteen minutes. The people back at work might laugh if you showed up with only one notch on a stick. Lost persons must always plan ahead.

The Big Fix

I had the opportunity the other day to ride in the perfect outdoor vehicle, namely one of those vehicles that belongs to somebody else.

In this case, the owner of the perfect outdoor vehicle was young Milt Thomas, a lad scarcely older than his car. Although I own a four-wheel-drive pickup, the road up to the mountain stream Milt and I intended to fish was so rough and terrible that I quickly realized that the only appropriate vehicle for such terrain was Milt's 1968 sedan. As he is still relatively inexperienced in outdoorsmanship, the lad was slow to perceive why his vehicle was the more appropriate one to meet the challenge.

"It's quite simple," I explained. "The Blue Creek Road is rough and dangerous, and requires a certain delicacy of motion to traverse. Your car just happens to possess that essential subtlety of traction provided by tires unencumbered by tread. See? Now shut up and drive."

Scarcely had we left the interstate and begun pounding up the Blue Creek Road than the wisdom of taking Milt's vehicle became loudly apparent. A horrible sound began emanating from beneath the sedan: *WOPPITTY WOP-PITTY WOPPITTY WOPPITTY!*

"Aaaaigh!" Milt cried. "A flat! Do you know what this means?"

"Oh no," I said. "You don't have a spare?"

"Sure, I have a spare," Milt said. "But we still have to change the tire. Then if we have another flat, we won't have a spare."

"Yeah, I already worked that out on my fingers," I said.

"We better change the tire and then go get your pickup," Milt said.

"Let's not be too hasty," I said. "Going thirty miles back up into the mountains without a spare, that's the sort of risk the true outdoorsman thrives on. Remember, Milt, it's risk that whets the edge of a person's life."

"Really?"

"Yup. Now, you hurry up and get that tire changed, while I have a cup of coffee and peruse the fishing regs pamphlet one more time. I'll be over there in the shade of that tree if you need any advice."

I would like to point out here that I eschew making the pretense that I am helping someone change a tire by standing next to him and occasionally handing him a tool that is no more than six inches from his hand. Such a pretense allows the stander-by to lay claim to a share of the work of the actual tire-changer. *"We* had to change a tire," he can brag. But think how much better it is to remove oneself entirely from the workplace and allow all the honor and glory to fall intact upon the person who does the real work, traditionally the owner of the perfect outdoor vehicle.

Unschooled as he is in logic and ethics, Milt failed to perceive the favor I was doing him. He seemed irritated even by my words of encouragement, such as, "Let's speed it up, Milt. Fish don't bite all day, you know."

As Milt shaped his mouth into its whining mode, I quickly offered inspiration. "Milt, Milt, my boy, you should look upon this bit of adversity as an opportunity to build your character."

"I don't see you building your character none," he retorted clumsily.

"That's because you fail to realize the strenuous mental labor required to comprehend fishing regulations pamphlets these days. Build my character? Why, just trying to understand the possession limit has put up four walls, roofed, and added a porch to my character in the short time I've been sitting here. My character's overbuilt, anyway. But to return to my original point, you should consider having to change a tire as an uplifting experience. Now *fixing* a tire, as they used to do in the old days, that was a journey of the spirit, Milt, a journey of the spirit, fixing a tire."

"Gosh," Milt said, "for a moment there I thought I heard background music. You kidding me? How could they fix their own tires in the olden days? They didn't even have VCRs back then."

"Yes," I said, "we are talking ancient times—pre-Columbian, pre-VCR. I myself was but a small child when I first was witness to a tire-fixing."

Tire-fixings were to become a regular and enlightening occurrence during the years of my early youth. My father was a man who believed that a spare tire ranked as a shameless luxury, an accessory serving no other purpose than evidence of conspicuous consumption. He apparently felt the same way about tire tread, if not the thin film of rubber coating the cords of his tires.

The typical tire-fixing occurred on remote dirt roads, where my father frequently took us on Sunday drives. Deprived as I was of almost any form of entertainment in those days, I looked forward to the drives with great anticipation, largely because of the excitement and adventure promised by the inevitable flat.

That first flat tire remains one of my earliest and most cherished memories. We were driving happily along, my father and mother in the front seat singing the forty-ninth verse of "The Old Gray Mare," my sister (the Troll) and I enthusiastically slugging it out in the back seat, when suddenly the joyfulness of the moment was shattered by an ominous sound: *WOPPITTY WOPPITTY WOPPITTY!*

"Oh dear, a flat," my mother announced. "Well, you will just have to get out and fix it. You really should buy a spare."

Dad responded by banging his forehead up and down on the steering wheel. "Women!" he snapped, in a tone suggesting the flat was Mom's fault. I wasn't sure how she had made the tire go flat, but supposed she had driven a nail into it when no one was looking.

We all got out and gathered around the flat, staring at it as though it were some aberration of nature. Dad kicked the tire a few times. That effort failing to inflate it noticeably, he heaved a long sigh. Hoping to cheer him up, I suggested that we could all sing "The Old Gray Mare" while he fixed the tire. Dad stared at me as though I, too, were an aberration of nature. After that I kept my suggestions to myself and concentrated on learning how to fix a tire.

A car jack apparently fell into the same category in which my father placed spares and tread. In any case, we never seemed to have a jack with us. Thus, Dad would go off in search of what he termed a "pry pole," usually one of the fenceposts a considerate farmer had stationed at intervals around his field for just such an emergency.

Dad returned with a pry pole and built a fulcrum out of rocks and pieces of rotting wood, giving no indication that he heard a word of Mom's lengthy lecture on the subject of jacks. Once the car was levered up into the air, Dad crawled under it and blocked up the axle, while the rest of the family sat on the end of the pry pole, bouncing it up and down to Dad's hearty cries of, "Steady! Steady! Steadeeeee!"

As soon as the car was precariously blocked up, Dad remembered that he had forgotten to loosen the lug nuts on the wheels, and so the whole process had to be repeated. This was the first time I realized my father knew a foreign language. "Sum glits um blotten putter fitzon mang fudder dits!" he shouted, although I can no longer remember the exact words.

Nowadays, lug nuts are welded to their bolts by fiends in garages using pneumatic wrenches, in the expectation that the tire might next be changed at the edge of a busy expressway at night in the rain by a pudgy middle-aged man using a hand-powered lug wrench. Pneumatic wrenches being unknown in the old days, lug nuts were held in place by rust, an early fixative possessing the qualities of both holding strength and cheapness.

Once the rust bond had been broken and the wheel removed from the axle, Dad set about separating the tire from the rim. To accomplish this, he used a tire iron—an instrument now unfamiliar to the average motorist—and a screwdriver. The screwdriver substituted for a second tire iron that was essential for removing the tire from the rim.

I studied Dad's technique carefully, to be ready for the day when I, too, would be old enough and lucky enough to fix tires on remote roads.

First, Dad shoved the tire iron between the lip of the tire and the wheel and pried a six-inch section of the tire up over the rim. Next, he stuck in the screwdriver and pried up a three-inch section of tire lip, leaving a gap about as wide as a man's hand between the screwdriver and the tire iron. Finally, holding the tire iron down with his knee, and the screwdriver down with his other hand, he thrust his fingers into the gap and attempted to jerk the rest of the tire lip up over the rim. That was when his knee slipped off the tire iron and the tire clamped shut on his fingers with kind of a slurping sound.

Mom gasped. The Troll emitted a frightened yelp. My father, not to be outdone in the dramatics of the moment, sprang to his feet and began to dance around in an impromptu impression of a foreign-speaking maniac, the tire swinging from his fingers like a vicious but toothless dog.

"Glop kitch feng dopper glitz!" Dad shouted, clasping the tire under one arm and wrenching his fingers free. His lighthearted antics had provoked me instantly to loud, delighted laughter, which was quickly smothered by Mom's hand over my mouth and a vague but ominous prediction as to my immediate fate should I persist. Nevertheless, I have long cherished the thoughtfulness of my father in taking time out from a dirty and difficult task to entertain his young son, a person generally regarded as somewhat peculiar by the family.

Eventually, Dad managed to eviscerate the tube from the tire. For those unacquainted with tubes in this day of the tubeless tire, I will explain that tubes consisted of a donut-shaped collection of patches held together by narrow margins of rubber. Dad hated tubes. The patching kit was equipped with a perforated lid used to roughen the tube surface so that a patch could be affixed to it. Muttering incoherently, Dad scraped the tube so vigorously as to make one think he was trying to torture out of it a confession of all its many crimes against him.

At last the tube was patched, reinserted in the tire, and inflated with a hand pump. Inflating a tire by hand pump, I learned from my father, is made easier by chanting a mantra as you pump: "Hennnn—UFF! Henn-nn-nn—UFF! Hennn-nn-nn-nn-n-n-n—UFF!" It works!

Two hours after the intrusion of the flat into our Sunday drive, we were back in the car heading home, Dad slumped behind the wheel in dense silence.

"There, there," Mom said consolingly, "that wasn't so bad, was it? Still, if we'd had a spare and a jack . . ."

"Women!" Dad barked, his tone speaking volumes in explanation. I knew then once and for all that women are responsible for flat tires.

Even to this day I am alert to any suspicious movements in the vicinity of my tires by my wife and daughters. Still, they manage to sneak by me from time to time and cause a flat. I guess they can't help themselves, and I try not to hold it against them.

"Hey," Milt called, rudely awakening me from a peaceful slumber. "Guess what caused the flat. A nail! How do you suppose a nail got in that tire?"

"Your wife put it there," I said.

"Wife? I'm not even married."

"Oh, that's right. It must have been your mother, then. Or your sister. If not her, possibly a neighbor lady. Women are responsible for all flat tires."

"But why?"

"Nobody knows, Milt, but they are."

I paused and shook my head for proper effect, just as my father had shown me so many decades ago, and then barked:

"Women!"

The Fine Art of Delay

Young Wally Whipple showed up at my house the other morning a whole hour late for the start of our hunting trip. The first thing he did was offer excuses.

"I'm sorry to be so late," he said, "but Retch wasn't ready when I got to his house." Here he jerked a thumb over his shoulder to indicate Retch Sweeney, who was grinning broadly and shaking his head in disbelief. "Retch wasn't even out of bed yet. Then, while he was making his lunch, he asked me if I would change a flat tire on his wife's car so we could get started sooner. After I got the tire changed, he still had to oil his boots and put new laces in them. So he asked me to pick up after the dogs that had knocked over his garbage can. Next he had to look for his sleeping bag, while I changed the bulb in his porch light. Geez, if I hadn't given him a hand, we wouldn't have got started on the hunt until noon. Now I see you ain't ready either."

"I suppose you are referring to the fact that I'm still in

my nightgown," I replied. "It just happens you guys were so late I thought you weren't coming, and I decided to go back to bed."

"You wear a nightgown?" Retch said, a note of suspicion in his tone.

"Of course," I replied. "Doesn't everyone?"

During the course of Wally's long harangue, I had scarcely been able to suppress a chuckle of appreciation at Retch's skilled performance. The man was a master of delay. I happened to know that Ernestine Sweeney's tire had been flat for three days, the garbage can had been the sport of dogs nearly a week earlier, and the porch light had been out for a year. Not bad, not bad at all. A delay of that quality and magnitude would be tough to top.

"I'll be ready in a jiff," I said. "Why don't you fellows sit down and have a cup of coffee while I get dressed? Oh, I nearly forgot!"

At this, Retch turned and headed for the door, mumbling that he didn't want any coffee and would wait in the car. As a master of delay, he can recognize one coming from a mile off.

"Hold it," I said. "We want to get this hunt under way as soon as possible, right?" Retch stopped, his shoulders sagging in surrender. "As I was saying, I nearly forgot that my wife asked me to perform an organ transplant for her before I left."

"Good grief!" Wally said.

"Yeah," I said. "The organ is in the basement rec room and she wants it transplanted up to the living room." I thought the joke pretty good, but it didn't get so much as a smile. "Just so we can get started a little sooner on the hunt, why don't you boys transplant the organ while I get dressed?"

As soon as they had disappeared into the basement, I whisked the nightgown off from over my hunting togs and started putting on my boots. A nightgown, for Pete's sake! I limited myself to a couple of brief chuckles as I listened to them grunting out what sounded like an off-color Gregorian chant as they hauled the organ up the stairs. An organ transplant beats a flat tire, a spilled garbage can, and a blown-out light bulb any day of the week. And Retch knew it, too, even if Wally didn't.

There are many reasons for hunting and fishing delays, other than getting help with a few chores around the house. Take, for example, my goose-hunting trip with two burly friends I'll call Keith and Gary.

I had been all but paralyzed by cold for the past hour, a particularly grim circumstance, since we were still in the car on our way out to the goose pits. Soon I would be crouched in one of the muddy pits, with icy rain rattling down on me like machine-gun fire. All I could think about was curling up under a nice warm electric blanket and dreaming that I had never heard of goose hunting. I needed to come up with a delay, one that would last until the rain at least eased up to a downpour.

"I love mornings like this," Keith said, throwing out his chest and beating on it with his fists. "It makes a man feel alive!"

"Yeah," Gary said. "It's invigorating. Grows hair on your chest. Some guys, all they could think about on a morning like this would be curling up under a nice warm electric blanket, the lily-livered sissies."

"Pardon?" I said. "You say something to me?"

"No, I was talking about lily-livered sissies."

"Oh," I said. "Hey, we're nearly to Greasy Gert's Gas

& Grub Truck Stop. Let's whip in there for a quick cup of coffee before hitting the ol' goose pits. Just take a couple of minutes. We can warm up a bit and give the hair follicles on our chest a rest. What say, guys?"

"I guess we got time for a quick cup," Keith said. "But just one, no refills."

It is important to note here the skill with which I eased my companions into the first stage of a delay. Both Gary and Keith are experts at delay themselves, and had neatly parried my utility delay back at my house, where I had tried a thrust at getting them to put the snow tires on my truck. Once on the road, however, they quickly relaxed their vigilance, and I was able to take advantage of the element of surprise.

As soon as we were seated in the restaurant, Gert herself came over to take our orders. "What'll ya have, fellas?"

"Three coffees, Gert," Gary said.

"And an order of French toast," I blurted out.

"We don't have time for French toast!" Keith snarled.

"French toast takes hardly any time at all," I said. "Besides, on an empty stomach I can't get the full enjoyment out of freezing off assorted parts of my anatomy in a flooded goose pit."

Twenty minutes and three coffee refills later, Gert returned with my French toast. I glanced out the window. Icy rain still pounded down.

"What's this white stuff on my French toast?" I asked Gert.

"Powdered sugar," she snapped. "What'd ya think?"

"I can't eat French toast with powdered sugar on it," I said. "Cook me up a new batch, plain."

"We don't have time!" Gary screamed. He reached

across the table, grabbed my slices of French toast, and wiped them across his pants leg. "There. Now your French toast doesn't have any powdered sugar on it. Eat!"

"Those pants clean? Okay, okay, put down the knife! I'll eat, I'll eat. Uh, say, Gert, you forgot my bacon."

"*YOU DIDN'T ORDER BACON!*"

"Did so!"

"Did not!"

I looked outside. The rain had stopped. Shafts of sunlight were breaking through the clouds. "Are we going to sit here and argue all morning, or are we going to hunt?" I said. "Let's go. Sometimes I think you guys would do anything to stay out of a goose pit for a few extra minutes."

Among the delaying tactics I've had pulled on me, the "roadside historical attraction" is the one I hate most, possibly because it is favored by my neighbor, Al Finley. We'll drive by a sign announcing HISTORICAL SITE ONE MILE.

"Historical site one mile," Finley says.

"I can read," I say. "But we're not stopping. Otherwise, we'll miss the peak feeding time."

"We're not talking fish here, we're talking history. Abe Lincoln, Thomas Jefferson . . ."

Knowing he'll give me no peace and probably even accuse me of being unpatriotic, I swerve into the turnout, where a rustic board sign hangs by chains from two posts. The printing on the sign tells us that at this very spot 150 years ago, the first white man to enter the region probably camped for the night, although it may have been a spot eighteen miles away, but it was easier to dig the postholes for the sign here.

"Isn't that interesting?" Finley says. "You can almost see him camped here, old Fletcher Malone. Hostile Indians finally did him in."

"Small wonder," I say. "I've never laid eyes on the man, and he's already made me hostile."

I have known many masters of the hunting and fishing delay, but none greater than Mr. Cranston, a tall, bald man who lived down the road from our place when Retch Sweeney and I were youngsters. Retch and I would be riding our bikes past his place and Mr. Cranston would call out, "Hey, you boys want to go fishing with me tomorrow? Be here at five in the morning sharp."

Retch and I would be at his place at five sharp. Mr. Cranston would stick his head out of his garage. "Be with you in a minute, boys. I've got to do a little work on my outboard motor's carburetor. Say, while you're waiting, would you mind pulling those nails out of the pile of boards by the barn? We can get away a little faster that way."

Mr. Cranston always had huge piles of old boards around his barn. Why the nails needed to be pulled out of them at this very moment, before we could go fishing, remained something of a mystery to us, but we never questioned him about it. About ten o'clock, Mr. Cranston would finish his carburetor work and relieve us of our five hours of free labor to go fishing with him.

We went fishing with Mr. Cranston several dozen times, but never once that he didn't first have to spend four or five hours tinkering with his carburetor.

"I sure wish Mr. Cranston would get a new motor," Retch would say, pulling his ten-thousandth rusty nail and tossing it into a coffee can. "Or at least a new carburetor."

"Me too," I would say. "He probably doesn't realize how much time he wastes fooling with that old thing."

After several years of pulling nails for Mr. Cranston, we finally caught on and found someone else with a boat to take

us fishing. Mr. Cranston didn't seem to mind. Every so
often, we would go by his place and see a couple of little
boys out by his barn, enthusiastically pulling nails.

"What you guys doin'?" Retch would yell.

"Goin' fishin' with Mr. Cranston," one of them would
yell back. "What does it look like?"

As I watched Retch and Wally stagger into the living
room to complete the organ transplant, I thought once again
of Mr. Cranston and what a fine old gentleman he had
been, taking the time to teach Retch and me so much about
fishing and, of course, the fine art of delay.

Gun-Trading

As my friends will be quick to tell you, I am normally this easygoing guy, practically brimming over with goodwill and love of humanity. It's only when I trade guns that I turn into a shrewd, hardhearted sharpie. Take last week, for example.

Gary Roedl called me up. "You want to go to the gun show tomorrow?" he asked. "Maybe we can trade a few guns."

"Sure," I said. "Sounds like fun."

I'm learning gun-trading from Roedl. Fifteen years ago he started out trading with a rusty single-shot .22 and has turned it into 47,000 guns. Roedl is shrewd.

The next morning when he picked me up in his truck, I was carrying my .48-caliber bolt-action, silver-inlaid, custom-checkered Thumlicker rifle with the digital readout sights.

"You going to sell your Thumlicker?" Roedl asked.

"Nope," I said. "This is my trading stock."

"Wow," Roedl said. "You're starting out in a big way."

"Right," I said.

"But you've got to be shrewd," Roedl said. "Let me see your shrewd look."

I gave him my shrewd look. Roedl shook his head.

"You've got to practice more," he said. "You still don't have the eyes right. Your squint is too tight. Well, forget that for now. Let me see your dumb look."

I gave him my dumb look. Roedl complimented me on it. He said it was so natural he would almost guess that I had been born with a dumb look, which pleased me. To trade guns successfully, you have to be able to do a good dumb look. Nobody wants to trade guns with somebody who looks smart.

Next, I did my yawn for Roedl, and he said that was pretty good, too. The yawn is one of the best weapons in the gun trader's arsenal. It works like this. You see a trader who is offering a deal so absolutely fantastic you want to leap in the air, click your heels, and give a rebel yell. Instead, you study the offered item with your look of casual disinterest—have I mentioned the look of casual disinterest?—and then you do your yawn. It should be a wide, slow, gaping yawn, the kind of yawn that implies that the deal being offered is so ordinary and boring that it's practically putting you to sleep on your feet.

Master gun traders like Roedl can even talk while yawning: "Hoooh-ah-you-ahh-hum-ever notice—yaaawph—that the barrel—ho-hummmm-on your gun there—unnnnh-ahhh—is badly warped—hummmm?"

I tried the talking-yawn once but it didn't come off the way I expected. A 300-pound gun trader snatched me off my feet, wrapped his arms around me, and began performing the Heimlich maneuver, almost crushing my ribs in the process. He stopped when a piece of meat shot eight inches out of my mouth, not realizing it was my tongue.

"What are you using for trading stock?" I asked Roedl.

"Four empty .30-30 shell casings and a brass belt buckle," he said. "I'm not in the mood to do any heavy trading today." He yawned.

The gun show was at the fairgrounds. We bought our tickets, got our hands stamped, and went into one of the buildings housing the show. A hundred or so tables had been covered with blankets. Artistically arranged on the blankets was every kind of gun I'd ever heard or read about. Tiny derringers rested in the shade of antitank guns. There were rifles, shotguns, revolvers, automatics, knives, hatchets, bows, arrows, shells, bullets, cartridges, shot . . . In short, just about every conceivable thing even slightly related to weaponry covered every flat surface as far as the eye could see. Actually, the eye couldn't see that far, because pressed shoulder-to-shoulder between the tables were hundreds of prospective gun traders, their trading stock in hand, all looking for that once-in-forever bargain. I jumped right in.

I stopped at a table where the trader, a grizzled old chap in a battered cowboy hat, had spread out his collection of fine old muzzle-loaders. He looked dumb.

"Is that an authentic Hawken rifle there?" I asked.

"Duh, I don't know fer sure. One gun looks about like another to me. All I knows is my great, great, great-grandpap owned it. I found it up in the attic. Think it's worth anything?"

The man obviously was so deficient I almost hated to take advantage of him. I yawned and stared off with my disinterested look. "Well, shucks, I don't know. I suppose I could take a chance on it." Then I put on my dumb look to set him up for the coup de grace. "I reckon I could trade you my Thumlicker here for it."

The trader yawned so long I thought he had forgotten I was standing there. "Oh, all right," he said. "I guess I could let you have this here gun, which might be an authentic Hawken for all I know, if you was to throw in a twenty-dollar bill with the Thumlicker."

Well, I could scarcely pull out my wallet and get the twenty-dollar bill, my hands were so slippery from the sweat on them. All the time I was afraid the trader would catch on to me and back out of the deal, but he didn't. He just sat there looking dumb and happy, without the slightest notion he was getting taken.

Shortly thereafter I made another fine swap, the Hawken for a knife once owned by Jim Bowie, with only one of the blades broken, and a nice little single-shot .22 rifle and a fine pump shot gun that some maniac had painted red, white, and blue. I calculated that a little paint remover would make it good as new, which is what I told the man I traded it to. By the end of the day, I'd made so many trades my jaws ached from yawning. But I felt exuberant and triumphant, and not a little shrewd. Gun-trading gets in a man's blood.

When I met Roedl back at his truck late in the afternoon, he seemed a little depressed.

"How'd you do?" I asked him.

"Not too well," he said. "I ended up with only three rifles, two shotguns, and a revolver. The stock on one of the shotguns has a small scratch on it, though. How'd you do?"

"Great!" I said. "I traded up from the Thumlicker to four empty .30-30 shell casings and a brass belt buckle!"

"Hey, all right!" Roedl said. "That's a whole lot better

than you did last time. You're starting to get the hang of gun-trading."

"No kidding? You really think so?"

"Sure," Roedl said. "No doubt about it."

Then he stared off at the horizon and yawned. Small wonder. Gun-trading can wear a person out.

Throwing Stuff

As far back as I can remember, I've had a compulsion to project objects through the air in the direction of a target of some sort. This compulsion peaked at about age eight and has been in slow decline ever since, although I still cannot pass up a good throwing rock.

My wife, Bun, and I were strolling along a beach the other day when I suddenly pointed in the direction of her feet and shouted, "Look!" She bounded into the air and performed a series of acrobatics usually associated with persons who have just stepped on a dead mouse with their bare feet. I admit to surprise at Bun's display of agility, something rarely found in a person of her years and demeanor.

"What! What! What!" she demanded in a voice not unlike the quacking of a startled duck. "What did you point at?"

"Why, nothing less than an absolutely incredible throwing stone, that's what," I replied, plucking the projectile from the sands. "Look at the way it fits perfectly the curve of my thumb and finger. Notice the texture, smooth but with just enough surface grain to provide good grip. The aerodynamics of its shape could scarcely be improved upon by aeronautical engineers. This is a throwing rock of rare quality, its equal not likely to be found anytime in the near future. Oh my gosh, there's another one! And another! Bun! Bun! We've struck the mother lode of throwing rocks!''

"Give me one of them," Bun said, blowing her hair out of her face and tucking her shirttail back in.

"Why?" I said. "There's nothing here to throw at."

"Let me be the judge of that!" she snapped.

Ever alert to possible marital pitfalls, I deposited the rocks in a pants pocket, safely out of the reach of persons unfamiliar with the dangers of accidentally discharging a throwing rock.

"Nope," I said. "Too dangerous. Gosh, that reminds me. I remember back when I was a kid . . ."

Bun rolled her eyes heavenward. "Please! Please! Spare me!" she cried.

I quickly assayed the area around us and, detecting no signs of threat to our well-being, concluded that Bun was merely a bit distraught from her recent fright. I hurried on with the little tale of my youthful experience with throwing things, hoping to distract her from the unfathomable horror that seemed to hold her in its grip.

As a boy of eight, I simply could not pass up a good throwing rock. I would pick it up, rub the dirt from it with my shirtsleeve, test it for heft and balance, and then deposit it in my pants pocket. At the end of the day, I would return home with my pockets so full of good throwing rocks that my pants would come slouching through the door a good five seconds behind me.

What did I do with the good throwing rocks? Well, I

saved them. I never wasted a good throwing rock by throwing it. Naturally, there was some expectation that one day I would come upon a target worthy of being thrown at with a good throwing rock. The problem was that every time I came upon such a target, all my good throwing rocks were stored in a box under my bed and unavailable. So I had to throw at the target with just any old rock that was handy. It was seldom if ever that a good target and a good throwing rock converged on the same point in space and time.

Thus it was that the rock collection under my bed grew and grew, until the floor joists under it creaked ominously, and any round object dropped anywhere in the house rolled in the direction of my bedroom. (I think it had something to do with Einstein's theory of relativity.) And then one day, I looked under my bed and the rock collection was gone!

"My rock collection's gone!" I shouted.

"Oh my gosh!" my mother exclaimed. "We must have been burgled! Is anything else missing? The furs, the jewelry, the silver?"

"We don't have any of that stuff," I pointed out.

"Thank goodness for that. I guess all the thieves made off with was your rock collection, terrible loss that it is."

There was something in her tone that aroused suspicion, but of course nothing could be proved.

Wonderful as rocks were to throw, there were things even more satisfying. Once my friend Crazy Eddie Muldoon and I found a nest of chicken eggs in a stump pile. We had no way of knowing how long the eggs had been abandoned by the hen who laid them, until, of course, we fired the first one against a tree. Then we were able to calculate that the eggs had been ripening anywhere from two months to two years. The rotten egg made an explosive *pop!* when it hit. The egg gunk splattered around the cottonwood and then began a slow slide down the trunk, eating away the bark as it went. The shock wave of poisonous gas arrived a few seconds later, smiting us almost to our knees. The odor was so potent and disgusting and nauseating that we could scarcely believe our good fortune.

"Wow *choke!*" Crazy Eddie said, wiping tears from his eyes. "This is *gag* great!"

"Yeah *rrretch!*" I exclaimed joyfully. "The smell almost *gasp* blinded me! Neato!"

We then set out to find targets of sufficient quality on which to expend our deadly ammunition. We blasted a few stumps, which seemed to shudder in revulsion upon impact. We defaced a large rock, probably for the remainder of its life. None of these targets, however, seemed truly deserving of being hit by such fine projectiles as rotten eggs. We looked around. Several of the Muldoon cows stared at us malevolently from the pasture. The thought crossed my mind that— But Crazy Eddie looked knowingly at me.

"No, we'd better not," he said, his voice tense from unaccustomed restraint. "My pa probably wouldn't like it."

"How about just one cow?" I said.

"Okay."

One of the nice things about Eddie was his willingness to compromise. But before we could execute our plan, the cows somehow got wind of it and galloped off.

"Hey, I know," Eddie exclaimed. "We only got six eggs left. You take three and I'll take three, and we'll play war. I'll hide over there in the woodlot, see, and you attack my position."

I stared at Crazy Eddie in disbelief. In all the years I had known him, he had come up with a lot of stupid and dangerous ideas, but this one . . . this one . . . Why, it was absolutely brilliant!

"Yeah!" I said. "Let's do it!"

As it turned out, I had the opportunity to charge Eddie's position only once. Crouching low, I ran along using some high brush for cover. Then I snapped a twig under my feet, and Eddie fired at the sound. An egg whizzed by my head and struck a limb three feet to my rear. The blast of odor lifted me off my feet and slammed me to the ground. I staggered out of the woodlot and collapsed behind a pile of brush, trying to collect my senses, although my sense of smell now seemed pretty well shot.

As I lay there recovering, I heard footsteps. Eddie! He was charging me! I snatched up an egg in my throwing hand and peeked over the brush pile. Much to my relief, I discovered that the footsteps weren't those of Eddie but his father. Mr. Muldoon stopped to fill his pipe, resting his double-bitted ax on the ground. I saw him sniff the air, turning his head this way and that, then holding his tobacco pouch to his nose and sniffing it. He shook his head, lit his pipe, put the ax on his shoulder, and strolled into the woodlot. I heard one of his big boots snap a twig.

Poor Eddie, I thought. If only Mr. Muldoon weren't carrying that double-bitted ax! I really didn't want to see this. Since I was already halfway home, however, it was highly unlikely I would.

I was somewhat surprised to see Eddie the next day, alive and in one piece. He said he had survived the disaster pretty well, considering, and figured that within a week or two he would be able to sit on hard surfaces again. He estimated it would be at least that long before his mother let his father back in the house, and in the meantime Eddie was enjoying the peace and quiet while he had the chance. His father, he said, got on his nerves a lot.

Certainly nothing was more exciting to throw than rotten

eggs, but dirt clods probably came in second in providing a satisfying throw. I think it must be at least twenty-five or thirty years since I've seen a really fine dirt clod, but when I was a kid we had trillions of them around. The road in front of the house, where we got the car stuck all the time in the spring, provided a sufficient supply of clods to last me all summer. The ruts would dry out and cake off into fine dirt clods, just the right size for throwing. The summer sun would bake them even harder. You could pick up one of these dirt clods and fire it at a tree, and it would explode into dust with a wonderfully satisfying *WHOP!*

One summer we had a chicken named Herbie, who was indistinguishable from all the other chickens, except he had a talent for getting out of the pen and digging in my mother's vegetable garden. One of the few chores I had consisted of running Herbie out of the garden. To do this, I would lob dirt-clod mortar rounds at him. Herbie would take off running as soon as he saw me, his neck stretched out and his feet churning like mad, and all around him the mortar shells would be going off, *WHOP! WHOP! WHOP!* I don't know if Herbie enjoyed the game as much as I did, but he continued to escape from the pen and raid the garden, so he must not have minded too much. Your average chicken leads a pretty dull life.

That summer my rich Aunt Alice came to visit from back east. My mother was particularly apprehensive about her visit, because, Mom said, Aunt Alice was a wealthy and genteel lady and unaccustomed to some of the rough ways of Westerners. Alice apparently held the opinion that gunplay still enjoyed a lot of popularity in our part of the country and that human life hereabouts was generally regarded as cheap.

Mom put on an elaborate welcoming dinner for Alice,

and we all sat around trying our best to act couth. In the middle of dinner, my sister, the Troll, went out to the well house for another jar of buttermilk. Upon returning, she reported disgustedly, "Herbie's out in the backyard again."

"Oh good," I said, sliding my chair back from the table. "I'll go have a little fun with him. Excuse me. I'll be right back."

"Oh, you have someone to play with way out here in the country," Aunt Alice said, smiling. "That's nice. I've always been partial to the name Herbert."

"Herbie's just a chicken," the Troll said.

Aunt Alice laughed genteelly. "My dear, don't be so quick to judge others. What we sometimes perceive to be cowardice often turns out to be wisdom."

Aunt Alice had a peculiar way of talking, so we all just smiled and tried not to look puzzled.

I excused myself and stepped out to the back porch. Herbie saw me immediately and made a dash for cover, his neck stretched out to its limit. Seeing I had only time for one shot, I snatched up a clod and, rather than mortaring it, rifled it at him, leading his beak by about six feet. Much to my astonishment, and probably even more to the chicken's, the sunbaked clod detonated right on Herbie's head. The chicken skidded along the ground in a cloud of clod dust, finally coming to a stop, with not so much as a feather twitching. I shrugged and walked back into the house, dusting off my hands.

"Guess what," I announced. "I just killed Herbie."

Aunt Alice's forkful of mashed potatoes stopped halfway to her mouth. "Wha—? Oh, I see, you're making a jest."

"Nope," I said. "I killed him deader than a doorknob."

"Are you sure?" Mom asked, buttering a roll. Do-it-yourself execution of chickens was a routine activity around our place, and not one to arouse much interest.

"Yeah, I'm sure," I said. "I hit him in the head with a dirt clod. He didn't even twitch."

"My gawwww . . . !" Aunt Alice said, turning whiter than her mashed potatoes.

I thought she must have a soft spot for chickens and decided to change the subject. "Boy, is it ever hot out!"

"Well, if you ask me," the Troll said, "it served Herbie right to get killed."

Aunt Alice's fork clattered into her dish, and Mom, too, noticed that she seemed ill, her eyes wild and blinking, her lips quivering as if she had unexpectedly found herself amid a band of cold-blooded killers.

"Enough talk about killing," Mom said. "This certainly isn't very pleasant dinner conversation. Alice, let me freshen that coffee for you, and then I'll serve the pie. Fresh huckleberry with homemade vanilla ice cream! Doesn't that sound good?"

Aunt Alice's head made a little jerking motion.

Reluctant to let go of the topic, the Troll asked, "You gonna bury Herbie?"

"B-bury?" Aunt Alice said.

"Naw," I said. "I thought I'd just chuck him on the manure pile."

"Enough!" Mom ordered. "Now go wash your hands before you eat your pie. You'll give Aunt Alice the impression we're nothing but a bunch of savages out here in the West. Right, Alice?"

"N-n-n-," Aunt Alice said.

About then, Herbie staggered by the living room window all goggled-eyed and grinning stupidly, which is about the only way a chicken can grin.

"Look, you didn't kill him after all," the Troll yelled. "Herbie's still alive!"

Aunt Alice gave a little jump and stared at the chicken. After a moment she whispered, "Thank you, thank you, thank you," although I wasn't aware that any of us had done her any particular favors.

Aunt Alice left a few days later, cutting short her visit by a week. She was a nice lady, if a little strange, but we weren't sad to see her go. We'd had about all the couth we could stand for one summer.

By the time Bun and I had finished our stroll on the beach, I had managed to collect a sizable arsenal of fine throwing stones. When we got back to our cabin, Bun still nursed a raging fit of feminism, merely because I had offered the opinion that women are incapable of appreciating the fine art of throwing stuff.

"Cramming all those dumb rocks in your pockets!" she raged. "That's the most infantile exhibition of macho . . . and your new pants, too . . . what about your new pants! Just tell me that! What about your new pants?"

"What about them?" I said. "We've only been home a few seconds. My pants will be along any time now."

Letter to Santa

Dear Santa:

For some time now, I have been in correspondence with one of your subordinates, a Mr. Elf Watson, Vice-President, Hunting and Fishing Gifts. As you are aware, most inquiries to your firm are now answered by computer. Thus it was with some relief that I finally received a reply from a real person, namely Elf Watson—assuming, of course, Mr. Watson is a person. (I confess my ignorance as to which species elves belong, if any.)

In the beginning of our rather lengthy correspondence, Mr. Watson impressed me as an amiable and ingratiating chap, and we soon arrived at a first-name basis. As time passed, however, Elf became increasingly surly and, in my opinion, even somewhat irrational. In his most recent letter to me, he lowered himself to outright insults, inquiring sarcastically, "What's a grown man like you doing writing letters to Santa for, anyway?" I am sure you don't approve of such belligerence shown toward your clientele by your employees and will take appropriate disciplinary action.

After my unhappy experience with Elf Watson, I decided to take my problem directly to the top, namely yourself. (I trust that by writing "personal" on the envelope, I have ensured that this letter will elude the computer and make its way to your desk.) Let me say, first of all, that I have generally been well pleased with my Christmas gifts for the past thirty or forty years, although there have been a few problems.

The insulated waders you brought me last Christmas were several sizes too small, prompting my children to laugh hysterically when I tried them on and my wife, Bun, to comment dryly that I looked like a roasted wiener about to burst its skin. I can understand how you and the elves might enjoy playing a little joke from time to time, but in the future I would appreciate a more serious attitude when it comes to filling my gift order.

You also made a minor error last Christmas in giving my wife a nice little side-by-side 20-gauge shotgun, since she doesn't hunt. But don't concern yourself about it. As I told Bun, even Santa can slip up on occasion, and there is no reason to hold a grudge against you. I think she is starting to come around, but I might suggest that this year, instead of entering through the chimney, perhaps you should just sling our presents on the porch as you go by. Okay?

Also, when I said I wanted fish scales for Christmas, I meant an instrument on which to weigh fish. Either there was a communications breakdown or Elf was pulling another of his practical jokes. True, Bun had a good laugh over the look on my face when I opened the package, but she stopped laughing when she had to vacuum the fish scales out of a shag carpet. So when you sling our presents on the porch, don't go "Ho, ho ho" or any of that stuff, and you'll probably be all right. It might be well to press the pedal to the metal on old Dancer and Prancer, even though Bun still isn't much of a wing shot.

But now to my point of contention with Elf. The Christmas in question was that of 1941. As you may recall—and I hope your memory's better than Elf's—I was six years old at the time and living with my folks in a small log cabin in a remote valley of the Rocky Mountains. The Great Depression was over by then, as I've since learned, but nobody had told my parents. They thought we were still poor. My father kept saying things like, "Well, it can't get any worse than this," and then it would get worse. "Now I know we have hit rock bottom," he would say, only to have the bottom drop out from under us once again. I had grown quite accustomed to my father's optimistic pronouncements and didn't pay much attention to them.

Then one December day over our breakfast gruel, he muttered something so ominous and frightening I forgot what I was doing and actually placed some of the gruel in my mouth.

"Pickings have got so slim," Dad said, "I kind of doubt whether Santa Claus will even be able to afford to show up this year. I expect he's busted just like the rest of us."

"Choke, petewweee, gag!" I said. "Wha—? What did you say?"

Dad repeated himself, staring at me glumly through the gruel steam. "But what the heck," he said, "you have lots of other Christmases ahead of you. You'll make up for it later. No presents one Christmas ain't gonna knock a big hole in your life, I guess."

Not knock a big hole in my life? It would kick down all four walls of it, that's what it would do, no presents for Christmas! If Santa Claus thought he could weasel out on me just because times were hard, he had another think coming. Why, I'd . . . I'd . . . Actually, there was nothing I could do, as you, Mr. Claus, are well aware. I probably could have given up believing in you, but I was only enraged, not crazy.

Now, you may think this is one of those maudlin stories where at the very last minute you, Santa Claus, do show up, and everyone stands around laughing and wiping away tears of joy and saying this was the best Christmas ever. Forget it. You, Mr. Claus, did not put in an appearance at our house that Christmas in 1941. I hope you are ashamed of yourself.

Sure, my father tried to get you off the hook by whittling me out a little toy boat and saying it had come from you. One reason I think he said it came from you was he didn't want to take the blame for the boat himself. Dad wasn't much of a whittler and lacked patience. The boat was a board with a point at one end, and a long nail pounded into it for a mast. The mast was too heavy for the boat and caused it to float upside down.

"This is the worst Christmas ever!" I complained.

"Shut up," my father said, "and go play with your boat."

So, the way I see it, Mr. Claus, you still owe me a Christmas, and I would like to collect. If you will check your records, you will see that in my letter to you in December 1941, I requested a tin boat that you put these little wax candles into and lit them and they generated steam and powered the little boat. Having computed the interest, compounded semiannually, on that little boat over a period of forty-five years, I find that it now amounts to a thirty-eight-foot sportfisher with twin diesels and a flying bridge. I would like you to pay up this Christmas, or I shall have to turn the matter over to a collection agency.

You needn't gift wrap the boat. Also, it would be best if you left it at the local marina, with my name on the gift tag. For gosh sakes, don't try to drop it off at the house! It might get peppered with stray birdshot.

Sincerely yours,
Pat

The Cabin at Spooky Lake

One dark and stormy night in 1953, I partici-
pated in a strange and frightening occurrence
at Spooky Lake in the mountains of North Idaho. Although
the exact cause of that inexplicable event remains unknown,
Birdy Thompson and Retch Sweeney advanced the theory
that we were attacked by an enraged ghost. I personally find
that theory to be sheer nonsense and even laughable. Sure,
the ghost may have been a little upset but he certainly
wasn't enraged.

The three of us were college sophomores at the time, and
had been granted an unexpected leave of absence from the
university. Somehow—and this in itself is amazing—the
mascot of a rival university got hold of a hacksaw, sawed
the lock off its cage, and made its way over twenty-five miles
of rough terrain, up the back stairs of the dormitory, and
right into our room, where it managed to conceal itself from
us for three days! As we told the Dean, it was a terrible
shock for us to discover that we had been sleeping in the
same room with a 200-pound mountain lion, old, moth-

eaten and toothless as he might be. We could certainly sympathize with the fright given the dorm counselor when he investigated our room as a possible source of strange smells, a more or less routine practice of his. The man apparently possessed an insatiable curiosity.

The Dean said our shock was certainly understandable and that he was giving us the rest of the semester off, to let our nerves calm down. We replied that we appreciated his thoughtfulness but that our nerves were already much better. He insisted, however, and thus it was that we were released on short notice from our strenuous academic labors.

As we packed our belongings and cleaned up the room, no small task as the result of the brief visit of the runaway mountain lion, we debated over the most profitable use to make of our free time.

"Maybe we won't have all that much free time," I said. "When our folks get the letters from the Dean, they'll probably kill us right off. I think what we should do is write letters home ourselves, explaining the whole misunderstanding and telling our folks that we are going on a camping trip for a week or so. Then we head up into the mountains and camp out until everybody has time to cool down. How does that sound?"

"Good," Birdy said. "Where shall we camp out?"

"You ever hear of Spooky Lake? Rancid Crabtree told me about it. Claims it's haunted. Ha! He says nobody goes there because they're afraid of the place. So Spooky Lake never gets fished. Rancid says it's full of huge old trout just waiting to be caught. Boy, it's funny how people can be so stupid and uneducated as to believe in ghosts."

"Yeah," Birdy said. "I hear Elk Lake is nice this time of year."

"Or Mirror Lake," Retch said. "I been wantin' to get back to ol' Mirror Lake for some fishin'."

"Nope," I said. "It's settled. We'll go to Spooky Lake, unless you guys happen to believe in ghosts and are too chicken to—"

"Naw, sounds okay to me," Birdy said. "Educated men like us don't believe in spooks, right, Retch?"

"Right," Retch said. "I still think Mirror Lake would be nicer, though."

That settled, we wrote our letters home and finished up the packing. I checked to make sure we had all our stuff: three shotguns, three .22s, two .30-06s and a .30-30, six flyrods, six casting rods, twenty fishing reels, three backpacks, three sleeping bags. "I guess that's about it," I said.

"Wait," Birdy said. "Where's the book?"

"Oh, yeah," I said. "We did have a book, a history of something or other."

"What the heck," Retch said. "We can always get another book if we have to. Let's go. Man, what a relief to get away from studying all the time!"

We stopped in our hometown long enough to stock up on grub at the mercantile, and then headed out to Rancid Crabtree's shack to get directions to Spooky Lake.

"Spooky Lake?" Rancid said. "You sure you fellers want to go up thar?"

"Why not?" I said. "Don't tell me you believe that story about the ghost that haunts the lake?"

"Course Ah do."

"Well, we don't," I said. "We're college men now, Rancid. College men don't believe in all the superstitious nonsense about ghosts. The phenomena people call 'ghosts' are quickly revealed to be nothing other than natural occurrences, if investigated by means of objective and rational thought.''

"Ah didn't know thet," Rancid said, "Ah guess the ghost Ah seen at Spooky Lake didn't know it neither.''

"You're joshing us, Rance. You didn't see any ghost.''

Birdy cracked his knuckles. "Know anybody else who claims to have seen the so-called ghost, Mr. Crabtree?''

"Oh, mebbe a couple dozen folks is all, most of them timid souls. Pinto Jack claims the ghost jumped him up near the old Spooky Lake cabin one day, but you fellers know Pinto. Can't believe a word he says. Swears the ghost gave him that white streak runs through his ha'r. Ah tells him, 'Good, It'll match the yeller streak runs down your back.' Ha! Well, thet riled him, and he comes back at me with—''

"Rance," I said, having heard about the exchange of witticisms many times before, "did you just mention a cabin?''

"Yup. Thar's a cabin thar all right, but Ah'd steer clear of it iffen Ah was yous. Got a bad feelin' about it, thet cabin. Belonged to an old trapper. B'ar broke both his legs. He drug hisself into the cabin, tied splints on his legs with some rawhide, climbed into his bunk, and died. Coulda saved hisself the trouble of makin' the splints. Now as Ah was sayin', Pinto comes back at me with . . .''

We spent the night at Rancid's shack and left early in the morning for Spooky Lake. I had asked Rancid if he wanted to go along, but he said his old legs weren't up to a hike like that anymore. He stood in the doorway and waved good-bye as we drove away. " 'Member what Ah told yous," he called after us. "Don't go n'ar the cabin!''

I laughed. "Rancid doesn't fool me. He's just as scared

of the Spooky Lake ghost as anybody. Did you hear that malarkey about his tired old legs? Last summer I saw him walk straight up Blacktail Mountain without even stopping to rest. I was glad to hear about the cabin. We can stay there. What say, guys?''

"I say we give Mirror Lake a try," Retch said, cracking his knuckles.

We left the car at the end of a logging road and started our climb up the mountain, according to the complicated directions given us by Rancid. If there was a trail, it had grown up with brush, and now was impossible to find. I began to wonder about the reliability of Rancid's directions, vaguely recalling a map of the area that showed a supply trail that ran to a Forest Service fire lookout station. If I remembered correctly, the trail offered a much shorter and easier route to where Spooky Lake was supposed to be. Still, Rancid knew this country like the back of his grubby hand, and there was no reason I could think of that he would deliberately give us bad directions. He did love a good practical joke, but this would be too cruel even for him.

After three hours of climbing through steep, thick woods, we finally broke out into the open on a rocky ridge. There, down below us, Spooky Lake sparkled like a blue jewel in the sun. Even from that distance, we could see the rings of feeding trout rippling out all over the surface of the water. I instantly regretted all the mean thoughts I had begun to harbor about Rancid.

At the far end of the lake stood a grove of massive cedars. In the shadowy, parklike area beneath the cedars we could make out the shape of the trapper's cabin. It didn't look the least bit scary. "The cabin seems fine from here," I said. "I think we're going to need it, too." I pointed to a mass of thunderheads looming over a distant range of mountains to the west.

"Yeah," Birdy said. "Looks like rain, all right."

"What are we standing here yacking for?" Retch said. "Let's go catch some of those fish for supper."

The fishing was fantastic, for half an hour. We hauled in one nice cutthroat trout after another, and soon had plenty for both supper and breakfast. Then, as is the case with most high mountain lakes, the bite ended abruptly. The lake grew still and glassy, and the rising thunderheads cast a soft, ominous light into the tiny valley. We headed for the cabin.

Up close, the cabin did not appear so fine. It looked as if it had been tucked away among the cedars for a hundred years, which probably was the case. The mud-and-moss chinking had cracked out of the spaces between many of the whitish-gray logs. Moss covered the thick shake roof. The door to the tiny cabin was massive, made out of split cedar logs. It leaned unhinged against the doorway, held in place by a stout limb someone had wedged against it. Retch kicked the limb out of the way and, grunting mightily, set the door aside, commenting that it was a good thing he was along, because Birdy and I between the two of us probably couldn't have moved it.

"Yeah, sure," Birdy said. "Well, give me brains over brawn any day. Yeeesh! Look in there!"

The cabin was a mess. Garbage, animal droppings, pieces of old clothes, a rusty tin plate, bones, and various other debris not easily identified cluttered the floor. "Looks almost as bad as our dorm room," Retch said.

"Well, at least a mountain lion hasn't been cooped up in here for three days," I said. "Let's get the place mucked out. We aren't at college now."

By evening, we had the place tidied up and a fire built in
the little tin-can stove, which, after Retch had set the heavy
door back in its opening, gave off the only light in the cabin.
The mixed aromas of sizzling trout and bacon and fried
potatoes with onions filled the air, as did the raucous sounds
of our mirth at recalling our surprise at finding the runaway
mountain lion in our dorm room. Quickly, the strain of
intense study vanished from our countenances, and a disinterested observer might never have guessed that we had
any college education at all, so quickly did the three of us
revert back to our true, carefree natures.

"Ah, this is the life," Retch said, munching a crisp trout
held in his fingers like an ear of corn. "You know what our
problem was at college? We was just getting too civilized,
that's what."

"Yeah," I said, blowing on a handful of fried potatoes.
"But a man needs an education. Now, you know, most folks
probably would be afraid to stay in this cabin, because of
all the ghost talk and all. We take the rational view, shrug
off all that superstitious nonsense, and we've got ourselves
a nice cozy cabin to spend the night in."

"Speaking of the ghost," Birdy said, "I wonder where
the old trapper was buried around here."

"What?" Retch said. "Buried? You don't suppose they
buried him around here, do you?"

"Probably wasn't much to bury," I said. "According to
Rancid, they didn't find him until ten or fifteen years after
he died. Found his skeleton in that bunk over there, with
the rawhide and splints still on his broken leg bones."

The three of us looked at the bunk. At that moment,
thunder shook the tiny cabin and slivers of light leaped
through the cracks between the logs. Big drops of rain began

splattering down on the shake roof. An eerie gloom filled the cabin as the fire sputtered lower in the tin stove.

"Throw another stick in the stove," Retch said.

"Good idea," I said. "It's, uh, starting to turn cool in here." I mopped sweat off my forehead with my sleeve. "By the way, who wants to sleep in the bunk?"

"Why, I think I'll roll my bag right out here on the floor," Birdy said.

"Me too," Retch said. "You take the bunk, Pat."

"Naw," I said. "Too cramped for me. I'll sleep on the floor."

Sleep evaded me. All my senses seemed to be standing guard in the darkness of the cabin, alert to every rustle and scratch. The fire died out. Minutes crept by like lame hours. Then I heard a strange thumping behind the cabin, as though some creature were trying to pound its way through the logs. A chill filled the inside of my sleeping bag. I wondered if I should disturb Retch and Birdy from their slumbers.

"Guys," I whispered.

"Yeah?"

"What?"

They seemed alert enough. "Do you hear that strange thumping sound?"

"Been listening to it," Retch said.

"What could make a sound like that?" Birdy whispered.

The sound stopped. We listened. All was still, except for the cracking of knuckles and dripping of beads of sweat. Then something climbed to the roof of the cabin. We stared up into the darkness, above which the unmistakable sounds of two feet crunched across the shake roof in the direction of the tin chimney.

"Something's on our roof," Retch said unnecessarily.

"Probably just a . . ." I said. I couldn't think of what it might be.

"Sure," Birdy said. "Th-that's all it is."

A hideous moaning came down our chimney: "Oooooooooahhhhhhhhhhh! Ooooooaahhhhhhhhh! Maw leeeeeeeeeeeggggggss! Ooooooahhhhhhhh! Mawwww leeeeeegggggggs! Ooooooooo . . ."

That at least was what the hideous moaning sounded like. It was difficult to hear it clearly because of all the hyperventilation going on inside the cabin. A few frantic moments passed. Slowly I began to collect my wits, even as my heart beat wildly.

"Let's calm down," I said.

"Good idea," Retch said. "No point in getting ourselves all worked up over nothin'."

"All we have to do is think this thing through," Birdy said.

"No need to panic," I said. "There has to be a rational explanation for this."

"Yeah," Retch said. "I got one for you. It's that old trapper's ghost!"

"Right," Birdy said. "It's his ghost."

"I know that," I said. "But what's the rational explanation for its wanting to bother us?"

At that moment we raced onto the rocky ridge above the lake and paused to see if we were being followed.

"You can drop the door now, Retch," I said.

"Well, shucks," Retch said. "So that's what was slowing me down!"

We got back to Rancid's cabin just before dawn, but he was already up. He was sitting in his underwear having a cup of coffee. His pants, shirt, and jacket were spread out around the stove, drying.

"What happened?" I asked.

"Fell in the crick," he said. "What brings you fellers back so soon? Thought yous was gonna stay up at Spooky Lake fer a week or so. You educated fellers run afoul of the ghost?" He wiped a big hand across his mouth, in a vain attempt to conceal his concern for us.

"Rain," I said. "Too much rain. We decided to risk going home early."

"I hate rain," Retch said.

"Me too," said Birdy. "Say, Mr. Crabtree, you know, that Spooky Lake is kind of, well, weird. I don't think I'd go up there ever again if I were you. Its name is pretty darn appropriate, if you ask me."

"It should be," Rancid said. "It was named after the trapper what built thet cabin—ol' Tom Spooky. Say, did Ah ever tell you boys about the turble thang what happened to poor ol' Tom? A b'ar broke his legs and—"

"Yeah," I said. "You told us."

Outdoor Burnout

I recently received a letter from a young fellow who has spent several months working in a state park. "It is a 27,000-acre park and wood reserve with three hundred head of American bison, deer, antelope, turkey, elk, and bighorn sheep, as well as nongame species such as coyotes, porcupines, coon, golden and bald eagles, and an assortment of ground critters." He went on to describe the beautiful lakes and streams stocked with brown, rainbow, and brook trout.

It seemed like a wonderful place to work, and I thought perhaps he was getting around to inviting me up for a visit. But then he said, "When I first arrived here I mentioned to my associates that 'it would take a lot of this to make me sick.' Well, I've reached my saturation point!"

In other words, he was fed up to the eyeballs with beautiful streams and lakes, forests, mountains, bison, bighorns, golden eagles, the whole sordid mess. I knew at once that he was suffering from a classic case of outdoor burnout.

Outdoor burnout, a term often used to describe camp

cooking, is actually a severe malady brought on by overexposure to beautiful scenery, wildlife, and wilderness in general. I have suffered from it myself.

By the time I was seven years old, I had spent most of my life in a log cabin surrounded by forest. Everywhere I looked there was nothing but trees—big trees, small trees, skinny trees, fat trees, green trees, brown trees, trees, trees, TREES! So many trees can drive a person mad, and very nearly did me.

Even the house was made of dead trees, trimmed and peeled but nevertheless retaining the unmistakable character of trees. At breakfast, I would glance up and there would be the trees, peering at me from all angles. "YAAAAAAAAAAAAAAAH!" I would scream.

My father would give me a quizzical look and say, "Son, if you're not gonna eat the rest of your gruel, pass it on over here." Dad was not a man to coddle a person suffering from burnout.

Such was my hatred of trees that if we happened to drive by a logging camp, I would yell out the car window, "Cut 'em all down! All of them! You hear meeeee?"

I loved a good forest fire. My father would come in from fighting a forest fire off in the mountains somewhere, drop his smoke-blackened self into a chair, and say, "We couldn't hold her. Fire topped out and jumped the line. Went up the side of Wolf Mountain like a blowtorch. Wiped out a lot of timber."

Delighted, I would gleefully clap my little hands. "Tell me again, Dad, how the fire burned up all the trees!"

Dad would pull back from me and say to Mom, "I tell you, the boy ain't right. We get some money we better take him in and get his screws tightened."

Eventually, we moved into open farm country, broken

only by a woodlot here and there, with the forests off at a sensible distance. I was amazed and relieved to discover that trees didn't blanket the entire world. It made life seem worth living.

After a while, I didn't mind trees as decoration, a patch of them here, a row there. I even developed an affection for a huge old solitary cottonwood out in the middle of our pasture. One summer day I took a picnic lunch out and ate it in the cool shade of the tree, listening to the wind rustling softly through the leaves. The tree seemed nice. I smiled up at it. The tree dropped a huge limb and tried to squish me. So much for trying to start a meaningful relationship with a tree.

As I grew older, of course, I learned to love the woods and the great outdoors in general. This was because I didn't live there, but made only periodic visits, to fish, hunt, camp, pick berries and mushrooms, that sort of thing. When I got tired of the wilds—five days was, and still is, about my limit—I went home. Sure, just as much as the next out-doorsperson, I enjoy sleeping in a dirty, soggy sleeping bag, freezing one side of me and roasting the other at the camp-fire, choking on woodsmoke, eating green hash and granite biscuits, and so on. No matter how much fun it is, though, after about five days the enjoyment begins to wane. I start to long for the roar of traffic, the smell of exhaust fumes, the clamor of shopping malls, and the haunting, melodic wail of sirens in the night. Then I know that outdoor burn-out is not far off.

Frequently, I run into people who spend their entire lives in the woods. As a general rule, I notice that their appre-ciation for their environment will have diminished. I spent a night recently with Sam Scuppers in his cabin up at High Meadows. In the morning, the first rays of sun softly illuminated the meadow, with patches of wildflowers dappling the delicate greens of the new grass. A rainbow hung faintly in the mist rising from the glistening steam, and standing in front of the rainbow were a beautiful whitetail doe and her twin fawns.

"Wow!" I said. "Come look at this, Sam!"

Sam got up stiffly, pulled his suspenders on over his underwear, and hobbled over to the doorway.

"Jeez cripes," he said. "It's just some fool deer." Grumbling, he hobbled over to the stove and put on the coffee. It occurred to me that Sam's outdoor burnout has been going on for about forty years now. I judged it to be terminal.

At the opposite extreme are some friends from Los Angeles whom I recently picked up at the airport and drove up to my lake cabin. As they were getting out of the car, Bert yelled at his wife, "Back in the car, Martha, back in the car or we'll suffocate! There's no air here!"

"Don't be silly, Bert," I said. "Of course there's air here."

"I don't see any," he said, panicky.

I explained to Bert that only in large cities can you see the air. In most other places, air tends to be invisible. Thrilled and amazed, Bert and Martha took pictures of the air to show their friends back in Los Angeles. "They wouldn't believe us if we just told them," Bert said.

I must confess that I myself have occasionally forgotten about outdoor burnout. Back in the days of my brief and unlamented career as a free-lance photojournalist, I came up with a great idea for a photo essay and queried a national magazine about it. "What would be the most wonderful place in the world for a boy to grow up in?" I wrote the editors. "Why a national park, of course! Just think of a youngster fortunate enough to grow up surrounded by beau-

tiful mountains, forests, lakes and streams, wildlife . . ."
And so on. The editors, no doubt looking at the air outside
their offices in a New York skyscraper, wrote back that the
idea sounded super to them and for me to go ahead and do
the photo essay.

My first problem was to find a boy about nine years old
who lived in a national park. I unearthed one, the son of a
park ranger, whose parents happily volunteered the kid to
be the subject of my photo essay. Terrific, I thought. This
essay is as good as sold. I'll go out and shoot a few dozen
rolls of film of the kid enjoying his wonderful and exciting
life among mountains, lakes, wildlife, etc. Nothing to it. My
reputation as a photojournalist would be made.

I drove a thousand miles or so to the park, found the
rustic house in the rustic compound provided for park employees, and knocked on the rustic door. The kid's rustic
mother answered. "Oh, Pithwood," she called to the kid.
"Guess what! The photographer is here to take pictures of
you enjoying your wonderful and exciting life growing up
in a national park. Doesn't that sound like fun?"

Pithwood, slumped in front of the TV with an unwaver-
ing stare, snarled, "How many times do I have to tell you!
I ain't going to do it!"

The free-lance photographer, who hadn't slept for days
and had just driven a thousand miles plus and whose fingers
were still frozen in the position of being clamped around a
steering wheel, laughed uneasily. "Ha ha. What does he
mean, he ain't going to do it?"

Wishing I had thought to bring along a power winch, I
finally managed to move the lad away from the TV and out
into the open air of the park.

Once outside and alone with the boy, I assumed that fake
cheerfulness adults use with children who refuse to believe

they are having fun. "Know what, Pithwood? We're going to hike over to 'Huge Billion-Year-Old Cedar Tree' and you get to climb up into one of its giant hollows and pretend it's your secret hideout while I photograph you! Hey? What say, guy?"

"You crazy? I ain't climbing no tree. I hate climbing trees. You can fall out of them. They're dangerous."

"Well, we can put that off until later. We'll start with something fun. You can sit on a rustic stone wall with the beautiful glacier in the background and feed some bread to the squirrels. Hey?"

"I hate squirrels, the dirty, fat, ugly little beasts, always nosing around for a handout. Forget the squirrels."

"I see, heh heh. Forget the squirrels. Well, Pithwood, perhaps you can tell me something you like to do in the park."

"Something I like to do in this crummy, stupid park? I can't think of nothing. Oh, wait! I got it!"

"Yes? Yes?"

"You could photograph me slurping down a milk shake at the Old Rustic Snack Bar, with a burger and fries. How does that sound?"

I told little Pithwood how that sounded, first checking to make sure his mother had gone back in the house, and then went on to explain that I would be happy to photograph him slurping at the snack bar as soon as we got the other photographs of him enjoying his wonderful and exciting life in the national park, photos by which my future fame and fortune hung in precarious balance. He reluctantly acquiesced.

After seemingly endless days of slogging about the park, shooting pictures, Pithwood and I one afternoon wearily made our way to the Old Rustic Snack Bar, as had become our custom after each day of shooting. We slumped down at a split-log table and ordered milk shakes and fries.

"Listen, Pithwood," I said. "I really appreciate your going through with this sham of letting me photograph you pretending to love your wonderful and exciting life in a national park."

"You're welcome," he said. "Just don't ask me to do it again. I hate this crummy park."

"No kidding, pal," I said. "What a rotten place for a kid to grow up in. By the way, if you could grow up anyplace in the world, where would it be?"

Pithwood's face brightened. "Disneyland!"

"Sounds good to me. Hey, smell that, Pithwood. Nice, huh?"

"Yeah," he said. "It comes from the parking lot. It's called car exhaust."

"I know. Back in the city where I live, you can smell car exhaust anytime you want. Especially in the morning, during rush-hour traffic, when the exhaust fumes come wafting over our neighborhood in nice thick blue-black clouds. And off in the distance you can hear the screech of tires and the blare of horns."

"Gee," Pithwood said, "I wish I lived there."

"I don't blame you, pal. Maybe someday, huh?"

I didn't bother to send the magazine my photos: Pithwood frowning at Bridal Veil Falls; Pithwood sneering at squirrel; Pithwood throwing rocks at deer; Pithwood littering patch of wildflowers; Pithwood yawning at Spectacular Canyon; Pithwood consulting his watch at Eternal Bliss Vista . . . .

Poor kid. You would think his parents would have had better sense than to raise him in a place like that.

Advanced Duck-Hunting Techniques

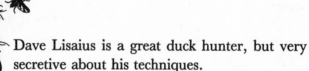

Dave Lisaius is a great duck hunter, but very secretive about his techniques.

"C'mon, Dave," I pleaded with him the other day. "Tell me. Is it some little trick you do with the call?"

"Nope."

"Okay, it's the way you set up the decoys, isn't it?"

Dave shook his head.

"You'd better tell me," I threatened. "Otherwise I'm not going to give you any more fishing tips."

He was instantly unnerved, or so I judged by his attempt to distract me by holding his sides and making raucous, annoying sounds.

But I was not to be put off. "Furthermore, I won't give you any advice on how to hunt whitetail deer."

"Stop! Stop!" he cried, holding up his hands. "You're killing me!" Then he emitted a weird, loonish shriek and beat on his thighs with both fists.

"As for my instructing you on the best procedures for hunting elk—"

"Stop! Please stop! Have mercy! I'll tell! I'll tell!"

"Good," I said. "I really don't like having to use threats about withholding my fishing and hunting expertise but—"

"I said I'd tell! Now stop! I can't stand any more."

As soon as he had composed himself, Dave went on to explain his secret duck-hunting techniques in detail. I have not had the opportunity to field-test them, but they seem highly promising to me.

"Deception," Dave said. "Deception is the key to successful duck hunting. Master deception and you've mastered the sport."

"I know that," I said. "I know all about camouflage, decoys, duck blinds, and duck calls."

"That's all secondary," Dave said. "Now to begin with, here is a little trick that almost never fails to bring in ducks."

He held up one hand with the fingers straight but clustered tightly together. Then, with his other hand, he began to fold down the clustered fingers one by one, all the while smacking his lips.

"Know what I'm doing now?"

"Yes, irritating me."

"This gesture simulates peeling a banana," he said.

"Right, first you pretend to peel a banana, then you put out the decoys," I said, not without a trace of sarcasm.

"No, you've got it backwards. First you put out the decoys, then you pretend to peel the banana. Got it?"

I nodded my head affirmatively. "Sure. What could be simpler?"

"I haven't known the ol' banana ploy to fail yet," Dave continued. "Many years ago, I noticed that even when I hadn't caught so much as a glimpse of a duck in over four hours, the instant I started to eat lunch, a flight would go whistling directly over my head. I started doing some research. I'd set my gun down close at hand, begin to unwrap a sandwich, drop it, snatch up the gun, and usually nail a double as the ducks went over. I'd catch 'em totally by surprise.''

But, Dave explained, using an actual lunch was messy. For one thing, until he became practiced in the maneuver, he used up as many sandwiches as shotgun shells. Other hunters would call out, "Hey, Dave, that's a big sack of decoys you got there," and he would reply, "No, this is my lunch. The sack with the decoys is the small one."

In the excitement of the moment, at first he had trouble keeping the procedure straight. Once he bit into a shotgun shell while trying to load a 10-gauge pickle into a 12-gauge gun.

Finally it occurred to him that ducks weren't all that smart. He tried just pretending to eat a lunch, and sure enough, here came the ducks. He eventually refined the technique down to the simple banana-peeling gesture. This alone provided him with the reputation of being a master duck hunter.

Not satisfied with mere mastery of the sport, Dave wanted to achieve greatness, and he went on to develop even more sophisticated techniques. Here are just a few of them:

The Long-Overcoat Trick—With this maneuver, the hunter wears a long overcoat, one that reaches nearly to his ankles. He makes a show of leaning his shotgun against a tree and walking away from it. The ducks will wait until he is about thirty feet from his gun. Then they will fly in and begin cavorting in the air above the hunter. At this point, he whips a second shotgun from beneath his overcoat and has at them.

Unloading the Gun—This bit of deception requires

sleight of hand, which should be practiced at home until the hunter becomes proficient at it. First the hunter shakes his fist at the duckless sky. Then he slumps his shoulders and hangs his head in the standard manner of skunked duck hunters the world over. He then makes a big pretense of unloading the gun and inserting the shells in his vest. But in fact the shells he inserts in his vest are shells he has palmed earlier. The gun is still loaded! Finally, the hunter walks in the traditional dejected manner back toward his car, occasionally kicking angrily at a rock or stick. He should remember to keep his head down so the ducks can't see his smile. Ducks can detect a smile on a hunter's face at six hundred yards, and even though they think his gun is empty, they will refrain from darkening the sky with their multitudes.

Toilet Tissue—It is a well-known scientific fact that a hunter scurrying out of a blind with a roll of toilet tissue in hand will bring in every duck within a ten-mile radius. The trick here is to have a second gun concealed some distance from the blind.

The Decoy—The hunter should obtain a mannequin from a department-store supply house and dress it in hunting togs identical to his own. An hour before dawn, he sets out his regular duck decoys, with the mannequin standing in the middle of them. While concealed in his blind, the hunter can pull a string that causes the mannequin's arms to move, as if it were still tossing out the duck decoys. As is well known, ducks will drop everything else they are doing in order to fly over a hunter while he is standing hip-deep in water arranging his decoys. Properly executed, the decoy ploy will provide excellent shooting.

On those days when absolutely nothing is moving, the

hunter may have to resort to drastic measures to bring the ducks over. Throwing the mannequin into the water and causing it to thrash around as though it were drowning brings fantastic results. Ducks will fly twenty miles out of their way to see a hunter fall out of his blind. If the weather is extremely cold and the hunter falls through a sheet of ice, ducks will *walk* twenty miles for a chance at such first-class entertainment.

The Cigarette Lighter—This is a simple but effective bit of deception. The duck hunter merely fakes the recommended procedure for thawing out his frozen trigger finger by holding it in a lighter flame. Since in this case the finger is already thawed, it is a good idea to use either a fake lighter or a fake finger. A fake finger is especially useful for veteran duck hunters whose real fingers have already been frozen down to nubbins. Finger nubbins are too hard for ducks to detect from a great distance. Ducks cannot resist coming in once they think a hunter's trigger finger has frozen up, and Dave recommends this ploy highly.

Fake Game Regulations—This device can be expensive, but Dave claims it is well worth the cost. You have a fake game regulations pamphlet printed up. In it you have set the official opening and closing times for the day's hunting fifteen minutes later and earlier respectively. Then you let the pamphlet appear to fall out of your pocket accidentally, making sure that it is open to the page where the ducks can see the times.

"During those fifteen-minute adjustments in the fake opening and closing times," Dave said, "you will have some of the best duck hunting you ever had in your life."

"C'mon, Dave!" I said, looking up from the pad on which I was scribbling notes. "You know good and well ducks can't read. Here you give me some good, sound, practical techniques for hunting ducks, and then you try to pull this on me.''

''You don't think ducks can read opening and closing times?'' Dave said. ''Well, then, you're never going to master duck hunting, I can tell you that right now.''

SPIDERMAN
ANANCY

Written by JAMES BERRY

Illustrated by
JOSEPH OLUBO

HENRY HOLT AND COMPANY · NEW YORK

For
Sista-Maud,
Cousn-Oley, Brodda-Hervan,
Sista-Neat, Alfie, Berry,
Ben and Doley

Text copyright © 1988 by James Berry
Illustrations copyright © 1988 by Joseph Olubo
All rights reserved, including the right to reproduce
this book or portions thereof in any form.
First published in the United States in 1989 by
Henry Holt and Company, Inc.,
115 West 18th Street, New York, New York 10011.
Published in Canada by Fitzhenry & Whiteside Limited,
195 Allstate Parkway, Markham, Ontario L3R 4T8.
Originally published in Great Britain in 1988
under the title *Anancy-Spiderman* by
Walker Books Ltd., 87 Vauxhall Walk, London SE11 5HJ.

Library of Congress Cataloging-in-Publication Data
Berry, James.
Spiderman Anancy / James Berry ; illustrated by Joseph Olubo.—
1st American ed.
Summary: A collection of twenty tales recounting the antics
of the West Indian trickster Anancy and his companions
Bro Monkey, Bro Dog, and Bro Tiger.
ISBN 0-8050-1207-9
1. Anansi (Legendary character) [1. Anansi (Legendary character)
2. Folklore—West Indies.] I. Olubo, Joseph, ill. II. Title.
PZ8.1.B4187Sp 1989
398.21'09729—dc20 89-33418

Henry Holt books are available at special discounts
for bulk purchases for sales promotions, premiums,
fund-raising, or educational use. Special editions
or book excerpts can also be created to specification.

For details contact:

Special Sales Director
Henry Holt and Company, Inc.
115 West 18th Street
New York, New York 10011

First American Edition
Printed in the United States of America
1 3 5 7 9 10 8 6 4 2

SPIDERMAN
ANANCY

FOREWORD

I want to thank Mother Africa for this wonderful character
of Anancy and for these stories and all the others Anancy
inspired. I want to thank my ancestors who travelled with
the stories and transplanted them in the Caribbean. I want
to thank my parents for keeping their links with the stories
and for passing them on to us in our Jamaican village, out
in moonlight or in dim paraffin lamplight, during rain and
storm winds, through empty-belly times or big bellyfuls. I
want to thank our folklorist Louise Bennett for writing and
publishing her telling of Anancy stories. I want to thank
Walter Jekyll for his resourceful collecting of these stories,
preserving their authenticity and providing a big body of a
printed record in his book *Jamaica Song and Story*. I want
to thank friends in England who have read my telling of
Anancy and given their helpful suggestions. I want to thank
the publishers for providing me with the pleasurable opportunity of writing *Anancy-Spiderman*.

*　　　*　　　*

Anancy, the spider hero of Westindian folk tales, originated in Ghana as the Ashanti Spider God. Sly and soft and sweet voiced, he can be anything from a lovable rogue to an artful prince. Often, he gets overwhelmed by a terrible greed he cannot help. Essentially both spider and man, his nature allows him to change as the situation demands. This ability to change himself, and leave the ground, vanish into a tree or into the housetop to hide, makes him godlike. That is also linked with the way he causes good and bad things to come into the world for the first time, continue to happen and become part of life.

On the face of it Anancy has nothing to use to counter the superiority of an opponent. You see, he relies on his wits and his cunning. His usual opponent is the mighty Tiger. Against that massive size, that destruction-capacity, little weaponless Anancy has to win, and survive, without physical combat. His opponents fall for his oiled and honeyed tongue – just like the way his audience sides with him – because, with his guileless approach, his innocent presence, his cunning is never suspected. Yet, Anancy doesn't at all always manage to impose his will and way.

Certainly, Anancy gets his revenge on Tiger at the dance contest at the "John-Canoo and the Shine-Dancer-Shine Event". But at the "Stump-a-Foot Celebration Dance" Tiger plays the game the wrong way and undermines Anancy's advantages and spoils his possible glory. Similarly, in "Anancy and Storm and the Reverend Man-Cow", Anancy's friends have to save him from the plot he cooked up which would lead to his own public disgrace. Also, in "Mrs Anancy, Chicken Soup and Anancy", Mrs Anancy deprives him of one of his big-feast moments and turns the eating into a charitable village act.

Some of the stories in this book are stories we had told to us as children and which we learnt from other village sources and told back to each other. I have expanded all of these. Other stories I have developed from traditional versions and themes. In an overall way, I have deepened, clarified and expanded the stories. I have brought in those parts of the stories usually left out in oral tellings. The ways of characters, their situations, motives, hopes, beliefs, were already known, well shared and well understood, by both audience and storyteller. Those parts were not brought out openly at all in a telling. It seemed to me that in cold print much of that left-out information was needed.

Right from the start I decided I would not keep Anancy confined within a restricted characterisation and narrative, which he had obviously outgrown. His inventive resourcefulness, his vocal zest and cunning, his outlandish ideas and ways all called out for an expanded staging. So Anancy here is the African Anancy showing his new Caribbean roots. He appears as the Caribbean mythological figure and symbol he has developed into. Familiar Caribbean characters with him – like Dog, Puss, Goat, Jackass – all come on to the stage with Anancy.

In spelling the name as it is – Anancy – I have kept the old Jamaican spelling instead of using the more recently appeared "Anansi" – the African way. My reason for this is emotional, aesthetic and cultural. In his new world the folk-hero character has taken on much that is new. For me, this familiar spelling has roots magic, a sense of originality, and an association with oral truth.

JAMES BERRY
June 1987

CONTENTS

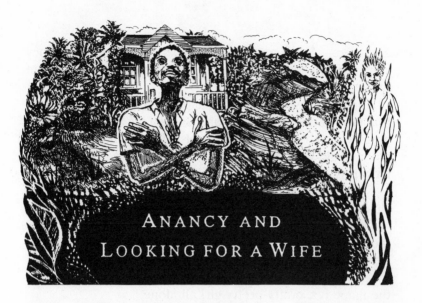

ANANCY AND
LOOKING FOR A WIFE

Anancy finds himself ready to have a wife. He has a lovely place where he lives. Anancy-Spiderman even has a clean stream running through his yard. But from the time wanting-a-wife stings Anancy, he begins to go funny.

Anancy sees Red Flowers together and Anancy gets fooled. Red Flowers are there close together dancing in Wind and Anancy thinks it's a girl. Red Flowers laugh at Anancy and say, "Can't you see we're just flowers and not a girl?"

Another time Anancy sees Rainbow in the sky and begs Rainbow to come down and become his bride. Anancy is there staring at Rainbow when Rainbow disappears.

Anancy goes walking through a green pasture. Everything is wonderful to Anancy. Sunlight is like gold surrounding him. Wind is the magic of a most fantastic wife who'll be beside him one day.

Anancy comes under a big spreading fig tree, where everybody usually stops and rests. But now, nobody is about anywhere. As if somebody whispers in his ear, Anancy stops. He looks round. Crickets and birds make noise in bright midday sun-heat.

Anancy sees a shining shape flickering, under low branches of the tree. The shape is like a big and strange bird preening itself. But the shape is also like a slender plant with blooms glowing. Then the shape is all a golden light flickering.

There is the crackle of a gentle fire burning. Anancy goes closer.

The fire is a pretty flame burning in the shade. As he sees the flame closer, a kind of magic works on Anancy. Bewitched, the Anancy-Spiderman steps up even closer yet.

Anancy sees. Anancy feels. Anancy understands now that the flame is a pretty-pretty girl all alone.

Anancy stares. He is lost to everything else. Anancy just walks round and round the pretty flame.

"Hello," Anancy says.

"Hello," Flame answers back, quietly.

Anancy is happy. Anancy is too-too impressed and excited. Such a big mark is made on him, Anancy can't talk. He bursts out singing:

"O, O! Palm trees have open arms.
O, O! Fire's a loving storm.
Rainbow—stay up high and far,
Red bloom is a red-red star.
Flame walks with me
Rain dries up round me, O.
Flame walks with me
Rain dries up round me, O.
  Dries up round me, O.
    Dries up round me, O!"

2

Anancy stops singing. He says, "Miss Flame. Oh, Miss Flame. Will you give Bro Nancy a visit tomorrow?"

With a gentle crackle in her voice, Flame answers in her quiet way, "I will come. I will come and visit Bro Nancy tomorrow." And now, Flame carries on talking.

Flame asks Anancy to be on his own when she arrives to see him.

"I'll travel on my own," Flame says.

But most important, Flame points out that for her to walk to his house, Anancy will have to prepare a trail. He'll have to put down a trail of dry sticks and twigs and dry leaves and dry grass. The trail should be laid through the woods, on through the gate of the pasture, on through the village, through his gateway and right on to the door of his house.

Next day, Anancy rises early. Quick and brisk, Anancy gathers up all the dry sticks, dry twigs, dry leaves and dry grass. And Anancy fixes the trail for Miss Flame to follow, all perfect-perfect.

Happy and excited, Anancy begins to sing and dance. Over and over Anancy sings this little song:

> *"Today! Today! It's to be.*
> *Today! Today! It's to be.*
> *Miss Flame – Miss Flame – a-visit me.*
> *Miss Flame – Miss Flame – a-visit me.*
> *I roll round and round and round the moon.*
> *I roll round and round and round the moon.*
> *Miss Flame is here soon-soon.*
> *Miss Flame is here soon-soon, O!"*

All the time Anancy is singing, Flame is coming along steady-steady. And mischievous Wind runs and runs in and out of Flame to help Flame. But mostly, Wind keeps arms

3

around Flame, pressing, helping Flame along.

All golden and beautiful, Flame's feet go on eating up the trail of dry sticks, twigs, leaves and grass. Flame comes steady-steady through the woods, through the pasture, through the village. Yet nobody sees Flame travelling.

Then, Anancy sees Flame coming down the road. Flame smokes and waves about in Wind. Anancy speeds up his dancing. And he sings louder:

"*Today! Today! It's to be.*
Today! Today! It's to be.
Miss Flame – Miss Flame – a-visit me.
Miss Flame – Miss Flame – a-visit me.
I roll round and round and round the moon.
I roll round and round and round the moon.
Miss Flame is here soon-soon.
Miss Flame is here soon-soon, 0!"

Flame turns into Anancy's yard-gate making the most awful whip-cracking noises. One look now and Anancy-Spiderman is worse than frightened. His face is terror itself. Flame is no longer little and beautiful. Flame is now a big and roaring and terrible Blazing-Fire.

Red-hot, Blazing-Fire is huge, fifty times bigger than little Flame. And Wind works with Blazing-Fire. Wind works whipping up Blazing-Fire, making Blazing-Fire increase in leaps and spread. And Blazing-Fire smokes bad-bad like a great pile of burning and moves quick-quick towards Anancy's doorway.

Anancy stands with arms spread wide, as if he can stop Blazing-Fire. He waves his arms about and shouts, "Go back! Go back! I change my mind about you. Go back. Go back, I say. I change my mind." Anancy has to jump back, to get himself away from the quick moving heat.

Oh, Bro Nancy works like six crazy men to save his house!

Fast-fast, Bro Nancy sweeps the trail of dry sticks, dry twigs, dry leaves and dry grass, away from his house. Bro Nancy shoves the trail away from his doorway, sweeping it over to the stream running through his yard. And all this time, oh, Blazing-Fire shoots out tongues of flames and sparks and smoke to cripple Anancy, but misses.

Not at all able to stop itself, Blazing-Fire is taken by the trail right over the edge of the stream.

Blazing-Fire falls straight into the pool of the stream. Oh, Anancy manages such a narrow escape!

Yet the dying Blazing-Fire spits out and splutters, keeping crying out. But Blazing-Fire goes smaller and smaller, drowning.

The Blazing-Fire becomes only a smell of burning. Blazing-Fire disappears. It goes completely. It could no more be seen.

From that day, water is used to stop fire. Anancy-Spiderman has a hand in it. All the same, Anancy doesn't stop. Anancy goes on looking for a wife.

5

ANANCY, OLD WITCH
AND KING-DAUGHTER

From the day King-Daughter is born, King-Wife decides she'll keep her girl child's name a secret. King-Wife sees that if her daughter's name isn't known, guessing it will be a test for the man who wants to marry her when she grows up. King-Wife smiles to herself saying, "Yes. That will be good. That will make him show how clever he really is. The first one – the first one who guesses her name – shall marry my daughter."

All servants at the palace become well warned. "Tell no one Daughter's name."

Every servant swears on oath. "Never ever will I let Daughter's real name come from my lips to anyone outside this big and beautiful palace."

6

King-Daughter is to be talked about only as "Daughter".
Then one day everybody begins to talk. "King-Daughter
is old enough to marry." "What?" "Yes, yes, yes! King-
Daughter is old enough to marry."

From everywhere, rich and famous young men begin to go
in their carriages to the palace, to guess King-Daughter's
name.

When Anancy hears what is happening, Anancy becomes
excited. Anancy walks up and down saying to himself, "Bro
Nancy, you have a chance. You know you have a good-good
chance to marry King-Daughter."

Anancy goes to see Bro Dog.

"Bro Dog," Anancy says, "suppose – just suppose – you
and me should play a game, could you be a first-class
partner?"

"Bro Nancy," Dog says, "you know very well I'm never
second class. Whatever I agree to I agree to."

"Well," Anancy says, "how smart a bad man beggar can
you be?"

"A bad man and a beggar together?"

"I think I'm thinking like that," Anancy says.

"I can try," Dog says. "I can try."

Anancy dresses Dog. Anancy works on Dog till Dog looks
like a scabby, ragged, dirty and smelly beggar.

"Bro Dog," Anancy says, "oh, you look perfect."

"Perfect what?" Dog says.

"Perfectly awful. Perfect bad man beggar to be scorned,
hated, despised."

"What?" Dog says. "Suppose I get hurt?"

"Bro Dog, all the time, we'll be together," Anancy assures
him.

Dog and Anancy take a short cut and come to a famous
royal picnic spot. They both hide themselves behind bushes.

Palace servants arrive ahead by themselves. They spread cloths and mats on the grass, put out picnic baskets together and sit awaiting the royal party.

Bro Dog creeps up behind the backs of the servants. He snatches the prettiest cloth, with DAUGHTER embroidered on it, and begins running about with it. Furious, the servants leap up and rush at Bro Dog.

"Drop it," they demand. "Nasty old mangy dog, drop it. Drop the cloth!" Dog rushes about playfully and then attempts to run away with the cloth. A royal maid runs after Dog. Really wild, she shouts, "Mangy dog, drop Princess Basamwe's picnic cloth!"

Dog immediately drops the cloth and runs away.

All the way home, Anancy sings:

"Nobody knows her name.
Nobody knows her name.
Then who is Princess Basamwe?
Who is Princess Basamwe, O?
Princess Basamwe, Basamwe, Basamwe."

Anancy becomes determined not to make any mistakes. It seems most important to Anancy that he should go and see Old Witch. But Old Witch needs money. Where can he get money?

Anancy remembers where money is. He goes and steals a gold piece from Bro Monkey. What Anancy doesn't know is that Monkey keeps the pile of gold pieces in the cave for Old Witch.

Anancy goes to see Old Witch in her plain earth-floor thatch-house. Old Witch sits surrounded by Snake, Alligator and a long leg Jumby Bird. Old Witch doesn't ask Anancy to sit, only to put down his piece of gold. Old Witch notices the gold but doesn't say she knows it comes from her own pile of gold pieces.

Old Witch works her tricks with Anancy. She tells him a certain time when he should start out for the palace. She tells him he'll find himself suited out with everything, at that certain time.

At that certain time next day Anancy can't believe his good luck. He suddenly finds himself dressed like a prince – perfect-perfect. He steps out of his door. And there a horse and carriage awaits him.

Carrying gifts, Anancy arrives at the palace in his shining open-top carriage. Anancy looks everything of a best-dressed prince. He stands proud-proud in his carriage at the palace gate and begins to sing:

> *"Nobody knows her name.*
> *Nobody knows her name.*
> *Then who is Princess Basamwe?"*

As Anancy calls the name Basamwe the palace gate swings open wide. Anancy's carriage drives up to the palace door. He stands in his carriage and sings:

> *"Nobody knows her name.*
> *Nobody knows her name.*
> *Then who is Princess Basamwe?*
> *Who is Princess Basamwe, O?*
> *Princess Basamwe, Basamwe, Basamwe."*

The King, King-Wife, King-Daughter and the whole royal family come out on the big veranda. As the stare of

King-Daughter's eyes touches Anancy, his horse and carriage vanishes. King-Daughter blinks; Anancy's top hat vanishes. She blinks again; his shoes vanish. She blinks again; his jacket, then his watch and chain, his walking stick, his trousers, all vanish. As he's going to be naked he finds himself standing in his own ordinary clothes, clutching his gifts of silver sandals, necklace and headdress. Anancy turns into spider and disappears.

Anancy hurries back to Old Witch.

Hurrying along, in his ordinary clothes again – without princely carriage, without princely dress – Anancy says to himself, "Oh well, nice things come, nice things go. Even day comes, day goes, like magic." But Anancy knows that somehow his stolen gold piece given to Old Witch has made her cross. Her angry spell has stripped him. Yet Anancy reminds himself, "Old Witch has done something. She's done something. She'll have to do another something!"

Anancy comes into Old Witch house and again stands on her plain earth-floor. Snake, Alligator and Jumby Bird are there with Old Witch. Before Anancy can open his mouth to speak Old Witch speaks. Not even looking at Anancy, Old Witch says, "Go and hand your gifts to the first three women you meet. Go, as I say."

Anancy leaves. And one after the other, Anancy gives away his gifts to women he meets, as Old Witch says. And, something the least expected happens.

The woman he hands his last-last gift to becomes Anancy's wife.

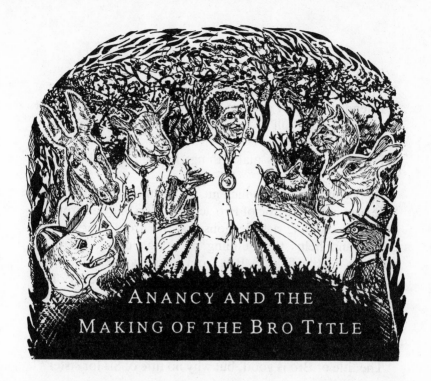

ANANCY AND THE
MAKING OF THE BRO TITLE

At the time, nobody is called Bro.

Anancy gets everybody to spread news that something special is ready to happen. It's ready to happen because everybody is ready for it. Come to the meeting in the village square. The big new happening will be revealed.

Anancy is pleased-pleased. A big crowd surrounds him in the early night. Anancy feels good and ready to make a sweetmouth speech.

"Friends," he starts, "you know and I know, everybody is a good-good person. But every person uses only a little goodness and a little bigness. People give teeny bits of gifts, a sprinkle of kind words, a pinch of this and a pinch of that. Friends, just think now of all the big extras that can come from making goodness work bigger and better."

"Hear, hear!" somebody says.

"Thank you, Dog," Anancy says.

"Friends," Anancy goes on, "make bigness work, and your fields are always full of harvest, your cupboards are always full of food."

"How can goodness make things happen just like that?" Rabbit asks.

"By becoming a Bro, which means Brother," Anancy says. "He who holds the title of Bro accepts everybody as brother. A Bro is building a little house; a Bro from every house comes and helps the building of a big house. A Bro is planting a little field; a Bro from every house comes and helps the planting of a big field. Drought is on; every Bro becomes rainmaker. It's hurricane; every Bro together clears up disaster. It's eating and drinking and dancing; every Bro and kinfolks are together in big merriment."

"Hear, hear!" Dog says.

"The title of Bro is good, but why no title of Sis for sister?" Anancy's wife says.

"Dear wife, thank you. But 'Bro' stands for 'Sis' as well."

"Dear husband, you well-well know Bro doesn't stand for Sis."

"Yes, dear wife, it stands for Sis, till one day, one day."

"Till one day, one day, what?"

"One day when you get your Sis title."

"Will we work on it together?"

"Yes," Anancy says. "We'll work on it together."

"And this is a good-good promise?"

"Yes, dear wife. This is a good-good promise, because everybody's ready to have their bigness, have their abundantness, their beautifulness, their wonderfulness!"

"Hear, hear!" Dog says.

"Friends," Anancy goes on, "take on the title of Bro in

12

front of your name and you have a mummah and a puppah in every house. No bad-mouth will hurt you and loved ones. No bad-mind will work on you and loved ones. No bad spell, no curse, no enemy will get you and loved ones. You are to be killed and everybody saves you. You are to be hungry and every family feeds you. You are sick and every family worries about you, gets you balm and heals you. Everybody is brother, everybody is friend. No enemies anywhere."

"Hear, hear!" Dog says. "Hip, hip, hooray!"

"Hip, hip, hooray!" the crowd say. "Hip, hip, hooray! Hip, hip, hooray!"

Anancy breaks into song:

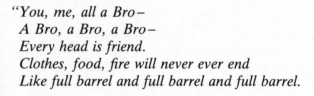

"You, me, all a Bro—
A Bro, a Bro, a Bro—
Every head is friend.
Clothes, food, fire will never ever end
Like full barrel and full barrel and full barrel.

I gi' you, you gi' me.
I gi' you, you gi' me.
Every head is friend.
Clothes, food, fire will never ever end
Like full barrel and full barrel and full barrel.

You, me, all, a Bro—
A Bro, a Bro, a Bro—
Make chain of full baskets,
Make chain of full baskets
Long-long, longer than day,
Long-long, longer than day,
Longer than day, O,
Longer than day, O!"

13

In noises and cheering, people rush forward. People want to be called Bro. Anancy puts his arm around Monkey. Anancy raises his other arm to the crowd and says, "Friends, I am your Bro Nancy. This is your Bro Monkey!" The crowd cheer them. Anancy gives Bro Monkey a big bag of corn. Rabbit becomes a Bro and gets two good cuts of cedar board from Anancy. Dog becomes a Bro and gets a shining necklace. Nearly everybody comes forward and becomes a Bro.

Next day early-early Anancy is ready to travel into everybody's country to spread the news about becoming a Bro.

In Anancy's yard, Bro Jackass stands there in the shaft of a cart. A garland of flowers is around the neck of Bro Jackass. Others with musical instruments sit in the cart. Bro Monkey has a drum, Bro Dog a banjo, Bro Rabbit a flute and Bro Puss a tambourine. Everybody is decorated with a garland of flowers or leaves. Peacock and Turkey have no instruments. Three other people are without instruments too; they are One-Eye Pig, Broken-Wing John Crow and Dropped-Leg Goat.

Though Jackass knows his way, Bro Nancy sits in the cart in front looking like the driver.

Bro Nancy picks up his sawn-off cowhorn and begins to blow it like a foghorn. That tells everybody something eventful is happening. In the sound of the horn, Anancy and his party start out with music and singing:

"You, me, all a Bro –
A Bro, a Bro, a Bro –
Every head is friend..."

With groups of people following them sometimes, Anancy

and his band of people travel till they come into Blackbird country.

Anancy begins to blow his cowhorn at great lengths to arouse the bird-people to the event of his arrival. And he and his band come to a road lined with Blackbird KlingKling-people cheering them and singing and clapping and dancing for them. In the sounds of the cowhorn and their music, they go on to a big square and find Chiefman Blackbird in official colours waiting for them.

As the crowd of Blackbird-people surround them, Anancy and his party play on and on and sing:

> *"You, me, all a Bro –*
> *A Bro, a Bro, a Bro –*
> *Every head is friend...*

As the music and singing end, Bro Turkey says, "Gobble gobble gobble gobble gobble!" Bro Peacock opens out his tail and spins. One-Eye Pig stares bright-bright, smiling. Broken-Wing John Crow and Dropped-Leg Goat flap and hop about in a little dance.

Anancy stands up in the cart and makes his speech about becoming a Bro.

In loud cheering Anancy steps down from his cart and embraces Chiefman Blackbird KlingKling. He declares Chiefman Blackbird and his people all a Bro.

Anancy hands out gifts, gets gifts himself and moves off again blowing his cowhorn, with his band, playing and singing, "You, me, all a Bro."

In the same way as before, Anancy and his party travel on and stop in Yellow-Snake country, in Monkey, Patoo, Rabbit, Hawk, John Crow and Ratbat countries, and then go on to Tiger country.

15

Here, in Tiger country, Anancy is to find more than usual resistance.

A great crowd of Tiger-people stand around Anancy and his party.

As usual, Bro Monkey bangs his drum, Bro Dog strums his banjo, Bro Rabbit plays his flute, Bro Puss shakes his tambourine. At the end of the music and singing, Bro Turkey says, "Gobble gobble gobble gobble gobble!" Bro Peacock opens out his tail and spins. One-Eye Pig stares bright-bright, smiling. Broken-Wing John Crow and Dropped-Leg Goat flap and hop about in their little dance. The Tiger-people clap and cheer.

Anancy gets going with his sweetmouth speech. The Tiger-people listen and listen keen-keen. Then sudden-sudden Chiefman Tiger stops Anancy, saying, "Anancy, I can defend myself. My people can defend themselves, in a group or as individuals. Why do we need this Bro business? I myself, I don't want to go and sit about with other people one bit. And you talk about getting hungry. We may get hungry, but certainly not for long. You talk about giving and getting. Why should I want to be given anything when I can take as I like?"

"Because as a Bro other Bro people won't be frightened of you," Anancy says.

"But I like other people to be frightened of me," Chiefman Tiger says. "I like people to hide when I walk past. It's great."

"Would it be the same," Anancy says, "if people didn't hide? If different people talked to you? And cheered you openly for your honour and your beauty and you knew that people talked about your good temper and the beautiful gentleman you are? Would it all be the same?"

Chiefman Tiger thinks, then in surprise he says, "Me a

beautiful gentleman? Me having some honour?"

"Yes," Anancy says.

"Nobody has ever said that. How else am I beautiful?"

"Well," Anancy says, "your coat – the coat of all Tiger-people – is a blessing. Your handsome head and strong-strong shoulders are all a blessing. The Bro title comes to you and all Tiger-people as a much later blessing."

"Is this true? Is all this true?"

"It's true. Bro title gives you a new status. With it you become Bro Chiefman Tiger. And once you're a Bro you can go on to become Mister."

"Me become Mister?"

"Yes," Anancy says. "You can even go on from Mister to Sir and on to Honourable."

"What will I become then?" Chiefman Tiger asks.

"You'll be Honourable Sir Mister Bro Chiefman Tiger."

"Wow!" Chiefman Tiger says. "With all the weight of that honour, I couldn't walk. I'd have to be carried."

A great laughter and cheering goes up.

"Tell me how I'll actually get all that honour," Chiefman Tiger says. "How I'll know I've got it. And everybody'll know I've got it. And tell me more about the good things about me I don't know and about all I'll get if I become a Bro."

"Well," Anancy says, "if you treat, say, Bro Monkey or Bro Rabbit or Bro Dog – all other people – like they are your own Tiger-people, the news will come back to me. And I'll see you get your honour in front of everybody."

Chiefman Tiger goes silent, then says, "But I don't want to be good to everybody. I want to be very bad to some people. I have a lot of badness I must use. Can I start being good to some people who aren't Tiger-people and go on being very bad to others?"

"Chiefman, Chiefman Tiger," Anancy says, "to be a Bro means everybody makes their own country a place of Bro, and so, at the same time, everybody makes all the countries one big place of Bro."

"Wow!" Chiefman Tiger says. "All this is new! Very new!"

"Yes," Anancy says. "Very new. But everybody is ready for it."

"I like the honour I'll get," Chiefman Tiger says. "I like the honour very much. But there is a spot of bother, I must admit. You see, as it is now, I can walk through anybody's country, and, apart from Lion, nobody, nobody can stop me. Or even challenge me. I have that safeguard already."

"Yes," Anancy says, "that's really so, Chiefman Tiger. But mightn't you get some news from Monkey-people or Rabbit-people, if when you walk through their country you were able to stop and have a chat, and have some refreshments they give you?"

"Hear, hear!" the Tiger-people say. "Hear, hear!"

Chiefman Tiger goes silent for a little while. Then he looks up and says, "Anancy, I'll join."

"Hear, hear!" the Tiger-people say. "Hear, hear!"

Bro Nancy comes and puts his arms around Chiefman Tiger. The Tiger-people become Bro. Anancy gives the people gifts. In turn, the Tiger-people pile on their gifts in Anancy's cart.

Anancy and his cart-band of people leave Tiger country in an uproar of cheering, cowhorn blowing and music and singing.

At home again, Anancy finds he has come into a new and difficult problem. How should he share out the cartload of gifts? Anancy tells his cart-band of people that silence has overtaken him.

"Silence has come upon me, friends," Anancy tells them.

"It is like a night a man must sleep in. Welcome in different countries make a man happy and sad. Unbrothers have become brothers. It calls for silence and fasting. I must have silence and fasting for seven days and seven nights."

Everybody is struck by Anancy's new mood. All agree to help Bro Nancy and leave him alone. "Let Bro Nancy deal with his deep mind," they say.

Anancy will have nothing to do with the gifts. Anancy lets his cart-band of people unload the cart and carry the bags of rabbits and birds, box of dried fish, barrel of crabs, barrels of different corned meat, bags of corn and dry beans, bags of yams, spices, bottles of rum and baskets of fruit and puddings and bread, and stack them in his kitchen.

The moment Anancy sees that everyone is really gone – and everywhere is quiet-quiet – Anancy leaps up and begins to dance and sing around the pile of gifts:

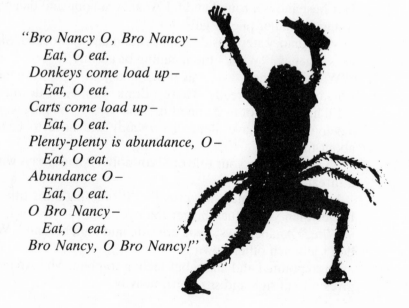

> *"Bro Nancy O, Bro Nancy –*
>   *Eat, O eat.*
> *Donkeys come load up –*
>   *Eat, O eat.*
> *Carts come load up –*
>   *Eat, O eat.*
> *Plenty-plenty is abundance, O –*
>   *Eat, O eat.*
> *Abundance O –*
>   *Eat, O eat.*
> *O Bro Nancy –*
>   *Eat, O eat.*
> *Bro Nancy, O Bro Nancy!"*

Anancy drinks rum and sings and dances. He begins to season and pickle different meats for keeping. At the same time, he cooks a sample of every kind of the meat and of everything else. And the more the kitchen gets stronger with the smell of cooking and spices and seasoning the more Anancy sips his drink, takes a taste of things and sings and dances.

Almost bursting with food and drink, Anancy falls asleep.

Anancy wakes up in his long furry gown. Anancy sings and dances round the gifts, and drinks, cooks, eats and falls asleep again.

Not caring whether it is day or night, Anancy drinks, dances and sings, cooks and eats and falls asleep for three days.

Worried about her husband, Mrs Anancy arrives at the kitchen doorway. She cannot really believe what she sees. Her husband is a round and fat Anancy singing and dancing round a smaller pile of gifts.

Mrs Anancy steps inside, looks round and is shocked. She asks Anancy, "What's the meaning of all this?"

"Wife," Anancy says, "sit down and join your husband. Lots of meals are ready. There's drink. Come, sit down."

"I'll have none of it. None of it," she says. "The gifts were never yours to have alone. Everybody will have to know about this."

"Shall I promote your title of Sis or not?" Anancy says with a threat.

"Not," Mrs Anancy says crossly. "Promoting a Sis title is bigger than you. Much bigger than you."

"Wife," Anancy says, "you are wife and I am husband. We don't let each other down."

Disappointed and angry but feeling trapped, Mrs Anancy gives a loud sigh and sits down heavily.

Somewhere, loud-loud, unexpectedly, Blackbird Kling-Kling begins to sing this little song:

> *"People, O people,*
> *Come and see Bro Nancy.*
> *People, O people,*
> *Come and see Bro Nancy.*
> *Come and see Bro Nancy, O!*
> *Come and see Bro Nancy, O!..."*

Other Blackbird-people begin to sing this same song, passing the news round the whole village.

Sudden-sudden, the yard is full of people.

Anancy's cart-band of people are the first to arrive. Immediately, Anancy says, "Oh, Bro Dog, Bro Monkey, Bro Jackass, and everybody, so pleased you've come! So, so glad-glad you heard the KlingKling call! Come. We'll put out long tables and benches. We'll put out the cooked meats with everything cooked. We'll cook more meat and everything else. We'll have all the drinks and get some more. We'll strike up the music. And Bro and Bro and Bro and everybody, when the merriment is on, and you see Anancy dancing, know that Anancy dances away his badness. With all his heart, Anancy dances away his badness."

That whole day and night, Anancy's yard becomes a place of great feasting and merriment.

From that time, leaders always try to cover up the lion-share of things they take for themselves.

ANANCY, DOG AND
OLD HIGUE DRY-SKULL

Bro Nancy doesn't go hunting with the hunters that day. It's Bro Dog and others who go hunting. And everybody shoots and catches something, except Dog. Every hunter has a bagful of birds and wild animals. Bro Dog alone turns home with an empty bag. Sad, tired and hungry, Bro Dog decides to hang back from the others and take a short cut home by himself.

Alone, halfway in the woods, Dog stumbles on something like a bone. Bro Dog can't resist a bone. Bro Dog stops, but is disappointed.

"Oh, blow it!" Dog says to himself. "Why couldn't it be a fresh bone with flesh? Why couldn't I have a meal?" Dog can't help looking at the bone better and seeing it's a dry-skull. He decides he'll just leave it, then finds himself thinking, "I'm so hungry. Might as well put it in my bag and have a bit of chew off it later." So Bro Dog picks up the dry-skull and puts it in his empty bag.

As Bro Dog walks on, he notices the bag hanging from his shoulder is getting heavier and heavier.

"Nonsense," Bro Dog says to himself. "How can my bag get heavier? I must be just hungry and weak."

But as Bro Dog walks on, his bag gets so heavy that his shoulder can't take the weight any longer. He has to rest the bag down. And Dog naturally has the urge to look inside the bag to see what's happened. Dog is dumbfounded. Dog can't open his bag. Dog struggles and struggles and no way can he open his own bag. Dog stops trying.

"Blow it!" Dog says to himself. "I'm too hungry and tired to bother with all this. I'll just leave it – the whole lot." Bro Dog takes his hands off the bag, stands up and begins to walk away.

"You can't leave me. You see me you can't leave me," a squeaky voice from the bag says. "Pick me up, Bro Dog. Put me on your back."

Bro Dog knows now he's really in trouble. He knows, he has picked up Old Higue Dry-Skull. Old Higue is the worst thing in the whole world. It holds you in its spell and takes your blood. Old Higue Dry-Skull is equally nasty and horrible and terrible. Dog could have died. All his bad-luck has come one day.

Bro Dog hesitates. But Bro Dog finds himself trying to lift the heavy bag.

"You can pick me up," the squeaky voice says. "You can pick me up. Put me on your back."

Bro Dog somehow manages to lift the bag onto his back and put the straps round his head.

Knowing he dares not stop, knowing too he doesn't know what he'll do with Old Higue Dry-Skull, Bro Dog walks and

23

walks with his load like a man on his back. Bro Dog comes out into the village wondering what he'll ever do with his burden or what it'll ever do with him.

The first person Dog is to see is Bro Anancy. Seeing Dog under his big load, Anancy's greedy eyes pop. And poor Bro Nancy can't help himself. He steps brisk-brisk up to Dog. Listen now to the sweet voice of Bro Nancy. "Oh, a good-good evening to you, Bro Dog. Seems for certain the hunt has favoured you with best-best of luck."

"I'm tired, Bro Nancy," Dog says. "Tired-tired! I have more on my back than I can manage."

"Bro Dog," Anancy says, "you know I'll help you. Let me help you."

"Oh, Bro Nancy," Dog says, "it's just what I need. I won't even bother to put it down."

"No, Bro Dog," Anancy says. "Just put your load straight onto my back."

"Thank you. Oh, thank you, Bro Nancy," Dog says, "for taking my load. So tired-tired, I'll just sit down right here a bit."

"That's all right, Bro Dog," Anancy says. "Now it's on my back, I'll just walk on. I'll take your load to your house. Or my house."

"Bro Nancy," Dog says, "it doesn't matter. I know where you live. You know where I live."

Bro Nancy goes off with Old Higue Dry-Skull. Relieved, Bro Dog merely goes off to his own house. Bro Dog well knows Anancy will take the heavy bag to his own house expecting to find a bagful of fresh meat. That is so. But instead of finding fresh meat Anancy finds trouble.

Bro Nancy opens the bag easy-easy. But Anancy jumps back. He can't believe his bad luck when he sees Old Higue Dry-Skull in the bag staring at him.

"You take me, you take me out the bag," the squeaky voice says. "You take me out the bag, Bro Nancy."

Anancy knows he's in the spell of Old Higue Dry-Skull. He knows Old Higue Dry-Skull lives on something alive put beside him every two days to quick-quick shrivel up and wither away. He knows, under his spell, you become his slave and can't go anywhere beyond a certain distance.

Anancy has to take Old Higue Dry-Skull out of the bag. He has to take on looking after him and becoming his constant companion. All the same, Bro Nancy is not a man to put up with anything.

Anancy racks and racks his brains to find a way to free himself of Old Higue Dry-Skull.

One day Anancy hears Chicken-Hawk excite his chickens outside. Anancy runs off from Old Higue Dry-Skull saying he must protect his chickens. Anancy sees Hawk eating one of his chickens on a tree stump. Hawk is about to fly off with the chicken but Anancy waves and gestures and calls in a panic voice. Hawk sees Anancy wants to talk to him badly. Hawk waits and listens.

Anancy tells Hawk he'll give him a whole coop of chickens if he'll do a job for him quickly.

You see, every day after twelve o'clock Anancy has to put Old Higue Dry-Skull outside to sun himself. Also, Anancy knows that open wings overhead drive terror in Old Higue Dry-Skull more than anything else in the world.

Next day, Anancy puts Old Higue Dry-Skull outside in the open and stands back in hiding to watch everything.

Chicken-Hawk comes overhead and begins to circle round. Hawk's shadow moves over Old Higue Dry-Skull and he's thrown into terrible terror.

"Anancy! Anancy!" the squeaky voice calls in panic. "Hawk's overhead. Hawk's overhead! Come and take me in. Take me in, Bro Nancy! You put me here. Come and take me in! Take me in!"

Hawk swoops down with open talons, picks up Old Higue Dry-Skull, flies off on and on and drops him in deepest woods.

To get even with Dog, Anancy takes Hawk and shows him an easy and quiet way into Dog's chicken coop. For seven days Hawk comes and carries off one of Dog's chickens.

Bro Dog complains to Bro Nancy about what Hawk has done.

"Ah, Bro Dog," Anancy says, "you know how people say 'Trouble there up at bush, Anancy brings it come at house.' But you see how poor Bro Nancy doesn't do all the bringing."

Bro Dog says nothing.

MONKEY, TIGER
AND THE MAGIC TRIALS

At the time, King Monkey and family are the royal family. But, you see, no doors, no walls, no soldiers protect the palace.

Also, the palace of King Monkey and family is made without a single nail or piece of iron. All rock and wood, the great royal home is like a hill with trees around it. Sun shines and the palace glistens with the shining sun. Moon shines and the palace glistens with the shining moon. But a magic gold stool that is there glistens most of all.

You see, wrongdoers are punished, or set free, by the way ten Magic Stools work and make an answer.

Anybody may well think nearly all the Magic Stools are just bulky looking like ordinary small rocks. Or they only look like short pieces of cut up wood-trunk. But remember, the Magic Stools work together. They work in ways that only a certain kind of person can understand.

They are always there, at the back of the palace, in the open shed of the Trial Place. You see the Magic Stools all the same size, side by side, in a row, on bare ground. Nine of the stools are dark and crusty with age. But the last stool, the tenth one, standing at the end of the row, on your right, is gold – pure shining gold.

Puss-Cousin happens to come to the palace, to be put on trial. Puss-Cousin comes marched up by Chiefman Puss behind him like a policeman.

King Monkey comes down from his top room. He comes down serious looking. He wears a special dress. King Monkey walks into the shed, on the bare ground of the Trial Place.

Puss-Cousin is put to stand in front of the ten Magic Stools. King Monkey stands behind him, and speaks.

"Puss-Cousin," King Monkey says, "wrong has been done. You are here on trial. If you are guilty, you will die. If you are innocent, you will live and go completely free. Do you understand?"

"Yes, King," Puss-Cousin says.

"Good," King Monkey goes on. "I want you to count the Magic Stools. Point a finger at each one as you count. Let the Magic Stools speak. Count the Magic Stools. Now."

Puss-Cousin points with his finger and counts, "One. Two. Three. Four. Five. Six. Seven. Eight. Nine. Ten." Puss-Cousin drops dead, exactly as his voice touches the word ten.

King Monkey steps back in a kingly way. Chiefman Puss steps forward. He picks up the dead Puss-Cousin. He puts him across his shoulders. He bows to King Monkey. He walks away carrying Puss-Cousin. The other Puss-cousins and friends follow him to the burial. All this time nobody knows Tiger hides in the bush, watching.

On the very next day, Dog-Cousin is brought for trial. Dog-Cousin is put in front of the Magic Stools. King Monkey stands behind him and commands him to count. Dog-Cousin counts the Magic Stools and drops dead. Chiefman Dog steps forward to pick up Dog-Cousin to carry him away. Tiger bursts out from hiding. In his rushing in Tiger knocks people down. Tiger grabs up Dog-Cousin. Tiger runs mad-mad away with Dog-Cousin to make a meal of him.

Oh, everybody is shocked. People at the Trial Place are beyond themselves. Oh, the awfulness of it! People shout at Bro Tiger. People run after Bro Tiger. Everything only makes Bro Tiger run faster.

King Monkey calls, telling Tiger to come back. No Tiger comes back. The people band together and go searching the woods. No Tiger is found. Tiger gets himself well-well hidden. Everybody has to give up the search, thinking, "Oh, Tiger can't be seen. He looks no different from air!"

Yet Bro Tiger lurks about in hiding.

Unseen, Bro Tiger comes back close. He waits. He watches to see if another wrongdoer comes and counts the Magic Stools.

Tiger waits around for two days. No other wrongdoer comes. Tiger gets hungrier and hungrier. On the third day Tiger's hunger bites him hard-hard. Tiger sees two royal children playing. Tiger rushes out. Tiger grabs a royal Monkey-child and disappears with him.

With all the hunts and searches made, Tiger cannot be found.

Every third day or so, Tiger manages to make a meal of a royal Monkey-person. Tiger does that. Bro Tiger does that till King Monkey, Queen Monkey, children, servants are gone. Only one son and one daughter escape. And in great hurry-hurry they go looking for Mister Anancy.

All during that time, Bro Tiger is sitting on the throne, laughing. Bro Tiger thumps his chest. He laughs big laughs and says, "King Tiger. King Tiger. Tiger is King Tiger!" He roars, laughing.

Tiger roams through the palace from room to room. Tiger looks at himself in mirrors. He then pulls faces at himself and roars with laughter. Tiger sleeps in a different palace bed every night. Then, getting hungry, Tiger comes out looking for wrongdoers or palace visitors.

Visiting the palace, Rabbit-Cousin walks up.

"I'm in charge now," Tiger tells Rabbit-Cousin.

"You?" Rabbit-Cousin says, surprised.

"You are doubtful?"

"No, no," Rabbit-Cousin says, a little frightened.

"King Monkey's away on holiday," Tiger says. "Long holiday. Might not even be back. I see to all business here. I'm doing a prize. A big prize. Come. Follow me. I show you."

Tiger takes Rabbit-Cousin to the Trial Place and says, "D'you know what is gold?"

"Yes," Rabbit-Cousin says.

"Show me gold."

Rabbit-Cousin points to the gold stool.

"That's the prize," Tiger says.

Not knowing anything about the Magic Stools, Rabbit-Cousin is excited. With this unbelievable chance of winning such a big block of gold, Rabbit-Cousin says, "Really? That really is the prize?"

"It is the prize."

"And I can win it?"

"If educated enough. Go on. Try it."

"What do I do?"

30

"Count the stools. In one go. In one straight go. Do it, and point at them."

Rabbit-Cousin counts the Magic Stools and falls dead. Tiger is seized with shaking laughter. It's all so easy, he can't believe it.

Anancy hears about what is happening at the palace. Hurrying, Anancy runs into Old Witch. Walking quick-quick across shadows of sunlit trees, Anancy has no idea where Old Witch appears from. Old Witch stands in front of him saying, "Anancy, you need me. You need me."

"Mrs Old Witch, I'm in bad hurry," Anancy says.

"Where are you hurrying to?" she asks, walking beside him.

"To the palace."

"To do with the Magic Trials?"

"Yes."

"Ah!" Old Witch says, full of knowing. "D'you know something is badly wrong, Anancy? D'you really know?"

"Mrs Old Witch, I'm Bro Nancy. I'm here on my way."

"Oh!" Old Witch says, getting cross. "You're rebuffing me. Anancy, you're rebuffing me. Because you want all the praises for yourself. But – you need me. You really do."

"Mrs Old Witch, I'm in bad hurry, I say," Anancy says and walks away quick-quick.

"Magic spells can be broken!" Old Witch shouts with spite, left standing alone. "Magic spells can be broken, I say!" she shouts again.

At the palace, in a comfortable bed, Bro Tiger yawns and stretches himself. He suddenly gets up and comes out into bright sunshine. Bro Tiger sees Bro Nancy sitting against a tree near the Trial Place.

Getting up to meet Tiger, Anancy greets him sweet-sweet. "Good afternoon, Bro Tiger."

31

"What d'you want?" Tiger says. "I'm in charge here."

"Mister King Tiger, I see you are in charge."

"I'm glad you see that. I'm glad you see you should call me Mister King Tiger."

"Position can make a man a big-big man."

"I'm doing a prize, with the gold stool. You're good at good-luck, and a bit of brain. Come. Try it."

"You know I'm not an educated man," Anancy says.

"I get on. You see that. Copy me. Hear what I say. Win the gold stool."

Anancy laughs at how clever Bro Tiger thinks he has become. He knows Tiger believes he'll count the stools and die. But Anancy doesn't say he knows Tiger thinks that. Instead, Anancy says, "You mean if I win I'll have gold and be rich. And you will be a king already. So both of us can be proud and be good friends. Do you mean that?"

"Yes. Yes." Tiger answers without thinking. Impatient, he goes on. "Come on then. Come. Count the stools. All of them in one go."

Anancy counts, "One. Two. Three. Four. Five. Six. Seven. Eight. Nine. And one more."

Tiger looks up surprised, puzzled and then gets cross. "That isn't proper counting."

"All right, Mister King Tiger. It's not a time to burn yourself out getting vex. I can try again."

"Right. But better this time. Better this time."

Anancy counts again. "One. Two. Three. Four. Five. Six. Seven. Eight. And two more."

Tiger leaps up and stamps about in a rage. "Stupid, fool-fool man. Stupid, fool-fool man. Can't count! Can't count properly!" Tiger turns round in his rage, carried away with his anger. He points to the stools, saying, "Fool-fool man, count like this, One. Two. Three. Four. Five. Six.

Seven. Eight. Nine. Ten." Tiger drops down, rolls over, dead, showing his belly.

Anancy looks round, triumphant, expecting to see a crowd of happy faces praising and applauding him. Instead, Anancy sees Old Witch grinning, with a spiteful satisfaction. And there, caught in surprise, looking at Old Witch, Anancy hears a shuffling movement beside him. He looks and sees Tiger getting up.

Tiger gets up, dusts himself off and walks away.

Old Witch disappears, laughing, saying, "I told you spells can be broken. Broken! Broken! Broken!"

Since that time, palaces have doors and gate and walls and soldiers.

TIGER AND ANANCY
MEET FOR WAR

Tiger sends Anancy a message. The message says he's coming round to Anancy's house to kill him. Anancy sends back a message telling Tiger to come. He should come any way he likes. But he should bring all his friends with him. He, Anancy, will be waiting with all his friends.

Tiger arrives. Tiger comes like a king on horseback, with weapons, with a crowd of Tiger-men around him. And every man carries weapons of different kinds.

Tiger and his friends stop at Anancy's yard-gate. They stop there. They see only one friend with Anancy in the middle of the yard. They see nobody else. They see that Bro Nancy has no weapon. They see his friend Bro Dog has no weapon either. They see Anancy lying down with his head on a piece of tree trunk.

They stand there at the gate. Bro Tiger and Tiger-men are puzzled. They wonder what trick Anancy has planned. They don't know what move to make.

Listen to the Anancy calling loud-loud. "Come on, Bro Tiger. Come on. Don't torture me. Come and chop off my head. Let the world know you are a brave-brave man. Let my head drop like a block of wood."

Tiger feels a fool. Bro Tiger sits on the horse with his head all confused. Listen to Tiger now. "Bro Nancy? You know I have no intention to kill you. Why should you mistrust me?"

Hear the Anancy's reply. "Come on, Bro Tiger. Don't stretch out your brave deed. Don't make it a bad torture. Come and do what you come to do. If you don't do it today, you'll only want to do it tomorrow."

"Bro Nancy?" Tiger says in a pleading voice. "You know I'm not that sort of man. You know that." And Bro Tiger gets down from his horse. Bro Tiger gives up his weapons to the Tiger-men. Bro Tiger says, "I'm coming, Bro Nancy. I'm coming to shake hands with you. I want the whole world to know we are good-good friends."

"If you say so, Bro Tiger. If you say so," Anancy says. Then listen how the Anancy goes on wrapping up his words in tricky traps. "You invite yourself to my yard, I don't say, Go away. You want to shake my hand, I don't say, Oh no."

Bro Tiger steps through Bro Nancy's yard-gate. Bro Tiger sinks. Bro Tiger falls straight down into a pit concealed with dry leaves, and has rocks at the bottom.

Every Tiger-man is shocked. Every one clusters round the pit. Every one works and works to get Bro Tiger out.

Bro Tiger is lifted out. He is lifted out all battered up with limbs broken.

And Anancy and Dog see nothing of the Tiger-men's fuss over Tiger's bad outcome. Anancy and Dog did just leave, just go away about their business.

Anancy and Dog don't see it's a bandaged-up Bro Tiger the Tiger-men take away, take away on horseback.

All the same, that day hasn't changed Tiger. It hasn't stopped Tiger from giving Anancy a bad challenge.

ANANCY AND FRIEND

It's holiday time, you see. Everybody is dressed up, out in the village square. Out there too are cakes newly baked, sweets newly made, other things freshly roasted and fried and cool drinks wonderfully brewed. All have a strong sweet smell in the square.

Everybody eats and drinks and talks and laughs. Everybody is in a merry mood. Anancy has more than one drink of rum in his head. Dog has more than one drink of rum in his head too. The truth is, Bro Dog is tipsy. Every time Bro Dog drinks a little too much he becomes the biggest boaster you ever hear. So everything Bro Dog does now and says is a big show-off.

Anancy has to say, "You know, Bro Dog, you can go on as if you're really the wisest man."

"I'm no fool," Dog says, staring at Anancy. "I'm no fool. Not like some folks I could name. I can't help that. Can't help it I'm no fool, can I?"

"Perhaps you have more senses than everybody else, Bro Dog," Anancy says.

"I have," Dog says. "I always know I have more senses than most people."

"How many senses do you have?" Anancy asks.

"Every worker-part of my body is a sense," Dog boasts. "My nose is one sense. My mouth is another sense. My legs are two senses and my arms another two. My ears are two. My eyes are two. And my voice is another sense."

"So, Bro Dog, you have eleven senses," Anancy says.

Bro Dog counts up on his fingers. "Yes," he says, staring at Anancy. "Eleven!" Dog laughs. "And I know some people with none at all."

"Well, Bro Dog," Anancy says, "I have only two senses."

"Well, I'm sorry for you." Dog laughs and asks, "Which ones are your two senses then?"

Anancy says, "My first sense is, I KNOW ME; my second sense is, I KNOW MY FRIEND."

"Then I beat you," Dog says, laughing. Dog counts up and laughs out loudly. "I beat you by nine! By nine, Bro Nancy!" Dog rolls about laughing and repeating, "By nine, Bro Nancy! By nine...!"

Bro Nancy doesn't say a word.

Everybody says, "Never mind, Bro Nancy. Never mind. Your day will come. You'll have your laugh another day."

The very next afternoon, coming round a corner into a lane, Anancy gets a big surprise. There is Bro Dog frightened out of his wits! Tiger is holding him. Tiger has a firm grip on Bro Dog, ready to eat him.

Listen to Anancy now, talking like the best neighbour, all easy and carefree. "Good afternoon, Bro Tiger. So good to see you on a good afternoon with a good meal in hand."

Tiger is irritated. Tiger stares at Anancy with all his hate in his worst looks.

Anancy stands looking pleased, as if he'd like to honour

Tiger for holding Dog. "Oh, Bro Tiger," Anancy says, "you do have a meal that calls for a respectable man's thanksgiving. You must at least make the sign of the cross. And say grace for this good-good thing you're about to receive. Then, Bro Tiger, a passer-by like me can go his way in peace, feeling blessed."

Anancy has meant to make Tiger confused. And suddenly Tiger does look confused, and even shamefaced. Tiger always dreads looking silly or stupid or just ignorant. Tiger lets go of Dog and makes the sign of the cross on himself. Oh, Dog makes such a big, desperate leap from Tiger that he knocks him over. Just for a moment, open-mouthed, Anancy watches Bro Dog break away like a frightened thief, running for dear life.

Then swift-swift Anancy turns into Spider. Anancy shoots up into the near tree and is lost in branches.

Anancy and Tiger don't become better friends. But from that day, dog respects a sense of friendship.

ANANCY AND THE HIDE-AWAY GARDEN

The garden belongs to Old Witch-Sister. Nobody is really ever supposed to see this garden. But Anancy keeps on hearing about the garden grown on rocks.

"It's the world's most glorious garden," people whisper to Anancy.

"If allowed at all, not more than one stranger is ever supposed to see the garden," people also whisper to Anancy.

Anancy sets out alone to find the garden.

Anancy finds himself in a desert of rocks. He climbs up a hillside of rocks. Getting up to the top, Anancy breathes like a horse pulling hard.

At the flat top of the hill, the garden is open to wide blue sky. Anancy stands fixed in surprise. Anancy is amazed.

"True-true. This is the richest garden in the whole world!"

Anancy whispers to himself. "The garden is growing, is fruiting, is ripening, is blossoming. Look at fattest vegetables! Look at shining fruits and flowers! Look at a garden of all reds, all oranges and browns, all yellows and purples!"

Anancy walks along the edge of the garden. Anancy can't help keeping on talking to himself. "What a garden of fat vegetables. What a garden of flowers that stay in your eyes. What a garden of little fruit trees ripening and blossoming. What a garden sweet-smelling of plenty-plenty!"

Anancy bends down. He examines the rocky ground. Roots are gone down, hidden in rocks, shaped like smooth mounds of earth.

Anancy stands. He looks in wonder at the colourful garden in bright hot sunshine. Anancy whispers, "Sunshine takes roots. Sunshine takes roots and grows like garden."

Anancy turns round. He goes back down the rocky hillside singing:

> *"Sunshine 'pon rocks gets dressed up like garden.*
> *Sunshine 'pon rocks gets dressed up like garden.*
> *Seeds get wings in a breeze-blow.*
> *Seeds get wings in a breeze-blow.*
> *Catch them, pocket them, plant them back of house, O!*
> *Piece-piece luck comes quiet in one-one.*
> *Breeze-blow seeds raise up stone-land!*
> *Oh, catch them, pocket them, plant them*
>   *back of house.*
> *Oh, catch them, pocket them, plant them*
>   *back of house.*
> *Sunshine 'pon rocks gets dressed up like garden, O!"*

Anancy stops singing. As he walks along, he begins to think again how the garden is rich and fat and colourful.

Anancy begins to think the garden should be his. He begins to feel how it feels having the garden. Anancy begins to count up what the garden can do for him. He reckons up that the garden can get mountains of praises for him. And in the heat of the day, he can lie back in a shade in the beautiful garden. He can stay there and listen to birds singing, and go off to sleep.

"Old Witch-Sister needs nothing beautiful!" Anancy says aloud.

Then Anancy laughs a funny laugh of excitement. In himself now he feels, he knows the Hide-Away Garden shall belong to him – Anancy!

But, Anancy remembers – nobody can just take away the garden, easily. For one thing, the garden has a Gardener-man. He cares for the garden. He's also watchman of the garden. Then, some mysterious ways work with the garden that cannot ever be explained. Any food stolen from the garden makes the eater keep being sick till the robber is found out. Then, of great-great importance, there is the flute playing by Gardener-man, who walks with a stick taller than himself.

With his stick lying beside him, Gardener-man sits on a comfortable pile of rocks at sunset every day. Sitting there, he plays his flute to the garden. He gives the garden his music till darkness covers him.

While the flute is playing, Old Witch-Sister always comes and listens. Dressed in red completely, Old Witch-Sister creeps up into the garden, unseen. Sometimes she just listens and goes away again.

Other times, she begins to dance straightaway, on a flat rock near the centre of the garden. But there is one big-big rule, you see, that must be kept.

Gardener-man must never-never play his flute over a

certain length of time. If Gardener-man should ever go on with the music over a certain length of time, he will not be able to stop playing. Also, if Old Witch-Sister happens to be dancing, she too will not be able to stop dancing.

Anancy goes and sees his son.

"Tacooma," Anancy says, "I want you to get Bro Blackbird KlingKling to get nine Blackbird KlingKling-cousins together with himself. I want them to do a careful-careful clever job. I want them to hide, to listen, to learn Gardener-man's music of the flute, exact-exact. I want them to learn, to know, to remember every, every slightest bit."

The Blackbird-people creep up and listen unseen, as Anancy asks. Bro Blackbird KlingKling and cousins have sharp ears. They take in every sound of Gardener-man's flute music, quick-quick.

Anancy sends a message to Gardener-man. The message invites Gardener-man to come and eat with him. But, you see, Anancy goes and collects Gardener-man himself. And because he's setting a trap for Gardener-man, just listen to that Anancy. "Oh, Mister Gardener-man, I just happen to be passing this way. And my good memory says we are eating together. And as you know, Bro Nancy isn't a man to miss a friendly company a little longer. So I come and call for you."

Gardener-man walks with his stick taller than himself beside Anancy, towards Anancy's house. At this exact time, Anancy's son Tacooma makes his way to the Hide-Away Garden.

Quick-quick, Tacooma collects up some food from the garden.

Sunset comes. The Blackbird-people come and sit in Gardener-man's place, on the pile of rocks. The Blackbird-

42

people begin to sing Gardener-man's flute playing, all to the garden.

The Bird-people work the singing in groups of three. When one group is stopping, the other group comes in smart-smart. Like that, the Blackbird-people carry on and on with Gardener-man's music, perfect-perfect.

With really sweet throats of the flute, the Blackbird-people sing and sing to the garden. Flute music fills the garden and the whole sunset evening, sweeter than when Gardener-man himself plays.

Dressed all in red, slow-slow, Old Witch-Sister creeps up into the garden. On her flat rock, Old Witch-Sister begins to dance, slow-slow. Her long red skirt sways about a little bit at first. The skirt begins to sway about faster. Then the skirt begins to swirl and swirl. From head to toe, with arms stretched wide, Old Witch-Sister spins and spins and spins. Darkness comes down. Darkness finds Old Witch-Sister swirling as fast as any merry-go-round.

Last to sing, on his own, Bro KlingKling takes over the flute-singing. As Bro KlingKling's voice spreads over the garden, Old Witch-Sister drops down dead, in a heap of red clothes. Then, at Anancy's house, Gardener-man is the only one to eat the stolen food from the garden. Same time as Old Witch-Sister, Gardener-man drops down dead too.

Anancy gets himself busy. Anancy sees to it that Old Witch-Sister and Gardener-man get buried as far apart as possible. He sees to it too that Gardener-man's walking stick is buried with him.

Then Anancy jigs about. Dancing, Anancy says:

"Sunshine 'pon rocks gets dressed up like garden.
  Catch them, pocket them,
    plant them back of house, O!"

43

Anancy begins to plan making a feast for himself, family and friends. He begins to plan too how he'll get Bro Dog, Bro Pig and Bro Jackass to work the garden.

Next day, early-early, Anancy starts out with Dog, Pig and Jackass and others to see the Hide-Away Garden.

They come to the garden. Anancy cannot believe his eyes. Every fruit and vegetable and flower and blossom is dried up. Every leaf is shrivelled and curled crisply. Anancy whispers, "The whole garden is dried up. The Hide-Away Garden is dead. Dead! Really dead!"

Anancy sings:

> *"Whai-o, story done, O!*
> *Whai-o, story done, O.*
> *The garden dead.*
> *The garden dead.*
> *The garden dead, O!"*

Everybody is sad. Even people who have never seen the garden get sad and very sad.

"That should never ever happen again," people say.

Nobody likes people who play bad tricks.

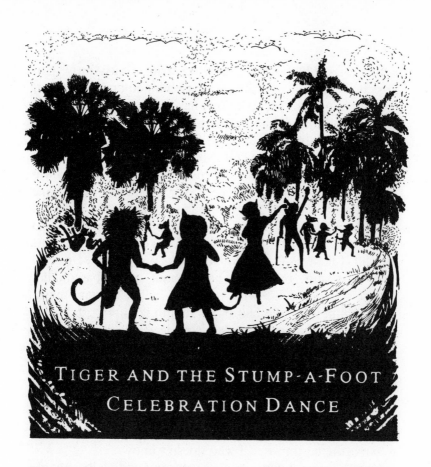

TIGER AND THE STUMP-A-FOOT CELEBRATION DANCE

Everybody really waits for Tiger to arrive. Bro Tiger is to come and challenge Bro Nancy as best dancer. But people enjoy themselves.

People dance inside the hall of bamboo-roof. People dance outside, in the yard of palm trees. Music rushes out of the hall, frolicking round the moonlight yard of people.

The dressed-up musicians sitting, playing in the village hall, have good fun. They grin. They nod to the beat. Every musician plays hard to play sweeter music than the other.

Bro Puss rubs his fiddle bow on strings, busy-busy. Bro Puss doesn't care at all his violin is chipped and tatty. And dressed like Mrs Puss, Bro Puss has the inside of his mouth capped, to look like he has no teeth. Bro Monkey rolls his head about, hitting his drums. Like his wife, Bro Monkey is padded to look humpbacked. Nodding hard, Bro Goat rocks about shaking maracas. Like his wife, Bro Goat wears a head-mask and looks like he has a bashed-in head. Bro Rabbit plays his flute, moving it from side to side. Like his wife, Bro Rabbit wears a black eye-patch. Strumming so swift-swift, Bro Dog plays his banjo like he wants to hurt himself. Like Mrs Dog, Bro Dog looks one-legged. Bro Pig, with eyes shut, rolling his head about, plays bass-fiddle. Dressed too like his wife, Bro Pig wears a snout-mask, making him look like half of his mouth is bitten off.

Everybody has come dressed up, looking like disfigured people. The hall has walls that are only halfway up, you see. And there are no doors. The music escapes freely. Dancing there in lantern light, dancers can see other celebration-people outside, in the moonlight yard of palm trees. People dance and talk and laugh.

You see, it's the big Celebration Dance that's on. Listen to what the custom is, all who doesn't know.

Once a year the dance happens. It's put on to allow people to become the same. That is, become like other people who have a dropped body-part, and have something missing or faulty. If you have no limb or eye or anything faulty, you can still come to the dance; but you have to make yourself look like you've lost something.

Nobody knows how disabled-looking Bro Tiger will arrive. Nobody knows how Tiger will look. Bro Tiger and Bro Anancy's dance challenge is the biggest happening of the celebration evening.

46

Like sweet friends, Anancy and Mrs Rabbit stand in the moonlight yard. In her long white dress, Mrs Rabbit looks marvellous. Of course for her disablement Mrs Rabbit wears her black eye-patch too. Opening her one-eye wide on Anancy, Mrs Rabbit asks uncertainly, "Is Bro Tiger going to come? Bro Tiger's never been to a stump-a-foot dance before, surely, Mister Anancy?"

"True, Mrs Rabbit," Anancy says with a shy face. "True-true. But, Bro Tiger will come." Anancy shuffles on his one leg. Then Anancy remembers he feels he's best dressed. He remembers he has on a stiff white front, with a cut-away black suit. Also, he has on his watch-and-chain hanging down. Anancy pulls himself up proud-proud and goes on talking. "If Bro Tiger's scared of a swift dancing foot, in the company of a wooden one, dressing up is even harder for poor Bro Tiger. But if hiding-away beats him, Bro Tiger well knows Bro Nancy becomes the winner."

"Bro Tiger likes himself looking strong-strong. Doesn't he?"

"True-true, Mrs Rabbit."

She goes on. "I'm sure Bro Tiger doesn't even like to dress up looking like he has a missing part."

"Clear vision," Anancy says, looking at Mrs Rabbit. "You can see deep-deep. All the same – not to miss my good-good chance – shall we go and dance?"

"Certainly, Mister Anancy. Certainly."

Anancy dances with his one-leg and crutch-stick. Mrs Rabbit dances looking out of one eye. People laugh at one another. People go on dancing, all around the hall, inside and outside. With their half-of-heads and half-of-faces, their one-eyes and one-ears, their one-arms and one-legs, they bob up and down and sway themselves and jig about. Now and then somebody tumbles over, and everybody laughs.

The music plays on and on. Then the music stops.

People crowd round Bro Anancy.

"Is Bro Tiger going to come, d'you think?" one-eared Bro Jackass asks.

"D'you ever know Tiger to just give up as loser against Bro Anancy?" Anancy asks, leaning on his crutch-stick.

Nobody answers. Instead, standing with Anancy's son Tacooma, Bro Blackbird KlingKling looks out of his one eye and says, "What loss-of-limb will Tiger come with to do his dance?"

Bro Dog answers sharp-sharp, "If Bro Tiger should come having ten legs, he'll still have no legs to stand on against Bro Nancy."

Everybody laughs.

Mrs Anancy comes up, brisk-brisk. Using lantern light, Mrs Anancy and other women have been busy cooking in little outhouses at the back of the hall. Mrs Anancy asks Anancy to put out more bucketfuls of drinks.

Though the people around Anancy want to talk to him, he leaves them standing. He leaves even truly disabled cousins, like One-Legged Peacock, Broken-Wing John Crow, Dropped-Leg Goat, Broken-Mouth Patoo and others.

Sitting down, standing up, people chatter. But everybody eats. Mrs Anancy and Dora, Tacooma's wife, and other helpful women serve food, inside and outside.

Smells of hot steaming food settle on the night. Steaming bowlfuls after bowlfuls go around. It's peppery soup with pounded vegetables and plantain fried. It's spiced-up barbeque meats and freshly baked bread. It's boiled pudding and rum-and-spice cake. It's more and more of all sorts of spicy nut cakes.

Full of food and drink, feeling good, Bro Dog does two clever tricks in front of the musicians' stand. Then again, unexpected, Bro Dog leaps up in the air, spins like a ball and falls great-great, on one leg. Oh, Bro Dog loves his big applause and praises! Rabbit recites a funny poem about Owl falling off a branch while having a daytime dream. Bro Anancy tells two funny jokes, one about himself and Tiger. Bro Pig gives a loud belch. Then, on his one leg, without a stick, Peacock does a strutting dance, perfect-perfect.

But biggest uproar of laughing comes when Alligator creeps in late, missing every bit of food. Alligator's disablement gets lots of laughing too.

Alligator wears a thin stretchable pink suit. Alligator wears the skinfit suit to make himself look like he has lost his thick leather-skin.

Just before midnight everybody comes in from outside. They all come in and cluster together with everybody else. Something different is going to happen!

A new mood has come. Everybody is frightened, but happy-happy with it.

You see, at midnight the Three-Legged-Horse is supposed to appear. It usually happens at every Stump-a-Foot Celebration Dance.

Everybody knows the Three-Legged-Horse isn't any ordinary ghost-horse. Everybody knows it's a duppy-horse – a really bad-bad ghost-horse. It will just blow off one big snort on you and kill you – anybody – for nothing!

All the same, not everybody can see the Three-Legged-Horse. But, there is agreement. All people who can see it agree. The Horse has one back leg missing. All agree that its tail, its mane, its whole body, is white like pure moonlight. Pure moonlight! But most of all everybody knows that in the presence of the Three-Legged-Horse, nobody – nobody – must ever talk. Nobody must ever say one single word.

The musicians begin to play and sing:

49

"Bro, O Bro,
People, O people,
if you see it come —
'pon three legs or 'pon one —
say not'n',
say not'n',
only quiet-quiet,
only quiet-quiet.
Bro, O Bro,
People, O people,
if you see it come —
with three eyes or with one —
say not'n',
say not'n',
only quiet-quiet,
only quiet-quiet,
 only quiet-quiet . . ."

The musicians go on and on and on repeating the song. Then they stop, sudden-sudden. Everybody knows the Three-Legged-Horse has arrived. The place is total silence. The people who can see it, see the Three-Legged-Horse. They see it come in backwards, moving in reverse, up, towards the musicians. They know it never turns round. It will go up and down the hall in a straight line.

Slowly, swishing its moonshine tail, dipping its moonshine head, it goes up the hall. Clop-pi-ti. Clop-pi-ti. Clop-pi-ti. It stops. It turns its head and looks at the people clustered on each side. It goes again. Clop-pi-ti. Clop-pi-ti. Clop-pi-ti. It stops again, looks on both sides then goes again. Clop-pi-ti. Clop-pi-ti. Clop-pi-ti.

As before, swishing its moonshine tail and dipping its moonshine head, it comes down frontways quicker. Clop-pi-ti, clop-pi-ti, clop-pi-ti. It looks both sides. It nods its head. It swishes its tail. Twice again it does its clop-pi-ti, clop-pi-ti, clop-pi-ti.

Then, at the hall entrance, the Horse disappears with the speed of a bird. As if he would smash up the country road in a terrible runaway clattering of hoofs, the Horse is gone like a hundred mad horses in the night.

Its clattering goes. The echo fades away. Everybody is relieved. Everybody talks crazily. The people touch one another, shake their heads and wave their arms about. They drag their hands over their faces. They rub their hands together. They scratch themselves. They laugh. They sing. They whistle. The people go on as if they are happy to be alive after something awful. But they are also stopping themselves from saying even one word about the Three-Legged-Horse. Everybody knows not one single word is ever to be said about the Horse.

So the people do all kinds of antics with their hands. And they talk nonsense. They go on like this:

"Did I ever come here tonight?"

"Oh no, no, no. But it's the brightest, brightest, bright moonlight."

"Did we eat? Did we eat tonight, last night, last week?"

"No, no, no. Last week I put no clothes on."

"Hoh, hoh, hoh! You do ask something you know I can't remember."

"We might as well have come without our heads."

"Don't you know? Don't you know we're here without heads?"

The people slap each other playfully and laugh. They go on like that. Nobody remembers the night is still far from over.

Sudden-sudden, Tiger rides into the hall on horseback. People have to leap out of the way, quick-quick. Tiger makes the horse dance about. Tiger has done nothing to make himself look disabled. Instead Tiger is dressed up like a plantation overseer. Tiger wears sun-helmet and riding breeches fitting tight down to his ankles. And he has his riding whip.

In the saddle, Tiger holds the reins of the horse strong-strong and stiff. He makes the horse arch his neck, dancing round the hall. More and more people move out of his way. Tiger makes the horse trot round, doing dance movements.

Unexpectedly, Bro Puss strikes up his fiddle-playing. And the whole band starts up playing. Tiger and the music get the horse to dance in with the beat. Everybody starts clapping to the beat as well. With Tiger on, the horse dances round and round the hall like that. Then sudden-sudden Tiger turns the horse round and gallops away, mad-mad into the night of moonlight.

Everybody can hardly believe what has happened. Bro Nancy is struck dumb, for once. People don't know whether to laugh at Bro Nancy or be sorry for him. But everybody – everybody – just laughs and talks and tosses their arms about with the joy—the sudden-sudden happening that Tiger put on. Everybody knows Bro Tiger has taken Bro Nancy by surprise and outsmarted him.

All the same, listen to the Anancy.

"Friends! Friends! That is a no-contest. A no-contest!" And the Anancy stretches out his arms wide. "Friends, I'll challenge Bro Tiger again. I'll challenge him again. And next time—next time—he'll be on his own, on his own-own two legs."

"Good idea," everybody shouts, laughing. "Good idea!"

So people begin to wait. People begin to wait for that next time when Bro Nancy and Bro Tiger will clash in a dance challenge.

MRS ANANCY, CHICKEN SOUP AND ANANCY

Mrs Anancy has six chickens she fattened up to sell. She wants the money to get a dress to wear to a special church service. Anancy makes himself believe Mrs Anancy has enough nice dresses already.

Anancy whispers to himself, "Oh, those fat and lovely chickens! They'll be much, much nicer in one special meal. Any good and loving husband deserves that. Any one! But, oh, there is the trouble. Mrs Anancy will never, never agree."

Bro Nancy works out a way for the six fat chickens to become his meal.

Anancy goes and sees Bro Dog. Anancy gets Bro Dog to agree to go and do a little trick job for him.

Bro Dog goes and hides himself in the doctor's surgery. He stays there hidden till the surgery is closed.

Just before night comes down, Mrs Anancy walks into her home. She comes and finds her husband close to death, in pain.

"Oh, my husband, what's the matter? What's the matter?"

"Oh, my wife – good-good wife – pain has me in its jaws. Pain chews me up. Pain cuts me up. Everywhere." Anancy clutches himself and rolls about in the bed.

"My poor-poor husband. Where is the pain? Where?"

"Everywhere." Anancy groans. "In my belly, in my throat, in my mouth, on my tongue, there's a blazing fire."

"I must get the doctor," Mrs Anancy says, all worried.

Anancy groans. Anancy sobs. Anancy gasps, "Wife – I'm getting a glimpse – a glimpse – of another world. A light – a light beckons me to another place."

"No, no, husband. Don't go." Mrs Anancy embraces her husband. "Hold on. Hold on. I'm going to the doctor. Right away. Right away."

Anancy keeps up his tired groans. Then, as Mrs Anancy is ready to rush out of the house, he says, "Good wife, you must hurry. But – but – but I'm getting terrible signs. Please. Please don't take any short cuts. No short cuts, good wife. None. There are pits hidden. There are trees with roots loosened. There are rocks on hillsides, propped by few rotten leaves."

"Every word is taken, good husband. Every word is taken. Now I must go." Mrs Anancy leaves the house in haste.

Then sudden-sudden Mrs Anancy stops. She doesn't want to leave Bro Nancy alone. She looks back at the house. A little way further along she looks back at the yard. In disbelief, she sees Bro Nancy rush out onto the road. He goes the other way, hurrying. He turns in on to the short cut.

55

Mrs Anancy is puzzled. She turns round and follows Anancy.

At first Mrs Anancy is worried. Her husband may be driven by his illness to do something crazy. Then she realises he's surely heading for the doctor's surgery. Wondering what Bro Nancy is going to do Mrs Anancy follows unseen. And to keep up with his speed she has to put in bursts of running.

At the surgery the place is closed. Then Bro Dog comes out and receives Bro Nancy. Both go back inside and lights are put on. Mrs Anancy stands outside in shocking disbelief. Nothing is wrong with her husband. He and Bro Dog talk happily inside.

Not knowing exactly what to do, Mrs Anancy stands outside waiting and thinking for a while.

Then Mrs Anancy goes to the surgery door and knocks. Doctor comes and asks her in.

Doctor is a bearded and bent-back little old man. Doctor wears dark glasses and a white coat. Doctor speaks in a peculiar croaking voice.

"It's my husband, Doctor," Mrs Anancy says. "He's at home in bed in terrible, terrible pain."

"Does he have pains everywhere?" Doctor asks in his peculiar croaking voice.

"Yes, Doctor."

"The pains come worst in the belly and throat and mouth and tongue?"

"Yes, Doctor."

"Common. Very common." Doctor shakes his head. "Some bad-bad cases about."

"Will he be cured, Doctor?"

"Yes, yes. Completely. But there's only one cure."

"Yes, Doctor? Tell me."

"Chicken soup. Go home, Mrs Anancy. Find six to eight of the fattest chickens. Make the tastiest soup you ever made. Give every bit of it to the patient, every bit of flesh and soup and seasoning. And leave him alone to eat, madam. Leave him alone."

"Thank you, sir."

Mrs Anancy conceals herself outside. She sees the surgery lights go out. She sees Bro Nancy and Bro Dog slip away smart-smart.

Mrs Anancy gets home. There is singing inside. She stands. She listens to every bit of Anancy's song:

> *"A big-big good lot*
> *Can make you fat-fat.*
> *Why be one of you*
> *And not two of you?*
> *Why be one of you, O?*
> *And not two of you, O? . . ."*

Wanting Anancy to hear her, Mrs Anancy goes inside noisily. Instant-instant, the singing stops. She goes into the

57

room. Anancy rolls about, groaning in pain.

"Any news? Any good news, good wife?"

"I'm to give you chicken soup."

"That'll cure me?"

"I'm to give you lots of it. Lots of it."

"Oh! Oh!" Anancy groans. "When will the treatment start?"

"Not tonight."

Early morning Mrs Anancy goes and sees Dora. She comes back, kills the six chickens and begins the cooking.

Mrs Anancy makes herself very busy. Importantly, she goes and opens Anancy's bedroom window. Mrs Anancy sets up her cooking just outside, under the window. The cooking steams up more and more. Tempting cooking smells drift in and fill Anancy's room.

With the delicious cooking under his nose, Bro Nancy turns and twists. He turns his face to the wall. He turns his face the other way. He turns his face towards the ceiling. Sometimes Bro Nancy sits up in bed. When he hears Mrs Anancy round at the back, he craftily takes a peep outside at the cooking.

Anancy lies down. Part of his song comes into his head:

> *"A big-big good lot*
> *Can make you fat-fat..."*

Mrs Anancy sets up a long table outside, near her cooking. She goes and closes Anancy's window. She tells him, "I don't want to tempt you any more. I don't want you to either see or smell the spiced-up soup. Everything is ready. Just wait."

Anancy continues his long wait.

Unseen by Anancy, Dora arrives with a party of village children. Dora settles the twenty-four children around the long table. Picked out as the worst fed, they wait with ravenous appetites.

Mrs Anancy dishes up every bit of the chicken flesh and soup and seasoning. All is put in front of the children. In no time every bit is eaten up. Every bowl is left clean.

Tortured by sounds outside, and his waiting-waiting, Anancy leaps up, swings the window open and rushes outside.

Anancy sees the children and their empty bowls. He sees the big empty iron pot. He sees everybody looking at him. Anancy holds his head and screams, "My chicken soup! My chicken soup!"

The children burst out singing:

> *"A big-big good lot*
> *Can make you fat-fat.*
> *Why be one of you*
> *And not two of you?*
> *Why be one of you*
> *And not two of you?*
> *Anancy, O!*
> *Anancy, O!..."*

Anancy storms out of the yard. But he doesn't stay away for long. He is simply too hungry.

RATBAT AND TACOOMA'S TREE

Spiderman Tacooma wants to be more than just being called the son of the great Anancy. He doesn't find that easy. All the same, on his own Tacooma can make strange happenings work, like magic.

Tacooma will sit under his fig tree and watch sunrise. He'll watch midday sun and watch the moon come up at midnight. Tacooma loves to sit and watch and listen or just think.

Tacooma will think on things like – the way an ocean lives there in the seabed it has; the way darkness is the only world of deep-sea fishes; the way fire is able to make itself burn; the way a seed changes more and more into a tree; the way webbed feet of flying frogs open out in flight like four little umbrellas...

Tacooma is sitting under his tree, listening to birds in it, and thinking. Then, from the little house next door, Ratbat his neighbour comes and complains about the noise in the tree that Tacooma sits under.

In his deep thinking, listening to the birds, Tacooma is surprised.

But Bro Ratbat and his Ratbat-people sleep in the daytime!

Unable to sleep, half sleepy, and not able to see properly in the bright afternoon sunshine, Ratbat has to come out wearing dark glasses.

Ratbat stands in the village road and complains loudly. He is cross about the feasting and frolicking of the noisy birds in Tacooma's tree. The birds' noise is keeping everybody awake in his house, Ratbat says.

It's true, the birds do carry on. The birds squawk and squeak and scream. And some coo, some caw, some cheep; some twitter, some whistle, some chatter, some gossip; some laugh, some cry; some sing prettier than the feeling tree-blossoms give off in sunlight.

Tacooma has been listening to those very different sounds the birds make.

"Listen to the noise!" Ratbat says. "Just listen to it! Beats me how some people think nothing, miserable nothing, about anybody else."

Tacooma explains that the crowd of birds only feasts and frolics because figs are ripening.

"Anyway," Tacooma says, "Bro Ratbat, you've never complained before."

"Past history!" Ratbat says. "All past history. These days noise gets to me. Noise shakes up my brains. It has to stop, Bro Tacooma. It has to stop. I can't stand it. I can't stand it..." Ratbat carries on complaining.

All the Ratbat-people come out on to the village road, wearing dark glasses. They flap their arms about complaining that hard-working night people can't have any proper rest. The Ratbat-people go on and on until they decide Tacooma's tree must be cut down.

"My tree!" Tacooma says. Tacooma stands up. "My tree! My tree will never be cut down."

"It will be put down," Ratbat says. "Big and bulky as it is, your tree will be cut flat – on its side!"

Hearing the argument some of the birds come down onto low branches, listening.

Bro Blackbird KlingKling arrives and says he and friends will collect up soft feathers to stuff all the Ratbat-people's ears.

"No Ratbat-person wants to sleep with ears corked up," Ratbat says.

Bro Woodpecker says he and friends will come and fit better doors and windows to Ratbat's house.

"No Ratbat-person will want to try to sleep with building noise around everywhere. Everywhere!"

Bro Nightingale says he and friends will come and surround Ratbat's house with singing.

"No Ratbat-person has ever slept any sweeter in Nightingale's singing," Ratbat says.

Sudden-sudden, Bro Nancy appears on the scene.

Bro Nancy holds his arms high up over his head and says, "Stop! Everybody, stop!"

There is silence. Complete silence.

"There'll have to be a decision," Anancy says. "There'll have to be agreement."

"Surely, there has to be a decision," Ratbat says.

"Agreed," Tacooma says.

Anancy begins with his order. Anancy says, "One – Tacooma must stop the noisy birds in three minutes' time. Or stop them tomorrow.

"Two–Ratbat must cut down the tree within three minutes. Or within three days."

Bro Tacooma begins to argue.

"No argument," Anancy says. "No argument whatsoever is allowed."

"Nobody can axe down a big tree in three minutes. That's crazy," Ratbat says.

"Nobody's going to axe down my tree in three days either," Tacooma says.

"Long before three days," Ratbat says, "it'll be down on its side – flat!"

Before Anancy disappears he calls Tacooma to one side. Quietly he says, "Tacooma, you didn't have to argue. You know you didn't have to. You know you have good friends who'll always defend you like sharp claws and teeth. You know that, don't you?"

And, as Anancy has whispered – reminding Tacooma he has friends to call on – the secret friends arrive. Like a small army, tough little trees come and make a strong fence around Tacooma's big tree.

Standing close together, looking like part rock, part wood, part weaponry, some guardian trees are covered purely with thorns sharp like cockspurs. Others also have thistle leaves needle-like as any porcupine's back. Others also have leaves of stinging nettles.

Next day at dusk, Ratbat comes through Tacooma's gateway with his six Ratbat axe-men carrying axes and machetes. They face Tacooma's tree. And the Ratbat men are stunned. They stand staring. They can't believe they see a tough guardian barrier right round Tacooma's tree.

Ratbat looks at his Ratbat axe-men. Everyone is alarmed. This fierce army didn't stand round the tree yesterday. And – it seems – nobody is at home.

Loud and cross, Ratbat calls, "Tacooma!"

There's no answer.

He calls again. "Tacooma!"

There's no answer.

"Where's that Tacooma?" Ratbat shouts. "Come on. Let's attack. Attack!"

The Ratbat men chop the guardian trees. But every time a Ratbat man chops, a branch bends quick-quick and lashes back, like claws, beaks, thorns and nettles together. Ratbat men chop; they're hit back. They chop, chop, chop; they're hit, hit, hit. They begin to itch. Except Ratbat himself, everyone drops weapons and begins to scratch tummy, legs, back, arms, neck, and all over.

Ratbat shouts, "Come on, attack! Attack!"

Ratbat men again chop, chop, chop and are hit, hit, hit. They notice their axes and machetes are blunted. And itching bites them. They fall about scratching themselves. Ratbat alone chops wildly taking his hits. Then Ratbat stops, and scratches and notices his axe is blunted. He finds every weapon is blunted as if it chopped a rock. Ratbat sees everybody bleeds and scratches. Ratbat himself bleeds as he scratches.

The Ratbat-people hurry away shouting and scratching their tummies and backs, legs and arms and everywhere.

Next day Ratbat comes back with fresh Ratbat-people.

Again he shouts, Attack, attack! Again they are hit. Everyone falls about scratching and bleeding. Again they hurry away shouting and scratching all over.

On the third day, Ratbat is bandaged from head to toe as he goes about begging for help. Nobody wants to be bandaged as he is. Nobody joins Ratbat to chop down Tacooma's tree.

Darkness comes down. The fourth day comes. Nobody sees a single thorn, thistle or nettle bush around Tacooma's tree that is still standing there.

From that day ratbats set up home in caves to hide from daytime noises. Anancy has a hand in the happening.

BRO TIGER GOES DEAD

Tiger swears he's going to crack up Anancy's bones once and for all.

Tiger goes to bed. Bro Tiger lies down in his bed, all still and stiff, wrapped up in a sheet. Bro Tiger says to himself, "I know that Anancy will come and look at me. The brute will want to make sure I'm dead. He'll want to see how I look when I'm dead. That's when I'm going to collar him up. Oh, how I'm going to grab that Anancy and finish him!"

Bro Tiger calls his wife. He tells his wife she should begin to bawl. She should bawl and cry and wail as loud as she can. She should stand in the yard, put her hands on the top of her head and holler to let everybody know her husband is dead. And Mrs Tiger does that.

Mrs Tiger bawls and bawls so loud that people begin to wonder if all her family is dead suddenly and not just her husband.

Village people come and crowd in the yard, quick-quick.

Everybody is worried and sad and full of sympathy. The people talk to one another saying, "Fancy how Bro Tiger is dead, sudden-sudden."

"Yes! Fancy how he's dead sudden-sudden. All dead and gone!"

Anancy also hears the mournful death howling. When Anancy hears it, listen to the Anancy to himself. "Funny how Bro Tiger is dead. Bro Tiger is such a strong and healthy man. Bro Tiger is such a well-fed man. Bro Tiger is dead and I've heard nothing about his sickness."

Anancy finds himself at Tiger's yard, like the rest of the crowd. Straightaway, Anancy says to his son, "Tacooma, did you happen to hear Bro Tiger had an illness?"

Tacooma shakes his head. "No, no. Heard nothing at all."

Anancy goes to Dog. "Bro Dog, did you happen to hear Bro Tiger had an illness?"

Bro Dog shakes his head. "No, no. Heard nothing at all."

Anancy goes to Monkey and Puss and Ram-Goat and Jackass and Patoo and asks the same question. Everyone gives a sad shake of the head and says, "No, no. Heard nothing at all."

The crowd surrounds Anancy. Everybody starts up saying, "Bro Tiger showed no sign of illness. Death happened so sudden-sudden, Bro Nancy. So sudden-sudden!"

Anancy says, "Did anybody call a doctor?"

The people shake their heads and say, "That would have been no use, Bro Nancy. No use at all."

"Before death came on, did Tiger call the name of the Lord? Did he whimper? Did he cry out?"

"He didn't have time, Bro Nancy. He didn't have the time," everybody says. "It was all so sudden."

Listen to Anancy now, talking at the top of his voice.

67

"What kind of man is Tiger? Doesn't Tiger know that no good man can meet his Blessed Lord sudden-sudden and not shudder and cry out?"

Tiger hears Anancy. Tiger feels stupid. Tiger feels he has made a silly mistake. Bro Tiger gives the loudest roar he has ever made.

Anancy bursts out laughing. Anancy says, "Friends, did you hear that? Did you hear that? Has anyone ever heard a dead man cry out?"

Nobody answers Anancy. Everybody sees that he is right.

By the time Bro Tiger jumps out of the sheet on the bed to come after Anancy, the Anancy is gone. Bro Nancy is well away.

Nobody even talks to Bro Tiger now. Everybody just leaves Bro Tiger's place without a single word.

ANANCY RUNS INTO
TIGER'S TROUBLE

Going about his business, Anancy hears a sound. Anancy
stops. Anancy listens.

The sound is heavy breathing.

Someone must be having a struggle. Somebody must be
trying hard to do something difficult. Anancy turns and goes
towards the sound.

It's Bro Tiger! It's Bro Tiger – trying to climb out of a deep
pit. Anancy can see the top of Tiger's weary head dipping
with his tired breathing.

Anancy's own head spins in dread and excitement.

What can he do? It's too much to ignore Bro Tiger!

He always wants to crush him up. Bro Tiger always wants to have him in pieces, always wants to have his body-bits round his nose.

Anancy bends over the edge of the pit.

Tiger is near the top. Poor Bro Tiger is tired. Bro Tiger is gripping on to parts of tree roots and a rock. His legs spread about in different ways. And, oh, Bro Tiger is thin! Bro Tiger is getting to look like an empty sack from days of hunger. He must have been in the pit for days.

Anancy sees the work of Tiger's attempts to get out. Tiger's feet have raked a fresh track along the side of the pit all the way down to the bottom. Anancy thinks, "Oh, poor hard-working man Tiger! Poor fallen-down-the-pit Bro Tiger has worked hard to get out! Bro Tiger has been stuck in the pit here. This is why Bro Tiger hasn't tried to kill him lately. This is why nobody brings him news that Tiger lurks about waiting for him!"

Sudden-sudden, Anancy gets a great idea.

Anancy puts on his sweet-sweet voice and says, "Oh, Bro Tiger, it's you! Fancy it's you, Bro Tiger. Looking so different from usual. Looking so, so unrespectable!"

Surprised to see Anancy, and tired and panting, Tiger says, "Yes, Bro Nancy. It's me. It's me, Bro Tiger."

Listen to the Anancy now. "Were you coming to see me, Bro Tiger, when this oh so terrible falling-down-a-hole happened and so battered you up?"

"Bro Nancy," Tiger pants, "I'm so weak – I feel so bad – so weak – all memory's gone. Gone. Gone away."

"Oh, poor Bro Tiger!" Anancy says, with his voice all sugary. "Such a beautiful man, a powerful man, turned into a striped bag of bones! But never mind. You're almost free, Bro Tiger. You see you're almost free. Almost out of the pit. You can see that."

70

Tiger groans. Tiger grunts. Tiger says, "Don't know. Don't know, Bro Nancy. Have been up here before. Only to slide down again."

"Don't give up," Anancy says. "It's not like you to give up."

Tiger tries. Tiger struggles. Tiger makes another big move to get himself out of the pit. But tired, Tiger's breathing is loud. Oh, Tiger's breathing is loud. Then Tiger manages to say, "Can't move, Bro Nancy. Can't move any more. Too hard. Too hard. What – what can I do?"

"Pray, Bro Tiger," Anancy says. "Pray. Pray hard. Put hands together and pray."

Tiger lets go, putting his paws together. Tiger slides down, down, right down to the bottom of the pit again.

Anancy lies down on his tummy. Anancy hangs his face over the edge of the pit and calls, "Are you all right, Bro Tiger? Are you all right down there? I'd come and keep you company but I don't want to become your dinner. Is that all right, Bro Tiger?"

No answer comes from Tiger. But Anancy knows Tiger will not give up. He knows Tiger will get out. He knows Tiger will be working out ways to catch him, to gobble him up.

Anancy remembers he has left home to go on business. Anancy steps off, quick and brisk. Anancy walks away fast.

MRS DOG FIRST-CHILD AND MONKEY-MOTHER

Mrs Dog's first-child is clever, you see. From when she is small-small she can stand on her head and catch things with her feet. Swing-Swing will catch a big unhusked coconut with her feet, her lovely little dog-child's feet. Lots and lots of difficult acts Swing-Swing-Janey can perform for herself alone, or for a crowd.

Then one day, just before sunset, Monkey-Mother happens to see Swing-Swing-Janey playing alone.

Passing by, going home with her tribe of many children, with one on her back, Monkey-Mother stops. She stands there with child on her back, watching Janey.

Swing-Swing carries on. Swing-Swing is in front of her house, there at roadside, practising her sticks-catching.

Swing-Swing tosses up four sticks and catches them. She

keeps on doing that. Monkey-Mother is thrilled. Monkey-Mother grins. Monkey-Mother puts down her child and settles down watching, with all her lots of children around her watching too.

Then so excited to have a crowd watching her, Swing-Swing-Janey starts up something different.

Swing-Swing tosses her ball up, then falls quick-quick on to her hands, throws her bottom end up, catches the ball with her feet, bends her knees, flicks the ball up again, half spins back onto her feet and catches the ball with her hands.

Seeing Swing-Swing's movements so precise, so perfect, the family grin and clap. And grinning and clapping Monkey-Mother says:

"O so right and so spry,
So nippy and so flippy!"

And grinning and clapping her lots of children say:

"O so right and so spry,
So nippy and so flippy!"

Swing-Swing-Janey repeats her act. Then Swing-Swing does lots of other things she can do.

The sun sets, and nobody sees Janey. Swing-Swing has disappeared.

Night comes down. No Swing-Swing-Janey is anywhere. Mrs Dog stands outside and calls and calls; no answer. No Swing-Swing comes home.

Mrs Dog practically goes off her head with worry.

Mrs Dog walks quickly to every neighbour and asks about Swing-Swing. Nobody has seen her child. Mrs Dog approaches everybody passing her house. Nobody has seen Swing-Swing-Janey. Nobody knows to where the child has disappeared.

Then just before bedtime, Mrs Puss calls and says, "I hear you lost your child. I have to say I did see your child. Monkey-Mother carried away your child. They all joked and laughed together, walking on and on together, like a friendly family."

"But where does Monkey-Mother live?" Mrs Dog wants to know.

Mrs Puss has no idea. Nobody knows where Monkey-Mother lives. She roams about; it is known. She lives miles and miles away; it is believed.

Mrs Dog begins to go about looking for her child, promptly.

Many strange villages see Mrs Dog for the first time.

Mrs Dog sees tailors making clothes, shoemakers making shoes, tinsmiths making vessels. Each time Mrs Dog asks the people, "Have you seen a dog-child with Monkey-Mother?"

"No," they say.

"Do you know where Monkey-Mother lives?"

"No," they say.

Every person or group of people Mrs Dog meets she asks the same questions and gets the same answers.

Mrs Dog keeps on going with her travelling and her looking. Other strange villages see Mrs Dog for the first time.

She sees basketmakers making baskets, carvers carving wood, potters making pots. Each time Mrs Dog asks the people, "Have you seen a dog-child with Monkey-Mother?"

"No," they say.

"Do you know where Monkey-Mother lives?"

"No," they say.

Every person or group of people Mrs Dog meets she asks the same questions and gets the same answers.

Mrs Dog keeps on going with her travelling and her looking.

Strange fields see Mrs Dog for the first time.

Mrs Dog sees people picking coconuts, she questions them. She sees people cutting stems of bananas, she questions them. She comes to an orange grove and sees people picking oranges. She says to the orange-pickers, "Have you seen a dog-child with Monkey-Mother?"

"Yes," they say. "Two days ago. We saw them mango-picking. The dog-child caught the mangoes picked and dropped. Sometimes she caught them with her hands. Sometimes she went down on to her hands, kicked up her feet and caught the mangoes and put them in the basket."

Anxiously, Mrs Dog wants to know where the mango trees are.

The orange-pickers tell her where.

Mrs Dog finds mango tree after mango tree but sees nothing of Swing-Swing or Monkey-Mother.

Mrs Dog goes home.

Mrs Dog weeps and weeps. Mrs Dog misses her first-child oh so much! And Mrs Dog is tired. Mrs Dog and husband and family wonder and wonder, "What may have happened to our Swing-Swing-Janey? Eh? Whatever may have happened to our little Swing-Swing?"

One after the other, everybody remembers how Janey has many busy antics, and makes them laugh. They remember how she comes to getting her name, Swing-Swing, from her father, from her leaping up to low tree branches and swinging from one to the next.

Mrs Dog starts out on her travels again.

A new river sees Mrs Dog.

She sees men in a canoe, river-fishing. She calls out, "Have you seen a dog-child with Monkey-Mother?"

"Yes," they say. "One hour ago they came back from the other side of the river. The dog-child swam and pulled the raft with Monkey-Mother and family."

Anxiously, Mrs Dog asks, "Where does she live? Do you know where Monkey-Mother lives?"

"Yes," the men say. And the men explain in detail where Monkey-Mother lives.

Mrs Dog comes to a rocky barren place. No trees are here. There are only rocks and hills of rocks.

Mrs Dog stands outside a kind of house of rocks.

Monkey-Mother and children come outside, into the yard.

Monkey-Mother waves her arm about and says, "She's not here. She's not here. Go away. Go away. I tell you—"

Before Monkey-Mother is finished speaking, Swing-Swing comes round some rocks, carrying wood. Monkey-Mother grabs her. She pushes her, bundles her round to the back, and locks her in.

"I want my child," Mrs Dog shouts. "I want my child!"

Monkey uncles and aunts and cousins all come out waving their arms about, telling Mrs Dog, "Hop it! Clear off. Get away. And don't you come back!" Oh, the Monkey-people are noisy and threatening!

Mrs Dog suddenly feels lonely and bullied. Mrs Dog feels bullied and lonely and hopeless and can't help crying. Mrs Dog begins to turn away.

The Monkey uncles and aunts and cousins carry on waving about and shouting, repeating, "Hop it! Clear off. Get away. And don't you come back!"

But, you see, just as the fishermen tell Mrs Dog where Monkey-Mother lives, they also tell Bro Nancy and Bro Dog. So, they arrive!

Listen to the Anancy straightaway, talking like the best of friendly visitor.

"To Mrs Monkey-Mother and all, a good-good and abundant afternoon!"

"Good afternoon, Mister Anancy," Monkey-Mother says, in a quiet voice.

Anancy notices everybody has gone quiet and goes on. "I know, there is no need to say, to most respectable strangers, good citizens come to meet good citizens not as a crowd, but in a small-small number of two."

"We are respectable people too, Mister Anancy," Monkey-Mother says.

"That's exactly why none of you can bark? Can any of you bark?" Anancy asks.

"No, sir," Monkey-Mother says.

Anancy knows the moment has come to let Swing-Swing hear him. At the top of his voice, Anancy shouts, "Well—who can bark, let her bark!" Anancy goes on even louder. "Bark now who can bark!"

Swing-Swing-Janey yelps, perhaps forgetting she can bark. Then Swing-Swing begins to bark like wild and crazy, like a terrible hollering in everybody's ears.

Looking badly shamefaced, Monkey-Mother holds her head down.

"Mrs Monkey-Mother, will you please let out the dog-child and let her come to us?" Anancy commands.

Monkey-Mother says nothing. Monkey-Mother only goes slow-slow and shamefaced and lets out Swing-Swing.

Swing-Swing-Janey comes to her mother, Mrs Dog.

Oh, child and mother are happy!

From that time, mothers don't like their children to get too friendly with strangers.

ANANCY AND STORM AND THE
REVEREND MAN-COW

Hurricane wrecks the whole countryside, you see. Almost
everything and everywhere is flattened and flooded. Nobody
is without damaged property. Anancy has his kitchen
chopped in two by a tree fallen across it. And the sky stays
gloomy.

Anancy-Spiderman is sad.

Anancy walks out with Mrs Anancy through the village.
He sees only storm-battered houses and trees and everything
and everywhere.

Anancy goes on and looks at his own lands.

Anancy finds his coconut and banana trees, his climbing

78

yam-vines on upright sticks–his fields of crops–are flattened. Some of his animals are dead.

"Oh, it feels bad to feel sad," Anancy says to his wife. "It feels so, so bad to feel sad."

"Husband, the sun will shine again," Mrs Anancy says.

"Wife, I can't believe how I can't believe that," he says.

Going back home, Anancy can hardly walk. Anancy and Mrs Anancy stop on a seat called Travellers Rest. The seat is fixed against a fig tree that grows and spreads itself in a stone wall.

"Wife," Anancy says, "an idea has come into my head. And I think it will help me get over my sadness."

"Will the idea really work?" Mrs Anancy asks.

"If I can get Bro Monkey to do a little job for me, the idea will be a wonder. It'll work so very, very well."

"Will Bro Monkey agree to do the little job?"

"Bro Monkey won't disagree," Anancy says. "Bro Monkey won't know everything. Bro Monkey shouldn't know everything. And he won't."

Now, Bro Monkey is sad about the hurricane too. But Bro Monkey is by himself, thinking. Bro Monkey is sitting right there, with his back against the same wall as Anancy. They don't see each other. But Bro Monkey hears all that Bro Nancy says. And right away Bro Monkey is suspicious, but waits to see what Anancy will ask him to do.

Brisk-brisk, Bro Nancy starts to work on his idea.

First of all, Bro Nancy sends a most urgent message to the Reverend Man-Cow, asking him to come and see him.

Quick-quick, the Reverend Man-Cow arrives in his long gown, carrying Bible and prayer book.

Anancy sits down on his veranda with the Reverend Man-Cow. And oh, the Anancy-Spiderman is sad. Listen to the Anancy:

79

"Oh, Mister Reverend Man-Cow, I don't know what to do. I'm not a man to feel so bad from feeling sad. It is a sadness that is a woeful hurtfulness. All my days have gone to waste. Even food has no taste. Sir, I don't eat. I have nothing to feel good with. I have nowhere, sir, nowhere, to draw anything nice from. All I have is feeling bad-bad from feeling sad. I try and find not one song will start in me. Any goat, sir, even the breeze, can break through me like a weaky-weaky fence. Hunger can kill me,  because I don't know it's there. Sadness can harden my heart, because I don't laugh. Sir, Bro Nancy is a stranger to himself and can't find Bro Nancy. All this, sir, is my grievous affliction. All this is why I have to call the Reverend to my house."

"Oh, dear, dear Bro Nancy! I understand," the Reverend says. "It's the storm, good brother. It's the hurricane that has created such a disaster in you and affected you."

"That's it, sir," Anancy says. "It has smashed up my kitchen and smashed up my field and smashed up everybody's everything."

"Yes, Brother Anancy. The Lord giveth and the Lord taketh."

80

"But, sir, why does he have to take so much?"

"Remember. You mustn't question the works of the Lord. You mustn't question."

"It will still be in my head, sir."

"Brother Anancy," the Reverend Man-Cow says, "I will pray for you. Let us pray."

The Reverend prays for Anancy. As the Reverend says, "Amen", Bro Nancy bursts out crying, saying, "Mister Reverend, I feel worse. I feel much, much worse."

"Then I will pray for you again."

"Perhaps, later, sir. For now, can we talk? Can I ask you something?"

"Yes. Ask me something."

"Mister Reverend sir, since your prayer didn't work I'm asking you to do something else."

"Ask me, Brother Anancy," the Reverend says. "Ask me."

"I'm asking you to put on a festival."

"A festival?"

"Yes, Reverend. A Festival of Shining Things. I'd like nobody else but you to be in charge of a Festival of Shining Things!"

"Why? Why a Festival of Shining Things?"

"Sir – most Reverend, Reverend sir – in my condition of loss, I don't want back only my beautiful fields. I long for plantations and estates and vineyards. I don't want back only my sound kitchen. I long for a Great-House or a mansion. For food crops I lost, I don't want back only a dinner. I want feast after feast to refill me."

"Keep heart, Brother Anancy," the Reverend says, "I understand your loss. I understand your longing to have something back. But how – how will a festival help?"

"Oh, sir – most holy Mister Reverend Man-Cow – the Festival will spread out all our shining things before my eyes.

81

The things will put a light into my heart, into my blood, into my body. The things will brighten eyes and hearts of all Brothers and family and everybody. Every eye will see we have things the storm did not touch."

"Splendid! Splendid!" the Reverend says. "I will do it. I will take it on. I will organise your Festival of Shining Things."

"Thank you, Reverend," Anancy says. "Thank you." But that was not everything. He Anancy alone must decide on certain arrangements.

For one, Anancy insists that all the Shining Things that people bring must be put on the spare bed in his and Mrs Anancy's bedroom.

On his side, the Reverend Man-Cow insists that on the day of the event, until it starts, Anancy should stay at his son's house; that people will bring their Shining Things on the same day of the Festival; that no name will be put on anything; that after everybody has seen everything on show, there'll be a thanksgiving prayer and song; and that everybody will file in afterwards and take back their own things.

Anancy goes off and sees Bro Monkey.

Anancy finds Bro Monkey cutting his son's hair in the backyard. Bro Nancy and Bro Monkey go and stand to one side together and talk privately.

Bro Nancy still doesn't know Bro Monkey has overheard his conversation with Mrs Anancy. And Bro Monkey isn't going to let on. Yet Bro Monkey isn't going to say no. Bro Monkey is going to handle matters in his own way.

Anancy tells Monkey the Festival will open just before night comes down. When it is dark enough Mrs Anancy will be in her bedroom getting dressed. At that time everybody at the Festival will be locked out and kept away from the room with the Shining Things. At that time, exact-exact,

Bro Monkey is to slip in through the backdoor, pick up all the gold pieces – the rings, the bangles, the earrings, etc., and again slip away.

Anancy insists on how Bro Monkey should remember that at the time – when it is made known to everybody that Mrs Anancy is getting dressed – everybody should see that even he isn't allowed in. He'll try to get in the room. But it will be arranged with Bro Dog that Bro Dog should stop him.

Last of all, Bro Monkey should remember, Bro Nancy isn't asking him to pick up wood, to pick up leather, to pick up shell or silver. Only gold. Only gold will wash away the sad-sad disaster self that cloak up Bro Nancy.

Bro Monkey asks nothing about a reward for his helping to steal the gold. But Bro Monkey asks, "What shall I do with the gold pieces when I have them outside?"

"Hide them," Bro Nancy says. "Hide them. Till everything cools down."

"But everything won't cool down. The loser of the valuables – and everybody else – will keep on wanting to know what's happened to them."

"Rely on bad memory," Anancy says. "Rely on bad memory."

"Suppose everybody's memory stays good and sharp? And all eyes fall on you, Bro Nancy?"

"Bro Monkey, eyes fall on me Bro Nancy?"

"Yes, Bro Nancy. Suppose eyes fall on you – as guilty?"

"Bro Monkey, dear-dear Bro Monkey, you mustn't put questions into my blank space. Just think of how you spoil everything. Spoil everything! Bro Monkey – I tell you – it's gone. I clean forgot you asked that question. Tell me you forgot you asked that question."

"Bro Nancy, we'll talk again."

"No. No, Bro Monkey," Anancy says. "When business is settled, business is settled."

Bro Monkey goes to see Bro Dog.

Bro Monkey finds Bro Dog clearing up his storm-damaged backyard.

Bro Monkey explains how Bro Nancy wants him to steal the gold at his Festival.

"Then we must spoil his plan," Dog says. "We must spoil it."

Dog and Monkey decide that Dog will take it on to let something unexpected happen at the Festival of Shining Things.

On the day, Mrs Anancy's green silk cloths – and gold one on her spare bed – are soon crowded with things people bring. So many things are brought, Mrs Anancy finds she has to put down her patchwork cloths on the floor round the room as well.

Anancy comes into the room.

Anancy sees that his bedroom is transformed into a wonderful place of Shining Things displayed. To Anancy, everything is truly wonderful.

Anancy's eyes are drawn first of all to gold and silver necklaces and pendants. His wide-eyed look moves over horn, silver and gold rings, over little boxes of beads, little boxes of gold sovereigns and boxes of rare silver coins.

Glowing with pleasure, Anancy's roving eyes gloat over large and small ornamental baskets with embroidered fancywork, decorated calabashes, decorated fans of bamboo and of straw, coconut-shell ornaments, painted nut marbles and stones, seashells of all sizes and shapes, alligator and goatskin bags, decorated sandals, decorated walking-sticks, little figures in carved wood, calabash and leather masks, decorated clay bowls and mortars-and-pestles, silver plates and spoons and forks, the many embroidered cloths and children's dresses.

Anancy's eyes glint with excitement. Anancy bursts out singing:

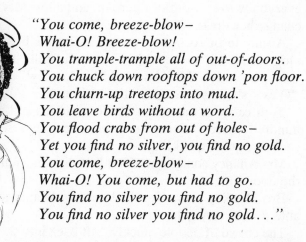

"You come, breeze-blow –
Whai-O! Breeze-blow!
You trample-trample all of out-of-doors.
You chuck down rooftops down 'pon floor.
You churn-up treetops into mud.
You leave birds without a word.
You flood crabs from out of holes –
Yet you find no silver, you find no gold.
You come, breeze-blow –
Whai-O! You come, but had to go.
You find no silver you find no gold.
You find no silver you find no gold . . ."

Anancy's house becomes like a garden-party of people. Everybody is dressed up and shows best behaviour with nicest words. Everybody smiles and touches one another and talks. The clusters of people go in and out of Anancy's room, looking at and liking every Shining Thing. People keep shaking Anancy's hand. They say, "Oh, Mister Anancy, you've lifted our hearts with your Festival." "Bro Nancy, it's good-good you're singing again." "Mister Anancy, you deserve every piece of Shining Thing in your room." "Shining Things, Bro Nancy, next time we'll ask you to get the moon for us and bet we'll have it."

Anancy is pleased. Reverend Man-Cow is pleased. Every contributor and visitor is pleased. All go on looking at things and smiling and touching one another and talking till darkness comes down.

85

Then Anancy begins to get fidgety. Anancy can't keep his mind on his conversation with people. Anancy's head is full of the gold he wants Monkey to steal for him.

Anancy goes and closes his bedroom door. He asks everybody to stay out of the room and allow Mrs Anancy to change her dress.

A minute or so, after Anancy closes his bedroom door, Dog rushes up to the locked door and calls in his loudest voice, urgently, "Mrs Anancy! Mrs Anancy!"

"Yes," she answers inside the bedroom.

"Your cakes in the oven outside exploded and burst into a hundred pieces! Come, please! Come and see to your cooking, quick-quick!"

Mrs Anancy comes out of her bedroom in a hurry, leaving the door wide open.

Bro Monkey comes forward, letting Anancy see he's not able to take any gold.

The crowd of people quickly drift back into the room. All over again, they start looking at the Shining Things, while touching one another and talking and laughing.

The Reverend Man-Cow comes into the room. The Reverend opens his wide arms and calls everybody to hymn-singing and prayer.

Thanksgiving over, and the eating starts, everybody keeps on thanking Bro Nancy for the wonderful Shining Things idea.

Bro Nancy sits and smiles and smiles, lapping up the sweetness of the praises.

Good people have always owed much to the help of their friends.

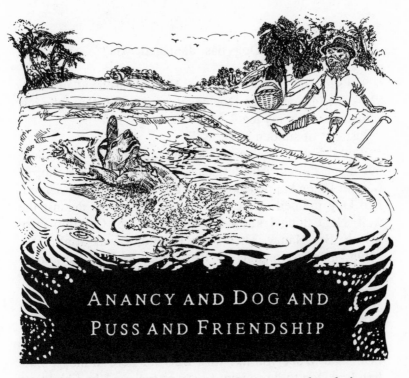

ANANCY AND DOG AND PUSS AND FRIENDSHIP

Bro Puss insists on doing the shopping, even when he's not at all fit and well.

Anancy sees Bro Puss walking down the road with a stick. Anancy can't believe it's Bro Puss with leg all bandaged up, hobbling towards him, carrying a shopping basket.

Anancy stops.

"Oh, Bro Puss, I'd say good morning. But all so hurt and bandaged up, how can it be a good morning for you?"

"You take notice, Bro Nancy," Bro Puss says. "You take notice. All the same, good morning, Bro Nancy."

"Good morning, Bro Puss. But—what bad luck has overtaken you with so much pain?"

"Ah, Bro Nancy! It's nobody else besides Bro Dog."

"Bro Dog? Bro Dog has damaged you?" Anancy is shocked.

Sad-sad, Bro Puss looks down. He nods his head and says, "Yes, Bro Nancy. Bro Dog has damaged me. Bro Dog has actually broken my leg."

"Just out of sudden badness?"

"Well," Puss says, "as you know, me and Mrs Puss share our home duties. And few days ago, I went to the shop. I waited. I then happened to point out I was first to be served. Bro Dog jumped on me. Held me. Tossed me against the wall. Next thing I knew I couldn't get up. Couldn't raise myself, Bro Nancy. Then I saw I couldn't walk at all."

"Oh, maddest madness!" Bro Nancy says. "Crazy madness! That's not like the Bro Dog I know." Bro Nancy shakes his head. "Not, not at all."

"But it is, you know," Puss says. "It is. Bro Dog's like that. I know. I know from experience."

"Bro Puss," Anancy says, "I'm sad. I'm sorry. Sorry to hear. Sad to see you like this. But – it's here in me, it's not like Bro Dog to be so vile. I have to believe a bad-bad tiger spirit rose up in Bro Dog and made him vile. Made him damaging."

"No, Bro Nancy. No," Puss says. "It's just him. It's just Bro Dog. It's just him... All the same – can you speak to him?"

"Speak to him?" Anancy says. "I'll go right now. I'll let Bro Dog answer to this damage he's done to you."

As Anancy speaks, his son Tacooma comes along. Tacooma says good morning to his father and Bro Puss and agrees that Dog has behaved very, very badly.

Tacooma takes the shopping basket from Bro Puss and walks to the shop with him. Anancy goes off straight to see Bro Dog.

Listen to the Anancy now, sitting down all friendly-friendly. "Bro Dog, I met a man today. You may call him Bro Kitten. And you know what has happened to Bro Kitten?"

"No," Dog says. "What?"

"Bro Lion has broken Bro Kitten's leg."

"Badness," Dog says. "Terrible badness! Lions are all the same. Wild and ignorant. What else can you expect? They get no schooling whatsoever. None."

"Bro Dog," Anancy says, "suppose I should say, the Bro Kitten is Bro Puss. And the Bro Lion is you. What would you say?"

Bro Dog goes quiet. Then Bro Dog says, "I'd say, I'm ashamed. Badly, badly ashamed."

"Ashamed enough to make the broken leg come good?"

"I can't mend broken legs. I can't, can I?"

"No, Bro Dog," Anancy says. "But you can mend a lot-lot by becoming friends."

"Me getting friendly with Puss? After breaking his leg? Would you even talk to me?"

"Bro Puss himself asked me to come and talk to you," Anancy says.

"Really?" Dog says, guilty and surprised, looking round at Anancy.

"Yes," Anancy says. "He asks me to come and talk to you."

Again Dog goes quiet, then says, "It's not the first time I hurt Bro Puss. You know that."

"Yes, Bro Dog."

"Yet," Dog says, "it seems Puss knows I feel bad I damaged him."

"Suppose," Anancy says, "both of you should meet, eye to eye, not too cross, cool-cool, with only a little bad-mind?"

"Would be all right," Dog says. "Would be good. If you can fix it up."

Anancy works as a go-between. Anancy gets the badness between Dog and Puss really cooled off. It even seems all their trouble has gone – disappeared.

Everyday now Bro Dog goes to the house of Bro and Mrs Puss. He gets wood for them. He gets water. He fetches and he carries practically everything. By the time the leg of Puss is healed up again, he and Dog are perfect-perfect friends.

Bro Dog and Bro Puss are seen together everywhere, doing jobs, or just enjoying themselves like old friends.

One day, Bro Dog invites Bro Puss to come to the seaside with him. Bro Puss hesitates, not really wanting to go, but still not wanting to be the first to refuse a friendly request.

They go to the seaside.

Dog promptly slips into the sea and begins to swim and dive and do all kinds of things in the water, enjoying himself. Puss sits under a coconut tree and watches Dog.

Bro Dog waves to Puss, calls him, "Come on in! Come on. The water's great!"

"I'll stay here and watch you," Puss calls back.

Every now and then Dog calls to Puss inviting him to come in the water. People on the beach become amused by Bro Puss and Bro Dog.

Every time Dog calls to Puss to come and try doing this or that, Puss calls back saying, "I'll stay here and watch you."

And Puss sits there and watches Dog float, dive, leap out and splash back in the water and swim in all different kinds of ways.

As Dog comes out of the water, Puss compliments him on being such an excellent swimmer.

"Anybody can do it," Dog says. "Anybody – who isn't frightened."

"It's a talent you have," Puss says, "and I don't. That's why I sit and watch you."

"Oh, come off it," Dog says. "Anybody can swim. Anybody who isn't frightened."

Bro Puss changes the subject. Bro Puss says nothing more about his lack of talent and feeling for enjoyment in water.

A few days later, at a holiday time, Puss specially invites Dog to a packed lunch at a well-used picnic and beauty spot.

Not having eaten, on purpose, Dog arrives hungry. All ravenous and ready to tuck into the special feast-lunch both Mrs and Bro Puss prepared together. Yet, Bro Puss hangs about, in no hurry to open up the lunch and begin the eating.

Sitting there under a tree, Bro Dog has to wait, listening to long drawn-out tales Bro Puss tells about his family.

Then, sudden-sudden, Bro Puss picks up the well-stuffed bag of food. He tosses the handle round his shoulders. He fastens himself against the tree. And, calm-calm, Bro Puss climbs himself up and up into the tree. Soon, Bro Puss is sitting at ease, comfortable, in the branches of the tree, with the bag of food.

At first, Dog doesn't understand what is happening. He's puzzled at what funny game Puss is playing. Bro Dog stands, looking up into the tree.

Bro Puss looks down and calls, "I have lunch for you, Bro Dog. Come and get it."

"What d'you mean?" Dog says. "You know very well I can't get up there. And you must know my belly's rumbling."

"Anybody can climb up," Puss says. "Anybody who isn't frightened."

Dog is shocked. Dog remembers using those words at the seaside. Dog looks down, thinking, "Oh! Puss is playing a game of teaching-a-lesson. Puss wants to trick me into seeing something!"

Dog is cross. Dog feels he has been tricked. He feels he has been invited to a special lunch so that he can be taught a lesson. Dog thinks back at the swim in the sea.

Dog remembers he hasn't made a call to Puss for a swim to put him down or to give him any lesson. He has made his call to Puss to come and swim – come and enjoy the swim with him – as he has felt it.

"Things are natural when they happen as they happen," Dog tells himself. "When something happens between friends as you feel it, that's natural. But when a game is set up to catch you out, or teach you a lesson, that's a trick."

Getting hungrier and hungrier, Dog walks round the tree, looking up, and says, "Bring the food down, Bro Puss. You invite me to lunch. Come down with it."

"Come up and get it, Bro Dog," Puss says. "Climb up and get it. Anybody can do it. Anybody – who isn't frightened."

Dog sees that Puss is sitting comfortably in the tree eating his lunch.

Dog leans against the tree. Dog sits down. Dog feels like waiting just to attack Puss when he comes down, and not bother with any of the food. But Dog is so empty, it hurts.

Dog knows he cannot leave the food. Dog knows too, he cannot find it in himself to attack Puss and eat his food.

Suddenly, Puss comes down from the tree. Puss hands Dog his lunch.

Standing there, Dog takes the lunch, looking really cross with Puss. A wave of madness comes over him to attack Puss. But, instead, an enticing smell of the cooked meat under his nose makes Dog want to eat more than attack Puss.

Dog sits down. He looks up crossly at Puss, sitting there. Bro Dog picks up the enticing meat; he gobbles it, crushing up the bones. And Bro Dog goes on eating his way through his lunch, not saying a single word.

"Have you got the point, Bro Dog?" Puss says. "Do you see now...that different people can do different things? And...we have much more...because different people can do different things? We have bird-singing...and frog-croaking. We have cow-mooing, and jackass-braying. We have horse-galloping, and kangaroo-jumping...Say you see the point. Come on, Bro Dog. Say you see the point. Some people can get about in water...Others can get up and around in a tree...Say you see my point. Say you see it!"

Dog finishes his lunch, gets up and says, "Bro Puss, if ever we are going to manage being friends, we better keep it on the ground. And not in the sea or up in any tree. All right?"

Bro Dog walks away quickly by himself, going off in a huff.

From that time, cats and dogs keep trying to be friends.

ANANCY AND
BAD NEWS TO COW-MOTHER

Cow-Mother is at her yard, eating alone. Anancy comes. Anancy disturbs Cow-Mother, saying, "Good morning, Cow-Mother."

Cow-Mother looks up surprised. "Oh! Good morning, Mister Anancy."

"And how are you this late morning," Anancy goes on.

"I'm very well," Cow-Mother says. "I'm very well."

Anancy's face and Anancy's voice all go sad-sad as Anancy says, "Cow-Mother, oh, Cow-Mother, you are not really very well at all."

"Of course I'm very well," Cow-Mother insists. "Why then, Mister Anancy, d'you tell me I'm not very well?"

94

"Cow-Mother," Anancy says, "you'll see you're not at all very well, when you know Tiger is coming to butcher you."

"What? Heavens above!" Cow-Mother says, in great alarm. "What are you saying? Is this true? Is this really true?"

Anancy nods. "Yes, Cow-Mother. Yes. Bro Tiger's coming to make meat of you. Only just a little later today."

Cow-Mother well knows Anancy has a way of finding out everything.

In great shock and horror and worry, Cow-Mother calls Cow-Daughter and shouts the terrible news.

Cow-Daughter comes, all shaking in terror and dread.

Cow-Mother and Cow-Daughter begin to beg Anancy, "Oh, Mister Anancy! Bro Nancy. Dear-dear Mister Bro Anancy! You must help us. You have to help us. Come on. Say you'll help us!"

Anancy well knows he has a plan worked out already. But listen how the Anancy shows himself careful-careful.

"Well," Anancy says, "I can only try. I can only try. But if I only try, it'll still be a hard-hard try."

"Try for us, Mister Anancy," Cow-Mother and Cow-Daughter say. "Try for us with a hard-hard try."

"Well," Anancy says, "to try and help, I have to use a little plan."

"Use the plan," Cow-Mother and Cow-Daughter say. "Tell us the plan. Tell us. Ask of us anything."

"Well," Anancy says again, "when Tiger comes, Cow-Daughter has to be left with Tiger, alone."

Cow-Daughter is thrown into panic. Cow-Mother yells in horror, "What! Leave my daughter with Tiger? Never. Never! How can I do that? Do you realise, Mister Anancy, that my young daughter is with child? Do you realise that?"

"Cow-Mother," Anancy says, "you should worry. But hear

Anancy. Stay cool-cool. Cow-Daughter will not turn into Tiger's flesh and Tiger's blood."

"How will you stop that? Just how will you stop that?" Cow-Mother asks, all beyond herself with worry.

Anancy begins to explain. Cow-Mother and Cow-Daughter stand quiet-quiet and listen.

Anancy explains that with his plan, mother and daughter have to be separated. Cow-Mother can come and hide away on his land. To pass the time away, Cow-Mother can occupy herself digging mounds of yam-hills.

Anancy takes Cow-Mother and walks her round a whole acre of his land to be dug. And Anancy gets Cow-Mother started on the digging of yam-hill mounds before he leaves.

At Cow's Yard, waiting alone, always looking out, trembling, Cow-Daughter sees Tiger coming up the track to her place. Tiger is arriving, coming, walking all slow-slow.

As Tiger comes into Cow's Yard, he hears Anancy's voice. "Good afternoon, Bro Tiger. And the very best of good afternoon!"

Tiger turns his face upwards and sees Anancy sitting in a tree branch over him.

Surprised, annoyed, irritated, Tiger asks crossly, "Where's Cow-Mother? I can't see Cow-Mother."

"Your sight is good-good, Bro Tiger," Anancy says. "Cow-Mother is away. But Cow-Daughter is here. Cow-Daughter is here, growing bigger and bigger for you every minute."

"Who says I want to wait on anything growing?" Tiger says.

"Ah! I see," Anancy says. "Bro Tiger can't wait. Does Bro Tiger know how people say, 'Can't-Wait Bro Tiger isn't at all Mister Bro Tiger'?"

"What d'you mean?" Tiger asks with a serious face.

Anancy knows Tiger will listen. Anancy knows Tiger hates to be seen as dim or stupid. Anancy knows he must engage Tiger and impress him and confuse him. Listen how the Anancy goes on.

"Can't-Wait Bro Tiger isn't at all Mister Bro Tiger. Can't-Wait is little boss of hungrybelly, ruling-ruling everybody, making Bro Tiger lose out in the end. Oh, so lose out in the end!"

"Lose out?" Tiger says. "How can I lose out? I never lose out. No little idiot can make me lose out. But–how d'you know people talk about me?"

"Bro Tiger–you are a thinking man. Think, Bro Tiger. Think."

"I'm a thinking man," Tiger replies crossly. "I think. I always think."

"Then, Bro Tiger, you should see, that rich man and clever man never eat big-bulk and big-bulk and big-bulk."

Tiger doesn't think whether that is really true or not. Tiger only goes silent. Then, softly, Tiger says, "There's something in that." And Tiger sits down.

The Anancy goes on. The Anancy puts it over on Tiger that rich man and clever man eat only nice dainty-dainty little lots of food.

Tiger suddenly says, "Anancy, I walked here with a total-total empty belly. I still have it."

"Of course, Bro Tiger," Anancy says. "Of course. But remember, you've eaten lots and lots of big-bulk before. And you walked here with a total-total empty belly. Rich man and clever man eat little dainty-dainty bits. And I never, never, heard a rich man or clever man complain of walking with empty belly."

Tiger is silent. Then Tiger says, "There's something in that." Tiger turns his face up towards Anancy in the tree and

97

says, "Anancy, you think I don't know things, don't you? You think I'm stupid? I'm not stupid."

Anancy sweetens up Tiger. He assures Tiger how he's far, far from stupid. Then Anancy tells Tiger how it's because people know he knows things why Cow-Daughter has gone through the trouble to prepare and keep a special dinner for him.

"Special dinner for me?"

"Yes, Bro Tiger. For you."

"Where's the dinner?"

Cow-Daughter, who all this time has kept herself locked up, calls out, telling that Tiger's dinner is in the kitchen.

Anancy comes down from the tree and goes with Tiger and finds the dinner. It is in a big wooden bowl on the kitchen table. The dinner has a spoon with it, and a pot of flowers beside it.

With Anancy watching him, Tiger sits at the kitchen table and eats up the food.

Anancy calls Cow-Daughter to come and shake hands with Tiger.

At first Tiger is all shamefaced, shy and reluctant to shake hands with Cow-Daughter, but eventually does.

Cow-Daughter goes and brings out a big dish of whole pudding and gives it to Tiger, with a spoon. Standing where he is, Tiger polishes off every bit of the pudding. Cow-Daughter turns her back to get him a mug of water. Tiger chuckles at how silly the big dish of sweet pudding makes him feel.

Anancy points out to Tiger that he can stay with Cow-Daughter and get regular meals.

Tiger chuckles, telling he prefers to have the job of watching Cow-Daughter getting bigger and bigger. Then Tiger chuckles at himself, again saying he'd like to watch himself everyday to see if the eating of high-up food makes him turn into a better man.

Tiger stays on with Cow-Daughter.

Anancy makes regular visits to Cow's Yard, at all sorts of times. He also goes and gives news to Cow-Mother regularly.

At first, if Cow-Daughter is cooking, Tiger is there watching her. If she is washing or ironing or doing anything in the yard, Tiger is there watching her.

Cow-Daughter sees that Tiger likes her cooking. She gives Tiger all kinds of extra and in-between titbits.

Tiger begins to help. Tiger gets wood. Tiger gets water. Tiger fetches and carries and does whatever task Cow-Daughter gives him.

One day when Cow-Daughter is coming up the hilly slope of the yard, carrying some food from the garden, Cow-Daughter gives birth to a baby. Suspecting that something is the matter, Tiger comes and finds that Cow-Daughter's baby has rolled halfway down the hillside. Cow-Daughter is by far too weak to move.

"Bro Tiger, please get my baby," Cow-Daughter asks him.

Tiger trots down the hillside, collects the baby, gives it to Cow-Daughter and helps her to get inside the house.

By now, Cow-Mother has dug all of Anancy's land into mounds of yam-hills. She has also organised his little hut and made it clean and tidy. Anancy has been taking all the news about Cow-Daughter, but Cow-Mother is anxious-anxious wanting to go back home.

Out on one of his regular walks these days, Tiger suddenly remembers how Cow-Daughter has become smaller, instead of going on getting bigger. Tiger doesn't understand that having had her baby – and no longer being pregnant – Cow-Daughter has reduced in size.

99

Sudden-sudden Tiger thinks how marvellous it would be without having to bother about Cow-Daughter. To be free of Cow-Daughter seems a most wonderful idea.

Tiger doesn't return to Cow's Yard at all.

Tiger leaves. All the same, Tiger turns away from Cow's Yard with a little malice in his heart against Anancy. Tiger feels Anancy has somehow tricked him. Bro Nancy knows that. Bro Nancy keeps his eyes wide open for Tiger.

MRS PUSS, DOG AND THIEVES

Bro Dog falls into hungry-time, bad-bad.

Bro Dog is starved. Every day Bro Dog gets thinner.
Hungry-time reduces Bro Dog to almost skin and bone. Bro
Dog's knees knock when he walks. All knock-kneed and
tottering, all looking and feeling terrible, poor Dog goes on
down the road and comes face to face with Mrs Puss.

Both Bro Dog and Mrs Puss stop. Bro Dog stares at Mrs
Puss with wide-open mouth, not able to say a single word.

Mrs Puss has to say, "Good morning, Bro Dog."

Still staring, Dog can't believe how well fed Mrs Puss
looks. At last Dog says, "Mrs Puss, you look so well, so
round, so shining! You look like a rich somebody, who
hungry-time hasn't touched at all. You look like you've just
landed from some foreign country."

Mrs Puss shakes her head.

"No, Bro Dog. I haven't been anywhere."

"Well, Mrs Puss, excuse me please," Dog says. "I have to
ask you, where d'you have your storehouse of food hiding?"

Mrs Puss gives a little smile and says, "Bro Dog, sometimes a thief from a thief makes even the good Lord smile."

"Mrs Puss," Dog says, "can't I smile too, even a little bit? Look how I'm all skin and bone."

Mrs Puss glances at Dog with a look of pity and says, "Oh, Bro Dog, hungry-time wasted you bad-bad. You're just not the same man." Then Mrs Puss looks about her, making sure nobody else overhears her secret. "Bro Dog," she says quietly, "it can't be a bad thing to share some goodness with a good friend. I'm going to tell you something. I've found a lock-up building where meat is kept."

"Meat!" Dog blurted loudly.

"Shuuh!" Mrs Puss says. "Not so loud. I believe only a few people are getting the meat," she whispers.

"Where? Where's the meat?" Dog asks impatiently. And Dog's ears practically stand up as he listens.

Mrs Puss explains that she believes the meat is stolen. She also believes the thieves use the little building as their meat lock-up store. She has seen the men bring meat. She has also seen them come and collect meat only. The men come and go only at night. She has discovered the unusual men from her sitting in the avocado tree, beside the lock-up building, eating an avocado in darkness.

The men do everything in whispers and careful-careful movements, never to make a sound. And, the big thing is, the men don't even use a key to lock up or open up the place. They use certain magic words.

Once she realises what the men do in the darkness, she makes it her business to come back. Again and again she conceals herself in darkness and watches and listens until she learns everything perfect-perfect.

She has learnt how to open the door, close it, collect her

meat, open and close it again and go, without any trouble.

Then, seriously, Mrs Puss points out, "One thing, Bro Dog, one thing, no liver must be touched. Not one little piece of liver must be touched."

Dog gives himself a hard smile and says, "Would happen, wouldn't it? Just because any time, anywhere, I'd give anything for a piece of liver, that's the meat mustn't be touched."

"Well, Bro Dog," Mrs Puss says, "I know how much you like your piece of liver, but I've listened, I've watched, I know what will cause bad trouble."

That night, after the men come and leave again, Mrs Puss slides down from the avocado tree and calls Bro Dog to come out of hiding.

Mrs Puss and Bro Dog stand in front of the door. Mrs Puss uses the magic words, ending with "Seven, eight, nine". Slow-slow, the door opens. Mrs Puss and Bro Dog slip inside. Mrs Puss uses the magic words again, this time ending with "Nine, eight, seven". The door closes and locks them in.

They light up a tiny oil lamp.

Quick-quick and brisk, Bro Dog and Mrs Puss fill their bags with meat. All kinds of meat are seasoned, corned, pickled and packed in barrel after barrel. The meat is ready in all kinds of cuts. There is a barrel of liver and a barrel of heart. Mrs Puss doesn't show Bro Dog the liver barrel. And still Mrs Puss doesn't see when Dog's nippy movement slides the lid of the liver barrel open; he has a peep, and slides it shut again.

Bags full of meat, the oil lamp is put out.

Dog and Mrs Puss come to the door. Again Mrs Puss uses the magic words ending with "Seven, eight, nine". The door opens. Both of them slip out quickly. Mrs Puss closes the door with the magic words ending with "Nine, eight, seven".

Dog and Mrs Puss hurry away in the night with their bags of meat.

Two nights later, Mrs Puss and Bro Dog come back again. They wait in hiding. Mrs Puss is sure the men are due to arrive. But they don't come. Afraid of being caught inside, with the barrels of meat, Mrs Puss and Bro Dog wait until almost daylight. Then they decide they are not going to go home with empty bags. They'll take a chance. But they know they have to be quick.

Mrs Puss opens the door and closes it again, using the magic words.

They light up the little lamp.

Working quick-quick, listening, looking, Mrs Puss and Bro Dog load up their bags with meat already cut into pieces.

"Are you ready?" Mrs Puss whispers.

"Yes. I'm ready," Dog says.

"Right," Mrs Puss says. "I'll put out the lamp." And she blows out the light.

Thinking Bro Dog is behind her, Mrs Puss keeps whispering to him. Mrs Puss opens the door, slips out, whispering to Dog, then closes the door again. Immediately, there is panic thumping on the door inside.

Mrs Puss uses the magic words. The door doesn't open. Mrs Puss calls to Bro Dog inside, telling him to use the magic words. Mrs Puss hears the locked-in Bro Dog using the magic words properly. But the door doesn't open.

Oh! What now? That greedy Dog is trapped!

"Did you touch any liver?" Mrs Puss calls. "Have you any liver in your bag?"

"Just one – well – two little pieces," Dog says, anxious-anxious.

"Oh, Bro Dog, you're in trouble," Mrs Puss says. "And putting back the liver now won't help one bit. In any case, it's nearly daylight. I'll have to go. I'll have to go, Bro Dog. I'll get some help. I'll try and get some help."

Mrs Puss hurries away leaving Bro Dog locked up with the barrels of meat.

When Anancy hears about Bro Dog's trouble, Anancy sends Tiger a message and keeps it a secret. All the same, Mrs Puss didn't know that the meat men sometimes come and collect meat in the daytime too.

The meat men come. To the meat men's great surprise they find Bro Dog locked up with their meat.

The morning sun is high up in the sky when the three meat men tie up Bro Dog in their cart, along with their load of meat. With Dog tied up, not able to move, not able to make the slightest whimper, the men begin to take him away.

The men come out on to the country road. Sudden-sudden the meat men hear a song. They don't see him, but it's Anancy. The meat men know it's Anancy with a message in a song. They cannot ignore it. The men stop the cart to listen. Hiding himself, Anancy sings this little song:

"There's a man who's no beggar.
Could it be the Bro Tiger?
No-beggar Bro Tiger?
No-beggar Bro Tiger?
Who for liver or leg
Just never learnt to beg
Who for liver or leg
Just never learnt to beg.
He never learnt to beg, O!..."

The meat men suddenly see Tiger in the road, coming towards them. The men become panic-stricken and bundle themselves off. They run away like mad, leaving their cart.

Tiger comes up to the cart in the road. Tiger unties a very grateful Bro Dog, who takes the liver out of his bag and leaves it for Tiger.

Bro Dog picks up his bag of meat and hurries off with Anancy, who waits for him in the road.

Tiger pulls away the meat men's cart of meat for himself.

When people hear about what has happened, each person says, "Oh!" and then exclaims the proverb, "A thief from a thief makes the good Lord smile!"

ANANCY, TIGER AND THE SHINE-DANCER-SHINE

Today now, the big happening is on. Tiger and Anancy meet in a clash, in the dance against each other. You can remember how Tiger did come in on horseback at the Stump-a-Foot Celebration and spoil that first competition. Well, everybody's been waiting to see the real honest contest.

Bro Dog's hard work has done everything to fix up the event. Everywhere, pasted up posters announce:

Big Christmas Event
MATCH OF SHINE-DANCER-SHINE
between the one
BRO NANCY
and the one
BRO TIGER

Choosing Christmas-time is clever too, you see. Plenty people will come out. But specially, it's the time when Great-House will give money to dancing events in Village Square.

The time has come now. Village Square is all noisy enjoyment. Usual Christmas dancers – John-Canoo Masquerade Dancers – did just finish fantastic crowd-pleasing dances. And everybody is glad some John-Canoo Dancers stand with the crowd. And chief dancer, John-Canoo himself, sits in with the musicians, who are all dressed up in rainbow colours.

Bro Dog puts down his banjo. He steps out and speaks. "Noise makers, and stiff faces, wow wow!"

"Wow wow!" the crowd chants back.

"Wow wow!" Dog repeats.

The crowd roars back, "Wow wow!"

Dog walks round in the circle the crowd allows. And loud-loud, Dog recites:

> *"Best-dancer will win.*
> > *Hear this, hear this, O!*
> *Best-dancer will have the bright-bright grin.*
> *Best-dancer gets Great-House prize money.*
> *I say, Great-House prize money.*
> > *Hear this, hear this, O!*
> *Nothing will go to what's half-dead –*
> *Better bring on John-Canoo Horse-Head.*
> *All is for dance and dancer.*
> > *Hear this, hear this, O!*
> *Bright-brightest ablaze with music-fire.*
> > *Hear this, hear this, O!"*

The crowd goes noisy with cheering for Bro Dog. He

waits. He goes on. "Starting off this revelation of rhythm, the joy of Shine-Dancer-Shine rivalry, here is best push-you-over-easy fellow, Bro Tiger!" In the crowd-roaring Bro Dog walks back and again picks up his banjo.

And with Monkey there on drums, Rabbit on fife, Puss on fiddle, Goat on maracas and Pig rubbing grater, all the musicians strike up music, swift and hot.

Bro Tiger starts with unexpected amusement. Tiger comes out of a lying-down barrel beside the musicians. Adding to that, he's dressed up in a floppy straw hat, in too-big blue jeans trousers with braces and patchwork patches, and heavy boots not laced up.

Tiger starts his dance.

To the hot music, Tiger jigs. Tiger wiggles his hips, missing the rhythm of the music, on purpose, going round and round the circle in the middle of the crowd. Soon, it is seen that Tiger isn't all beef and no brains. Tiger has a plan.

Tiger begins to clown. Tiger begins funny mime dances, showing off that he's really a big country buffoon.

Tiger stoops. Tiger plays he's milking a cow, with all sorts of clever movements. Unexpectedly, Tiger imitates getting kicked over by the cow, swift-swift, flat onto his back. Tiger's hat falls off his head; he ignores the hat.

Tiger gets up, shakes himself off, then begins walking all droopy-droopy, all half-dead, dragging himself along, doing a lazy walk-dance, on how a lazy countryman walks. And with the crowd cheering, Tiger goes into mocking the climbing of a tree. With all lazy movements, out of beat with the music, Tiger barely manages to get one foot up against the side of the tree. It's too much hard work. He gives up. He mocks trying to get his leg back down, but even that effort is too much. Again Tiger falls flat on his back.

All this time, wild with roars, shrieks and whoopee whistles, the crowd claps with the musicians, and sings with them, this song:

"Poor Tatty-Tatty Pappy.
Poor Pitchy-Patchy Pappy—
Lost yesterday, lost tomorrow.
Doesn't rent, doesn't borrow.
Finds a fine-fine blackskin gal
She finds a better-better pal.

O, they cuss him and cuss-cuss him.
They cuss him and they cuss him.
Whai-O, they cuss-cuss him!
Can't guess any riddle-mi-riddle
But what a John-Canoo-man, John-Canoo-man,
John-Canoo-man, John-Canoo-man,
*   John-Canoo-man, O!*
*   Tatty-Tatty Pappy.*
*   Pitchy-Patchy Pappy . . ."*

Tiger goes on. Tiger mocks how somebody falls about under the weight of heavy load. Tiger's mocking dance has him with one hand up holding the load. His legs are rubbery, his body wobbly. And he staggers about till his load falls on top of him, leaving him panting, half-dead.

With having the crowd noisy with enjoyment, Tiger begins to mock how a man and a woman quarrel. Doing his wiggles, Tiger stretches his neck. Tiger does snappy high-pitched yaps and grumbles. He does the man answering back, chest-beating himself, jumping up and down, with deep-voiced barks and growling.

All this time, the music with the clapping and the singing goes on:

"...*Poor Tatty-Tatty Pappy.*
Poor Pitchy-Patchy Pappy—
Lost yesterday, lost tomorrow.
Doesn't rent, doesn't borrow.
Finds a fine-fine fairskin gal
She finds a better-better pal.

O, they cuss him and cuss-cuss him.
They cuss him and they cuss him.
Whai-O, they cuss-cuss him!
Can't guess any riddle-mi-riddle
But what a John-Canoo-man, John-Canoo-man,
John-Canoo-man, John-Canoo-man,
  John-Canoo-man, O!
  Tatty-Tatty Pappy.
   Pitchy-Patchy Pappy, O!..."

Tiger sits down, suddenly rolls onto his head, kicks up his boot-clad feet into the air tiredly, like somebody without strength to pedal a bicycle properly. Tiger gets up. One of his boots falls off. He picks it up, jigs and wiggles and waves the boot about round the circle.

The music stops. Tiger bows. The crowd cheers and cheers him till he disappears. Anancy knows Tiger has done well. Everything he does must better Tiger.

The crowd goes silent, waiting.

Then, Bro Nancy doesn't wait to be announced. Anancy comes out wearing a long gown of brown sugar bag sacking. The music and the crowd welcome Anancy big with noises. The musicians start up another song. And straightaway, Anancy-Spiderman goes into a dramatic fall-on-your-face sort of dance.

Anancy bends forward, stretches one arm down and tries to make his face look long. And, head dipping, bottom pushing sharp, an arm hanging down like a horse's front leg in movement, Anancy does a Three-Legged Ghost-Horse dance. His movements, his feet, make the three-legged sound, clop-pi-ti. Clop-pi-ti. Clop-pi-ti. Clop-pi-ti. The crowd groans, as if it thinks this is magic. Head dipping, bottom pushing sharp, arm hanging down, Anancy goes round and round the circle doing his "clop-pi-ti, clop-pi-ti" dance, to the music with clapping, and singing of this song:

> *"Number one golden-tailed monkey goes –*
> *Monkey named Molenggen-Spanneh.*
> *Monkey flies, he flies, he flies, he flies –*
> *He flies, O.*
> *Ante du du du du du –*
> *Clean gone, O!*
> *Ante du du du du du –*
> *Gone O Moleng..."*

Round and round this song is kept up, with the music and clapping. And Anancy doesn't stop.

Anancy imitates the way the Ghost-Horse looks at an audience. Anancy stops. He bends his ghostly long neck, looks at the crowd on one side and slowly dances – clop-pi-ti. Again, he bends his ghostly long neck, looking at the other side of the crowd and slowly dances – clop-pi-ti... The music is carrying on.

> *"Number one golden-tailed monkey's gone –*
> *Monkey named Molenggen-Spanneh.*
> *Monkey flies, he flies, he flies, he flies –*
> *He flies, O.*
> *Ante du du du du du –*
> *Clean gone, O!*
> *Ante du du du du du –*
> *Gone O Moleng!..."*

Dancing backwards now, like the Ghost-Horse, Anancy, head-dipping, bottom-pushing, round and round the circle, goes on with his weird clop-pi-ti, clop-pi-ti, clop-pi-ti. Clop-pi-ti, clop-pi-ti, clop-pi-ti... Then the crowd notices that the Anancy is going on with something else.

While still dancing, smart-smart, the Anancy works

himself out of his gown. The Anancy now shows off short trousers with a tight-fitting coat of glittering stars, all military looking. The tunic has red shoulder flaps. It has a red sash, like a belt over his shoulder and across his chest. The dress brings out Anancy like a grand military man. But, best of all, the dress glitters with pasted-on silver-paper stars, close together over it. This then must be the shining glory! This must be it! As the people see the Anancy's star-shining coat, their roar is unbelievable.

Didn't the posters announce "Shine-Dancer-Shine"! Bro Nancy's interpretation is all-sensational. Whistles and shrieks and roars make the people one big deafening body.

Like the Ghost-Horse taking off, Anancy wants everybody to believe he's as swift as a bird. He opens his arms wide and runs round the circle, till the music stops.

Bro Dog comes out and says, "Wow wow!"

"Wow wow!" the crowd answers back.

Wearing his masquerade mask again, with his enormous horned headdress, the John-Canoo chief dancer comes forward beside Bro Dog and shouts, "Who's for the prize?"

Everybody knows. Everybody shouts, "Shine-Dancer-Shine man, Bro Nancy!"

By this time the real Pitchy-Patchy of the John-Canoo Dancers has come back with a collection of money from the crowd, for Bro Tiger.

But Bro Nancy walks away with the most – with Great-House prize money.

From that time, all who perform for a crowd like to wear a most shining glitter-glitter costume. Anancy has a big hand in it.

ANANCY, LION AND TIGER'S LAST DAY

This is a last meeting story – a terrible last meeting story. It's also a warning. It says, should you ever happen to hear Tiger and Lion fighting, oh, you shouldn't look. The sight is too terrible. Bro Tiger and Bro Lion have equal strength. They have it in themselves to fight to a kill, if nobody stops them.

It's such a wonder how Anancy knows when something awful is happening. And this now hits Anancy just after he has kindly offered to deliver a pan of oil – still hot – to a good neighbour. Anancy turns round swift and brisk and arrives on the scene.

Bro Tiger and Bro Lion damage each other worse and worse. They are all fight noises and eyes and weapons and blows. Their coats are ripped. Their faces and necks and bodies are cut. Lion and Tiger bleed. They smear each other all over on and on and don't care. Standing to full height, heads and arms busy, they damage each other.

"Gentlemen!" Anancy shouts. "Gentlemen, stop it!" Anancy puts down his vessel of oil. He walks round the roars and blows and blood. He raises his arms in despair and shouts, "Bro Lion, Bro Tiger, stop it, please!"

Lion and Tiger fall to the ground, locked to each other. In grips giving each other pain, they struggle onto their feet again. They stand to full height, with arms round each other's shoulders and mouths open with rage. Unexpectedly, Anancy tosses the warm oil onto their faces. Each one closes his eyes and lets go of the other.

"Enough is enough – Gentlemen!" Anancy says.

Lion and Tiger give each other one last long, terrible stare. Tiger turns slowly and walks away. Lion goes too, slowly, in the opposite direction. Both are hurt, tired and sad.

Anancy stands, thinking. He doesn't know how long Lion and Tiger have fought. He doesn't know what has started the fight. But both have their coats cut like rags. Both are dirty with smears of blood. Tiger seems to Anancy to be the sadder of the two. Unexpectedly, Anancy feels sorry for Tiger. Anancy wants to comfort Tiger. Oh, Bro Anancy wants to comfort Bro Tiger! He looks round and Tiger is gone. Anancy calls, "Bro Tiger! Bro Tiger!" No answer. And no sign of Tiger. Anancy begins to run after Tiger, where he has disappeared.

Anancy travels on all night. After sunrise Anancy sees Bro Tiger and Mrs Tiger ahead, going along. Anancy walks quicker. He catches up with Bro Tiger and Mrs Tiger and settles with walking beside them. But nobody speaks.

"Bro Tiger," Anancy says, "I'm happy you're walking well, after such a fight." Tiger walks on, taking no notice. Anancy goes on. "A giant fighter. A giant fighter you are, Bro Tiger! And only me saw it."

Nobody else speaks. On and on without speaking, Anancy and Tiger and Mrs Tiger keep on walking till late afternoon. Suddenly Anancy knows he must go back. He should go no further. He stops. Unexpectedly, Anancy hears a sound, a strange sound, as if the sea rages about like thunder in caves underground.

Anancy knows something is going to happen. He watches Tiger and Mrs Tiger going on and on alone, up a hill, never looking back, never sideways or even ahead. He watches them go over the hill and disappear onto the other side.

A sudden burst of flame splits the side of the hill where Tiger and Mrs Tiger have passed. Quick-quick, other bursts of flames open the hill into a glowing fire. The hill rolls and roars belching up burning land. Then, unexpectedly, the sea rushes in from everywhere. Bulk pieces of a broken and burning hill ride on the inrush of sea. Big glowing rocks begin to drift. Next moment the sea has swallowed every glowing spark. All is a level of sea, as if the sea has always been there.

Anancy is amazed. Then Anancy looks and sees Tiger and Mrs Tiger on level land on the other side, still going on and on.

"Goodbye, Bro Tiger!" Anancy shouts. "Goodbye!"

Brother Tiger turns and waves goodbye.

"Bro Tiger's in another land," Anancy whispers to himself.

He gets home. And Bro Nancy is surprised how much he misses Bro Tiger. Anancy decides, to keep the memory of Tiger, he'll tell stories about himself and Bro Tiger.

Spider Anancy hides in bedrooms and whispers stories like dreams. Anancy remembers more and more stories and tells them like dreams.